MW01518585

Turtle Tushies in the Land of Banana Beer

A Peace Corps Memoir

by

Anita Pauwels
(aka Cooper Hill)

Copyright 2015 Anita Pauwels

2nd edition 2019

All rights reserved

Dedication

This is a story for all people around the world--no matter their race, creed, color, or origin. It is the story of 'us'--human beings who struggle to come to terms with our differences. And it is a salute to all peacekeepers who bring hope, friendship and light to a world coming out of the darkness.

"You pray for rain, you gotta deal with the mud too. That's a part of it."
Denzel Washington

"Peace does not mean an absence of conflicts; differences will always be there. Peace means solving these differences through peaceful means, through dialogue, education, knowledge; and through humane ways."
Dalai Lama XIV

"Peace is a daily, a weekly, a monthly process, gradually changing opinions, slowly eroding old barriers, quietly building new structures."
John F Kennedy

Peace cannot be kept by force; it can only be achieved by understanding.
Albert Einstein

"My dad grew up in a mud hut and studied by candlelight. He was 14 when he got a scholarship to Russia. He was super clever--the cleverest person. He landed in 5 ft of snow, and was alone at 14, studying science and engineering. He didn't have a bed and he slept on a table."
M.I.A

Table of Contents

Table of Contents (Cont.)

Table of Contents (Cont.)

Foreward

One person can make a difference, and every person should try.
JFK

This is the story of us, of how we came to honor, respect and love a people in Africa within a fragile political and difficult physical environment as Peace Corps Volunteers

We have waited long to tell this story, for on the verge of telling, the great troubles began and the story seemed suddenly unimportant in the face of such loss, annihilation, sadness and fear.

But this is not a book about conflict or genocide. It is not a book about poverty.

It does not purport to 'fix' things or judge a people for their past, or their struggles to define who they are in this new century.

It also does not contain many of the stories from the wonderful volunteers and ex-pats that made our work all the richer for having known them, for theirs is not our story to tell.

It is simply a story of us: Of love and laughter, and hard work: Of learning to embrace a culture and a people not our own: Of learning to laugh, deep from the belly, at the simplest and most beautiful things in life: Of learning that hard work and working hard can sometimes be the same thing, and that each can yield rewards and disappointments.

As the terrible years of war have too slowly diminished, and as repatriation and reconciliation now occasionally or slowly take root, we can finally offer this story, based on letters home at the time, as our hope; that through our eyes, the world will at last see the luminous, joyous, industrious beauty of a new nation and a people determined to grow and redefine themselves in a world moving both too fast and too slow.

Even after these decades of sadness, we continue to hold out hope for a people and a country still rich in the promise of things that count: the sheer joy in greeting a morning sun, the courage to face each day with a smile, the beauty of extended family and community, a strong work ethic, forgiveness, reconciliation...and caring.

* * *

To the people of Burundi,

Thank you for everything that you taught us, for all that we learned from you. We see you from afar and yearn each day for you to become a whole people in a united country.

We wish only good for you, that every heart in your nation will find peace, hope and balance.

We wish for you to thrive, to know that you are cherished as a part of the whole, and to know that we are all One.

Jim & Anita Pauwels

Preface
Reflections

"I heard the geese today," he said.

"Really?" I looked up in surprise. "They're three weeks early! How high were they?"

"High enough so I never saw them, just heard the honking."

"Neat. That means an early spring. Just like the year we left for Africa."

"Yeah. Brings back memories."

"Do you miss it?"

"Almost ever day. I miss the people. And I miss the intensity of living life for each separate moment."

I sighed. "Yeah. Me too.

Chapter 1
Ode To A Grape

Dear Carol,

You asked how this happened? Well...Not too long ago or far away, it all began with a dead grape. We were in the car on our way to one of my art shows, talking about the future. You know--is there life after marriage? Even second marriages? Should we even get married? Responsibilities, choices, commitments. We talked of doing something together, a work, something for somebody else. But what could two successful, approaching middle-aged, totally opposite strangers do together? Jim mentioned his Peace Corps service in India of twenty years earlier and how neat it had been and would I be interested in something like that? Of course the idea intrigued me. Romance, idealism, visions of saving children and building bridges swam into view.

That's when he asked for something to munch on. My hand reached behind, down and under his seat for the pretzels, and there it was-- something soft, wrinkled--and wet--"Oh, yechhh!!!!!"

"What is it?" he asked in alarm.

"Oh, yechhh," I repeated and withdrew my hand, the squashed forlorn something dangling from a finger, "It's a dead graaape!"

* * *

That marked the beginning. We were married. For two years we struggled, we laughed, we fought, we had fun and we adjusted. And all along something kept pulling at us, asking us to let go of our rat race, to do something unique and have fun on the way to the earthquake. So we did. We put our house on the market, sadly found new homes for the pets (the very hardest, emotional part), took leave from our jobs and joined the Peace Corps.

Easier said than done. We were told it takes anywhere from three months to a year and a half to complete all the paperwork, physicals, background checks and interviews. We have never really decided if this

is a part of the screening process to see if you're sincere, or just another
bureaucracy in progress.

You also need the following:

-Marketable skills (i.e. marketable to the developing world, as in
education, agriculture, medicine, technology, economics, conservation,
construction, mechanics, etc.)

-Great teeth (i.e., no cavities, no ongoing dental problems)

-Reasonably good health (yes, having a decent, no-problems body
helps, though they are more lenient on that than they are on teeth.)

-Proof of good citizenship (i.e. will you make a good representative
of the American people?)

-Great teeth

-No connection with the CIA or other anti-civilization
organizations.

-Great teeth

-Flexibility, patience, good sense of humor, adaptability, and a
sense of what Peace Corps is about.

-And, oh yes, did I mention it before? Great teeth.

* * *

Now, the only program a mechanical design engineer and a
biologist-turned-artist appeared equally qualified for, and that had an
opening for a couple in the same country (very important that we go to
the same place at the same time), was the Inland Fisheries Program, and
that, only if we could both pass their rigorous ten-week training
program. This consisted of a military style form of harassment and
mind-games where 'trainers' picked on perceived weaknesses to toughen
us up--or wash us out--so we didn't waste precious allotment money.

The one outstanding segment we did receive in the training was
from a County Extension Agent, J. M., who taught us pond surveying
techniques and also gave us the most important how-to advice for
anyone who wants to impart new information and knowledge to another:

1. Tell them what you're going to do
2. Show them how to do it
3. Tell them what you did.

Three repetitions and they have it for life. Oh, and another gem he
gave us, always get credentials from the people you meet, find out who
they are, how they can help or hurt you and proceed with cautious
enthusiasm.

At close of our ten weeks training, we thirty in-training-survivors
(one guy dropped out early on) gathered to learn the country
assignments where we would be posted. As countries were announced

for individuals and teams, excitement and anticipation filled the hall. Then they introduced a guest speaker, the Peace Corps Country Director (PCCD) for Burundi (OUR country), an Uber-cool lady named Chris, who just happened to be stateside. She gave a welcoming speech of encouragement and congratulations on our respective assignments and all went well until she put up the slides of Burundi. I have to say, they were so beautiful and her descriptions sounded so much like the land of OZ, there was more than a bit of jealousy from some of the volunteers posted to more challenging climates.

The only other important memory of the ten stress-filled weeks (beyond meeting some really great people) is that we made it--along with twenty-eight other fisheries-volunteers (fishies) to be dispersed and sprinkled round the world.

Jim and I were officially primed for adventure, selected as part of a six-person team, ramped up and ready to go--until they told us we might be going elsewhere, that the situation in our country was uncertain. As Peace Corps worked on the details, we were sent home for a week to hurry-up-and-wait and re-pack a dozen times.

* * *

Not being regular travelers, packing perplexed us. Our first efforts resulted in a floor-full of so much stuff we would have required the plane's entire cargo hold for transport. Face it, when you are accustomed to luxuries like shampoo and toothpaste and you are facing two unknown years in the African jungle or bush, what is essential?

Should we go 'macho' like some of our fellow volunteers with just the small army-green backpack, beat up shorts, and walking shoes, or try to take everything including the corner hardware store? We felt we compromised. And still, our four nylon suitcases (though two of them were stuffed full of official fish-farming and pond equipment), a really big duffel bag of books and two backpack carry-ons weighed in around the proportions of a medium-sized elephant.

In training, some of our fellow volunteers had sworn we'd packed enough for ten people, rolling their eyes and whispering to each other:

"What on earth are these tourists doing here?"

"They'll never make it!"

"Do we have to sit with these guys?"

--But all criticism was forgiven and forgotten as we finally got word of approval and headed for Central East Africa and our new assignment in the tiny mountainous country of Burundi. Excitement reigned as we met up with the other four of our team in New York, Dann, Mary, Michael and Sarah) for the first leg of our journey, had a twelve-hour stop-over in Frankfurt, Germany (we had great walks through nature gardens, the zoo, and terrific camera stores) and a short stop for inspections (off-load/on-load) in the Addis Ababa airport, Ethiopia (beautiful people–but lots of guns showing), then finally on to Burundi.

The excitement. The unknown. What was in store for us? What lay ahead? Would we all make it through the next two years or would some of us not be able to handle the culture shock, the stress, the language barriers and physical hardships...the bugs?

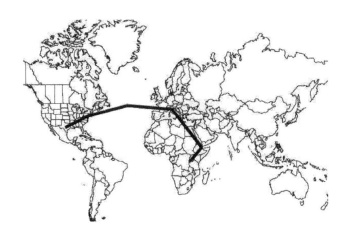

More later, love and a hug,

Anita & Jim

Chapter 2
Africa!

Dear Folks,

We flew over Lake Victoria into eternity and the foothills of Lake Tanganyika today.

Yellows, browns and greens light up the savannah, and everything sparkles vibrant and warm under a bright African sun. Eight thousand miles from home. This is where Stanley found Livingston, and 'Texas-close' to where my heroes, the Leakey's, found Lucy, one of humankind's oldest remains in Olduvai Gorge, Tanzania. Excitement reigns!

Let's see. First impressions:

-Land--red-brown, dry, hot, dusty, windy

-People--friendly, stare, point and laugh a lot

-Food--terrific. Fresh lake fish, rice, beans, fries, salads, great veggies, warm sticky-sweet sodas, cool beer and not nearly enough boiled, filtered water.

Too tired to write any more. Twenty-four hours on an airplane and you feel like you were born and raised there. We will have a week to acclimate to our new environment then it's off to language training for another eight weeks of school--French and Kirundi this time. Sounds like fun, huh? Whoopee!

* * *

Impressions:

A few days later: Just a few notes about our country, Burundi:

The Capitol: Bujumbura (hereafter known as **Buja**) is a large modern city with paved streets, a large downtown, and an enormous central market with buses, cars, trucks, and people, people, people everywhere.

It is the dry season. Heat and dust prevail. They say in the rainy season the air is so clear you can see the mountains of Zaire. Or is it Tanzania? Or both? Across the lake or down the lake? No hint of either of them now, of course, as a bright, dry-white haze has limited visibility to less than two miles, so up, down or sideways is about the same.

Buja lies at approximately 2,000 feet altitude, on a flat plain at the foothills of the Nile Crest (where begins the ultimate source of the Nile). Steep mountains arise only ten minutes out of the city and honestly, Mom, we have never seen anything so beautiful. Every square inch is covered in coffee, banana and manioc (cassava) trees. Green everywhere. If they have this much green in the dry season, the rainy season ought to be spectacular when all the underbrush and grasses are renewed.

People; very friendly, work and play hard and have the curiosity of ten cats, just like home. Questions posed to and about us are non-stop. Just wish we knew enough of any language to answer. We are definitely fish-out-of-water at this point.

Dress in the city is both Western and traditional, depending on the social class. I wish we could tell you more about the populace, but we don't speak any of their multiple languages yet, except Smile and Wave. The food is great and Peace Corps is stuffing us like there is no tomorrow. I can see us getting fat and fatter during language training, what with studying all day, eating three meals whether we need them or not, and no exercise. Already feel like a blimp.

Better get to bed now. We are installed in a hotel at the moment, hot running water (most days) and fans for sleeping at night. Will write more next week after our fish-trip up-country to meet Provincial Governors, tour valleys and mountains, and assess the current status and potential of inland fish culture.

More Later
Love and a hug,
Us

Chapter 3
Up Country

Dear Mom and Dad, (alias folks, alias Dottie and Dick),

We are back--and still shaking the dust off after two showers. Paved and in great condition, the two main highways are excellent, but we didn't spend much time on the excellent part. Take six fresh new fish-volunteers-in-training; stuff them sideways into the back of a Landrover on un-padded metal seats; add one hundred plus miles of stop-and-go dusty red-dirt roads in the hot and dry season; shake well and stir violently into all possible potholes before baking and what do you have? One dusty, red-baked bunch. Red hair. Red clothes. Skin permanently tinged. And sore tushies (bums--rears--behinds and bottoms).

But not for naught did we coat our lungs with silty powder. The Provincial Governors seem pleased that we are here and impatient for us to get to work building fishponds. And the people, in particular the kids, were a delight. Everyone was so friendly--waving, laughing and shouting as we drove by, mobbing us the moment we stopped. We wanted so badly to communicate but were forced to endure the embarrassment of interpreters, so we are all anxious to acquire some language skills. For Jim and me, that means wrapping our slow Texas tongues around two new languages that are pure fluid, grace and speed.

* * *

Interesting week. Good word--interesting. We will be using it a lot in correspondence as we have been warned repeatedly not to say or write anything that could be considered controversial about the country, its people or each other as mail is opened and read frequently. Any perceived criticism could get us sent home, and our program cancelled.

* * *

Today, we met the three Peace Corps voc-ed guys who have just arrived. They will be teaching machine shop, heavy equipment and road construction--in classrooms only as there is no heavy equipment available yet.

Interesting crew. Oops. One's already being medi-vac'd out to
Nairobi, poor guy. Appears he ruptured a vertebral disc three days
before arriving here and no hope for him to stay. Too bad, as he seemed
like a nice guy.

The eight math and science teachers Peace Corps expected were
denied entry at the last minute for unknown reasons and have been
shipped elsewhere (no one will say why or where--I hope they show up
somewhere). Interesting. We shall miss them...and we didn't even
know them.

Speaking of language training, we start tomorrow. Then, we can at
last ask important things like,

"Where's the bathroom?"

"I'm lost, how do I get outta' here?"

"Hello"

"Goodbye"

"How do you say "_____" in French?"

"See you next Tuesday"

--And similar profound deep dialogue--with questions by the mile.

Till next time, take care, with love and lotsa hugs,

                          Jim and me,
                          Au revoir

Chapter 4
Immersion

Dear Mom and Dad, alias parents, teachers and friends,

What have we gotten ourselves into? Man, this hard. A boy's technical boarding school (let out for the summer) located some five kilometers outside the small village of Gitega (Gih-tay-gah) is to be our home for the next six weeks.

The moment we stepped off the bus, they allowed no more English. All talk, all questions, everything from morning to morning is in French. It's called Immersion, and might be the best way to learn a language, but they forgot to tell us which way to the bathroom, chow or bed before they switched off the English. Really forces you to learn stuff fast, so you don't go dirty or get locked out of the dorm.

The professors are all Burundian teachers, really smart and super-friendly. (One of the stipulations of accepting our fish program was that Peace Corps would use local professors and support the economy here instead of packing us off to the established language school in Bukavu, Zaire for eight weeks.)

Unfortunately for some of us, the professors don't speak any English and they teach French like they speak Kirundi. You hear the first syllable and sometimes the last, but all the stuff in the middle is connected and run together without enunciation breaks. Oh, yes, and said very softly with the head lowered so you can't lip-read, and the last four or five words of every sentence drops off so you can't hear them at all (even with my super-sonic ears), as that's a part of the culture, a sign of an educated, informed person.

But with the eight new Peace Corps teachers not coming in, we have a two-to-one ratio student-to-teacher, and will have lots of individual attention. So eventually we'll 'get it'. Just hope it's before our two-year tour is up.

Jim and I are the only couple in the group of eight volunteers (Six fishies and two technical teachers for the school). We were assigned the only private room (with a door), while the others will sleep in the gender-divided dormitories of half-walls and half-curtains, along with the professors. Sounds considerate and neat for us, except that we are automatically excluded from the late-night gab sessions and practice conversations in French, which we desperately need for 'ear-training'.

Speaking of ears, Jim has an excellent ear for everything and anything mechanical, numbers or engines, but no ear for languages or music, so learning a musical (tonal) language is especially hard on him. If we had the choice, even now, think we would opt to separate for the duration of language training just to insure no distractions or tension and more practice.

My class may start Kirundi in a week or so, in addition to the French. I keep reminding myself we came to Africa to slow down. Hope it happens. Well, enough of the doom and gloom. A little about where we are:

* * *

First off, we're in the mountains at almost six thousand feet, and is it ever cold. The first three hours of class each morning are frigid and none of us brought enough warm clothes. If anyone had told me last year that I'd be freezing my tushie off in Africa, I'd have said they were nuts. Down to around forty degrees Fahrenheit in the mornings, it only heats up to fifty-five or sixty degrees by noon. Everyone is asking for more blankets.

--**The kamikaze**, no-see-um-mosquitos drive us crazy. They don't bite, or at least you can't feel them, but they have this maddening habit of jumping off the bureau and dive-bombing your ears till the wee hours of the morning. Nniiinnngggg... Nniiinnngggg...

--**Showers:** The showers are outside open-air stalls with privacy walls. Concrete throughout. Very clean. No hot running water. I can't find our pond thermometer, but I'll lay odds the water temperature never creeps above forty degrees F. We splash our faces with a drop or two at the sinks to wake up, but wait till the noon break to bathe.

Even then, it takes some major courage to undress on that cold concrete with the wind whipping round and about, turn on the water and step under dripping icicles. All the teeth chattering is enough to bring down the 'walls of Jericho' and expose everything, and some days we just skip the entire ordeal.

Food: Meals alternate between American and local traditional food. Peace Corps expected double the number of volunteers, so they engaged three cooks, five professors and lots of food.

The Continental breakfast is good and consists of fresh bread, fresh-churned butter, fresh strawberry jam, boiled eggs (strong tasting--not anemic like factory eggs), and hot tea or coffee, and we are learning simple vocabulary for them in both French and Kirundi daily. That's easy--one word at a time. The chore is to string the words together using proper grammar, tense and gender into sentences or questions that makes sense.

Most of the available food offerings are terrific but there is one of the local favorites I'm not yet excited about. While they don't eat termites or grubs as in West and Central Africa, they do eat a tiny fresh-water smelt-like-thing that is sundried whole (as in complete with all the Lord gave them). They're called ndagala (in-duh-gah-la), and they smell like dead, dried fish, which is what they are.

The dead fish are served up with a lump of swelled-up boiled stuff made from manioc flour (man-ee-ahk, same as cassava root in other parts of the world) called fóe (pronounced 'phoo')', but that I call foo-foo, because it tastes and smells like really bad milk after four or five days in the sun (at least to me). They say the taste grows on you and that you don't notice the smell after a while. We'll see. (Some of the volunteers actually like it and have said it's the same thing as poi in Hawaii, but I believe that is made from Taro root, and while the consistency may be the same, I hope the odor and taste are not, as I've always wanted to visit Hawaii.)

At any rate, you scoop off a gooey portion from the lump of foo-foo, dip it in various hot sauces, grab a dead fish, and pop it all in your mouth where it swells up some before you swallow it. Then it swells up some more in your stomach till you think it's going to pop, and the dead fish resurrects and swims half the night.

--On the American side, our food coordinator and a former Peace Corps volunteer, is making up for the foods she missed during her service by serving many-too-much of them to us: pizza, spaghetti, beef stew, and really rich desserts. Even moderating our portions, without exercise we're all getting fatter and bigger, like 'sheeps to the slaughter'.

We've discovered there's a huge variety of local food available, just hope we can afford some of it once we are official volunteers and on a small monthly living allowance: rabbit, goat, beef, chicken, pineapple, avocados, tomatoes, onions, cabbage, beans, plantains, rice, bananas, sour oranges, sour limes, potatoes, spinach (a coarse, hairy variety), lettuce, strawberries, blackberries, mango, papaya, manioc leaves (it tastes like spinach but with a long prep-time to get the cyanide toxins out and yields an astringent cooked veggie similar to wild poke weed or dock), eggs, butter, delicious-and-tart-no-sugar Belgian yogurt, an elongated thin white sweet-potato, and too many more to mention.

Meats are very lean and generally as we expected so we are glad we don't have any bridges or dentures. It also makes us appreciate the Peace Corps requirement for 'good teeth'. (The small-just-right-for-two pressure cooker you sent should really come in handy once we're posted up-country.) The local rice is great, except when they boil it in manioc-flavored water, and then--well--it tastes and smells like upchuck. Yummm.

As sugar is an expensive import, local desserts are few and mostly something to do with fresh fruit. They serve a broiled, candied banana that is delicious--and oh, my favorite--maracuja juice (passion fruit), a delicious drink, strangely and magically distilled from a rough brown-and-round leathery ball filled with large black seeds and small amounts of slimy orange-fruit-stuff. (Have promises from one of the kind Burundian chefs to show me how they make it.)

Avocados are plentiful--in season--tree-ripened, and cost about three cents each. Burundi also grows the best AAA tea and Arabica coffee in the world. We'll send you some of each as soon as we have a free afternoon to walk to town.

Volunteers usually lose weight in language training, and if we were eating only beans and rice with fried termites like the volunteers in Zaire, it might be true, but such is not the case here in our perfect Land of Oz. Please don't worry about us, or our food, unless you want to send diet pills.

We hope to 'tone it down and firm it up' after language school when we have control of our lives once more. But for now, we could each double as the Goodyear blimp!

                              * * *

The ankle-length shirt-dress you made for me, Mom, is perfect for cold mornings and evenings. Many of the women wear something similar called a 'panya', which is just four yards of wide brightly-printed cloth wrapped round and round with an end tucked into the fold. No hems, seams or buttons that I can see. The shirtdress helps me fit in without worrying about sudden exposure if the 'tuck-thing' slips.

I 'slip' it on at night when I have to trek to the 'faire le nécessaire' (fare-luh-ness-is-sare) (out-houses or 'squatters' as they're affectionately called) (and I have been making quite a few trips recently). Two others of our group have not adjusted yet to the local intestinal flora and fauna and had 'it' really bad and have been laid up for several days now. My 'it' is more just a nuisance and dehydrator.

Females are required to wear dresses in class, so I'm glad I brought the one utility brown cotton skirt, but it's wearing out quickly! I'll be so very glad when we are free and at our posted sites so I can wear jeans again. (We were even required to wear dresses to visit potential pond sites--now how does anyone think we're going to ride motorcycles or climb mountains in a dress? And I really don't think I can stay upright to pedal-shift a motorcycle sidesaddle.)

* * *

--**French**--We don't have favorites, because they're all good, but we do have two professors we relate better to, Godance (female) and Barnaby (male), mostly because they are willing to slow their speech way down for us until we comprehend the words and sentences.

But even they laughed today when I said 'j'entendre le poullet a quatre-heure cette matin," which I thought meant, "I heard the rooster at four o'clock this morning." What I really said was, "I heard the dead chicken this morning." Turns out a poullet (poo-lay) is a chicken for eating, with the head, feet and innards gone already. I should have said, "...le chant de coq," (luh-chawnt-deh-cock) the song of the rooster-- Much prettier, yes?

We are all still making lots of mistakes and Jim and I have simply been out of school and in Texas far too long. But the days are moving fast and soon we'll be free.

* * *

The canvas suitcases are showing some wear and tear. Five tons of stuff shoved and pulled daily from under the beds is beginning to wear the threads and zippers out. And no matter what it is we want or need, or where we think we saw it last, it's always at the bottom of the last suitcase we drag out. Murphy's Law is alive and well and living in our bags. We'll be ever so grateful to have a permanent place to hang our hats soon, even if it's a tent.

'Nuff for now. Love and a hug,
Hey You and What's-her-face

Chapter 5
Language Training
July - First Year

Dear Uncle Con and Aunt Dorothy,

Our country is beautiful. Green mountains and long wide valleys are decorated with dozens of rivers, waterfalls, flowers, fields, springs and streams. Though deforestation from population pressure has caused major destructive changes in the ecosystem, reforestation, terracing and better agriculture projects promise to reverse some of the damage.

The huge valley-wide peat bogs may eventually offer an alternative source for cooking and heating fuel, leaving the trees to their purpose of protecting the watershed and producing oxygen instead of becoming charcoal. There's a wild and funny Irish team in-country finishing up two years of testing and documenting to see if a peat project is feasible.

--One would think the air would be clean and pure, what with no major industry and a limited numbers of vehicles. But inversion layers from the mountains trap the smoke from cooking fires, the dust from the roads and hills, and the practice of slashing-and-burning the fields after harvest and leaves the atmosphere in a constant state of hazy blue. Plus the inversion layers are worse in the big dry season (now).

Almost every square inch of arable land is farmed. Erosion, due to torrential rains and lack of terracing, is massive. Their only compost comes from weeds gleaned from the fields, coffee hulls, and straw after harvesting of food crops. There are no commercial fertilizers available (too expensive to produce or import into this remote landlocked country). Tests show, too, that even if fertilizers were available, the soil suffers from excess acidity and high aluminum toxicity. Fertilizers so far, don't look like the solution to the problem.

Aluminum toxicity ties up food receptors on the roots and prevents plants from taking up existing nutrients. Thus, yields are low and the weakened plants are susceptible to disease, plus they are missing essential nutritional elements. No studies done yet on the affect of all that aluminum on the human population. Can't help but wonder what it does to the brain.

The entire family pitches in to do the backbreaking work of hoeing and planting. But economically, the sides and tops of hills are generally reserved for the men's business: cash crops of coffee, tea, manioc, bananas, avocados, pineapples and peanuts.

Women and girls are relegated to the valleys (rich peat bogs that turn into huge papyrus marshes during the rainy season--the season of hunger--so less food can be grown at that time-as it is the bogs where they grow the family staples of rice, beans, peas, and sweet potatoes.

They've recently adapted to growing more umuzungu (u-moo-zoon-goo--stranger, non-Burundian, or white-man) foods to sell in the markets, and thus are learning to eat it themselves. Things like onions, potatoes, tomatoes, parsley, cucumbers, cauliflower, broccoli, cabbage, corn, squash, lettuce, and carrots. But, because mothers are working all day in the fields and because they are generally trying to sell what they can at market for extra income, there are still many malnourished kids (significant poochy bellies, dry, brittle red hair, thin limbs--called kwashiorkor).

Also, the yields here are far less than in many neighboring countries because the pH of the soil is extremely acidic at 2.5 to 4.5 (volcanic), which, along with the aluminum, is also not good for plant growth. The lack of nutritional knowledge, the time to carry it out and poor soil, coupled with horrendous tropical diseases and parasites, finds families all too often attending funerals for their children. Only one in five reaches the age of five. There are almost enough of the right kinds of foods, just a lack of time or knowledge of what to do with it, and lack of a stable economy and support system to encourage change.

* * *

A daily visual event which still amazes us each time we venture out is that everything is carried on the head, balanced on a two to three-inch thick circle of woven grass or banana leaves called an 'ingata' (in-gah-tah). What can't be carried on the head or loaded on a bicycle is too big to worry about.

I can't believe the weight they do carry, though! The tiniest kid will balance a five-gallon jerry can full of water on his head and walk-run straight up a 60-70 degree hill like it was nothing. And we regularly see a guy with ten or fifteen handmade wooden captain's chairs balanced on his head on his way to market. The best one though, was the man with five mattresses, a bed, a table, and a bunch of chairs, headed for Sunday market like he was out for an afternoon stroll. Amazing. Market days are colorful, noisy and the highlight of everyone's week, including ours!

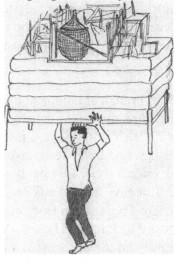

* * *

Our language school is outside one of the few villages, with only ten towns or so in the entire country. Traditionally life was based on individual family 'rugos' (roo-goze) on a hillside with a 'living fence' of trees or brush surrounding the compound of three to six thatched mud-brick huts, and each hill or group of hills was occupied or owned by a particular clan with the valleys belonging to the government.

Even now, for people to use the bottomland for any project, permission must be obtained from a ministry office. The government is also encouraging families to establish and move into small central villages for better distribution of services, and we see the beginning signs of that here and there. But erasing hundreds of years of tradition and culture in a single generation is proving difficult. Time will tell if it is a good thing.

Animals are not traditionally used as beasts of burden. With the Bantu heritage, cattle and oxen are revered as part of one's fortune or money, (and you don't work or eat your money, right?). Thus there are also few carts or laborsaving devices with wheels. Or could it be that no one wants to pull the same heavy loads UP the steep hills as ran-away down them?

We're told that education for the masses is slowly becoming a reality, but with a lack of natural resources, industry or exports, the government can't really afford to over-educate people beyond the country's ability to provide employment.

With over-population and insufficient food production being the two largest problems, education in sustainable agricultural techniques, water management, nutrition, and housing are their number one priorities. The only recent export hope for the economy was AMOCO's oil exploration on Lake Tanganyika, but it doesn't appear to be working out.

* * *

Everything is still in French at language training and we're having a very hard time attuning our slow Texas ears to the Burundian professors, who are wonderful, but VERY soft-spoken, fast-speaking, and their French runs altogether into one long word, just like their Kirundi.

We do get a break once a week for health class, which we present ourselves, in English. Jim gave a good talk on treatment for shock from the First Aid book, Where There Is No Doctor.

My topic was first aid to fractured bones. We made a 6' 4" dummy out of bed sheets, pillows and towels, stuffed a pair of socks for the feet, dubbed him Claude, and he flopped around just like he had broken lots of something's. He was a very cooperative patient and didn't scream much as I demonstrated splinting techniques.

* * *

Some of us have added lessons in the local language of Kirundi, a musical 'Bantu' language with lots of vowels and noun classes, and tonal, like Chinese, so the way you pronounce or emphasize a word can change it's meaning, tense, and distance in time. Verrrry difficult. (Bantu is a sub-branch of the Niger-Congo language system, and contains over two hundred Bantu dialects, the largest of which is Swahili.)

--Don't know where our professors find the patience to deal with our slow learning abilities and Texas accents and not sure that I will ever progress past baby talk in the Kirundi. The French is coming along, but just OK.

Everything else is actually pretty terrific here except for the cultural isolation and lack of news from the outside world. Of course, there's always the radio: the BBC (anti-American), or the VOA (pro-pro-pro-American), and a few French stations (criticize everyone including themselves), but we usually just tire of the static and trying to make out the words and await with great anticipation for the Peace Corps office weekly edition of Newsweek or batch of letters from mail-call to arrive.

* * *

Our immediate boss, Mona, APCD (Assistant Peace Corps Director–everything has an acronym) is great. She is from Oklahoma and the former roommate of your assistant-pastor, Shirley, whom we met at your church. Small world--we traveled 8000 miles to meet a next-door neighbor!) Mona works hard to make things right for the volunteers, buffers us against any and all things political, and has really been encouraging Jim and me to get involved in some small secondary projects in relation to fish culture, just in case our primary objective doesn't pan out or fish won't grow here. Huh?

We trust her, though, and taking her advice, we've been looking up info on growing earthworms, making clay pipes for pond overflows, raising rabbits (meat for families, rabbit poop for composting the ponds or family gardens, rabbit skins for craft-work), tanning hides, and solar projects).

The P.C. office has a terrific micro-fiche library with specifics on just about every kind of development project that we can think of to research, from capping springs to building oil expellers, and digesters that use human waste to produce methane for cooking fuel (a current project in Nepal). Much better than TV.

--So far, the most impressive thing about the country is its people. Haven't seen such an industrious society--ever. They work hard the full twelve hours from dawn to dusk and we have yet to see any attitude of idleness or despair, though they live constantly at the edge of poverty in a life-challenging environment.

The government has a five-year program to double the number of roads, hospitals, schools, teachers and doctors. (Hope it works better than our own government's five-year programs!) Education for the masses may become a reality one day, but their biggest problem is a lack of natural resources. No precious metals or minerals so far, so no big foreign investments or large industries to kick-start the economy.

* * *

Also, if you have an extra prayer handy, the church here could use it (predominately and nominally Catholic). Like most places in the world today--whatever the denomination, the church is finding itself at odds with governments over civil liberties and supreme authority, to the sufferance of both the church and the government, with the people caught in the middle. All are losing out as the lines are drawn for battle over who has the power.

* * *

Is there anything to complain about in this Land of Oz? Oh, well, yes. One or two minor things, maybe. In addition to the frigid showers and a few of the local recipes, there are the school toilets. Definitely not designed with people in mind. (Especially female-type people). They have been constructed in a unique fashion that is guaranteed to make your day:

The 'squatters' as we affectionately call them, are nearly flat, porcelain-covered steel plates imbedded in the ground, with two dimpled footpads on either side and a slight slope to a tiny hole at the back, all surrounded by narrow cubicles of cement walls. Unfortunately, when you turn around, place your feet on the dimpled footpads and squat to do your business, three things happen:

First, ten million huge, dive-bombing kamikaze mosquitos hiding in the shadows home in on your bare bum;

Second, the steel plate makes a perfect splash pan and everything tends to bounce right back up toward whence it came, while very little seems to go down the hole.

And third: it's "LOOK OUT, NOAH!" when you pull the chain to the water tank, because a veritable flood comes shooting out to follow where your feet have been. You feel compelled to dust your behind with repellent before--and take a shower after each trip to the 'petit coin' (petty-qwah, which means little corner--and it is).

Most fun? Three a.m., when you have to crawl out from warm covers, dress, put shoes on, find toilet paper, exit room without waking husband, stumble blindly to facilities in the dark because the flashlight has disappeared again, squat, splatter, stand, flush, wash splattered legs by climbing into large concrete sink and splash with icicle- water, stumble back to room, wake husband with cold wet feet--YIKES--and try to get back to sleep.

Well, enough fun and games for now. Have to go study.

With love and two hugs,
Two Red Bums in Burundi

Chapter 6
Swahili and Frogs
August something

Dear Laura, Bill, and Boys,

Thanks for such a neat letter! Got a kick out of all the kindergarten news.

As for here, four weeks of French has our heads spinning with present and past participles, grammar, tense and gender. Some of us start the local Bantu language of Kirundi next week.

But for the following five days we are visiting fish projects in the country next door, Zaire. Stuffed inside the back of a Landrover on metal benches and facing sideways over rough, red dusty terrain for eight to ten hours is enough to wish for more personal padding.

--After each visit to a volunteer's pond site we are invited to either the farmer's house or a local pub for kasiksi (kuh-seek-see--means banana or sorghum beer):

The banana beer is interesting.

Take tiny ripe sweet bananas (3-4 inches long) and hang them high above the cooking fires in the home hut.

Smoke them for up to a week.

Peel or squeeze the banana juice and fruit out into a huge earthenware pot, drop in a little yeast cake or two, add water and ferment the whole thing for almost a week. The resulting mixture is a milky white liquid with lots of residue on the bottom and thick foamy 'stuff' floating on top.

It tastes a bit like sparkling lemonade and leaves the arms, legs and head feeling warm and fuzzy. It's also somewhat of an insult if you don't partake, so we've learned to accept the offered gourd dipper, blow the 'floating stuff' over to one side, smile and swallow, knowing we must be really boosting our immune systems with all the flotsam and jetsam.

* * *

--We were at a Zaire farmer's pond yesterday when someone spied two frogs in the water in the process of making baby frogs. (Frogs are wicked invaders to a fish farmer because they **EAT FINGERLINGS** (baby-fish) and they compete for some of the same foods as the fish). The volunteer we were visiting asked for a machete from his farmer and, in Swahili, told everyone to step back. Of course, none of us rookie umuzungus (ooh-moo-zoon-goos--means 'whites' or strangers) understood.

We were about five feet away when he sliced the water. Safe distance, right? Wrong. The machete entered at a perfect angle for a wall of water, frog insides, and mud to come flying up, out and all over us. The locals got a big kick out of this and fell on the ground laughing, and to be culturally sensitive we all did the same.

One thing we're finding out--as long as you are not mortally wounded, anything is fair game for ridicule, laughter and making the day fun. Really helps keep the ego in check!

Another thing. We are already weary of being called **umuzungu** (white man) at every turn, as if we had no names or individuality. There's no discrimination made between male--female--European--American--Chinese--we are all lumped into one big category of 'white man' or stranger, as in non-local.

Can now empathize with minorities in the states who are classified as Blacks, Asians, Hispanics, Natives, etc., instead of simply as people worthy of having names, or even just Americans. Somehow it becomes more personal when it's directed at you, and you are made to feel the difference every minute of the day. We will have to come up with an alternative response to keep them laughing and still make the point.

Well, gotta' go now,

Love and a hug,

Us (alias white-men, soon becoming somebodies)

Chapter 7
Death and Taxes

Dear Mom and Dad,

Well, here we are, still in Burundi, still in language training, still shivering through cold showers and still fighting off the mosquitos. The mosquitos, by the way, support equal opportunity in both the regular and the Chloroquine-resistant malaria, so each week we take Chloroquine and Fansidar tablets, which we are told, strangely enough, also affects the melanin in your skin and won't allow us to 'tan', but doesn't protect us from UV rays. Hmmm.

After visiting some fish volunteers in Zaire last week, we are not likely to forget the preventatives. They said if they missed their pills by even a day or two, they'd come down with a weeklong case of bone-wracking malaria. Apparently it rests in the liver as long as you take your medicine. Without, it progresses rapidly to the blood-stream stage, which gives the chills and fever.

Speaking of tired, we are keeping up in training, but the pills seem to make us really tired and for the first time in our lives, we require a full eight hours sleep, or maybe it's because we're on the equator and our blood hasn't thinned enough yet to push the energy envelope?
Once we finish our service and head home, we'll take a triple-dose of a super-drug cocktail for six weeks to get rid of the dormant liver-stage little buggers. The medication is toxic over time, (great, right?) so we have to wait till end-of-tour for this all-in-one dosage.

Let's see--as long as we're talking about death and taxes: We volunteers are asked (not required) to take gamma-globulin (GG) shots on a quarterly basis to keep our immune systems up (they say), and man, are they big injections in the bum--makes a big hard knot there for days! Please let me know your wisdom on taking the GG shots and what if any, are the side affects? Are they necessary or are we being used as guinea pigs? We've already had our second boosters for tetanus, typhoid, yellow fever, cholera and a host of others I don't remember.

We're even taking rabies boosters? Now that's scary. But so far, the
only thing we've seen foaming at the mouth is the two of us after too
much banana beer.

* * *

--One of the things it does hurt to see is the number of polio victims
in the local populace with no source for treatment or rehabilitation, no
braces, no wheelchairs, nothing. (Another project for a volunteer or
Doctors Without Borders). When we asked, we were told the
government has recently begun an obligatory inoculation program for all
childhood diseases and is already seeing a decrease in infant mortality.

My generation forgets how things like Polio, Whooping Cough and
T.B. crippled and took so many lives before vaccinations came along.
Makes sense unless or until it's your child who has a reaction to them?
Still...

* * *

On a lighter note, we had a small talent show one Friday evening.
Jim and I (jimani) donned red bandanas, powdered our faces and hands
with flour and did a mime of two wind-up dolls in a store window with a
'Punch and Judy' twist at the end. Was great fun, but don't think we'll be
quitting our day-jobs--Oh, that's right--we already did!

All of Peace Corps made a short trip this last Sunday, August 18, to
see the National Drummers (Tambourinaires, tam-boor-ee-nairs), who
had just returned from a 28-city tour in Europe.

Twenty or so guys with enormous carved and hollowed out tree-
trunk-drums entered the arena, drums impressively balanced on their
heads on the traditional woven grass circlet called an ingata (in-gah-tah),
dancing, twirling, whacking, drumming and chanting. Had no idea
hollowed wood could make such a phenomenal amount of noise.
Vibrates right through to the soul.

The drums were set down in a semi-circle as the drummers began a
series of individual and duo high-jumping acrobatics while the others

kept up the beat. Wish you'd been here--You would have loved the performance!

Both youth and adult teams practice the same drumbeat all over the country--in schools and for local celebrations. We awaken to the sound of them in the mornings, and on weekends they go long into the night and will be one of the lasting memories we carry home with us.

Hope this finds you both well,

Love and lotsa hugs,

Jimani--white faces becoming volunteers.

Chapter 8
Dull Boring Dodders

Dear Folks,

Guess what? You raised a dull, boring dodder. At least, that's Peace Corps staff's assessment of me and all the other trainees. (Peace Corps hereafter referred to as P.C.) Yep, they say we are too serious; that we don't have enough fun or get into enough trouble; that we only study, study, study, and think about work.

Maybe. But if true, I think it might be because we're an older group (the mean age is 32, and I mean that as an average, not unfriendly). Plus, we're all worried about knowing enough of the language to be accepted not only into the program, but to survive and do well in our work. (If we don't pass language tests, they send us home!)

Well, these dull, boring dodders had fun last night playing cards with some of our professors. We taught them rummy, Euchre, and poker. Most of them picked up on the rules very quickly, but one kept making wonderfully disastrous plays that had us in stitches, (like laying down all his cards to show us a Full House and asking if that was any good--before the bidding began--or bidding the max on a Euchre hand when he had nothing to back it up)--it was great!

Could it have been our instruction? Or maybe it was the consumption of beer purchased from the local 'Boutique Scholaire' (boo-teak scole-air, or bar by any other name) for the soiree (swahr-ay which means party)?

I know what you're thinking: I don't drink beer, but this is pretty good stuff. It doesn't take long to tire of the extra-sweet, (they add a higher percentage of syrup in Africa) sticky hot Coke®, orange, and lemon sodas, and there never seems to be enough filtered water boiled up, so beer fills the space between.

We are also learning to drink beer because almost all important social and political happenings at the local level take place at a bar or on a porch over a bottle of beer. It's the favorite pastime next to playing

soccer or drumming, and our prof's drink it like water with about as much effect. A Belgian brand, made and bottled locally, Amstel is rich and dark and gives me a headache; but the Primus is mild, smooth, and tastes great--even warm. Only trouble is, the Primus comes exclusively in quart bottles and it takes two of me to finish one, else I see two of everything. That night I saw many, many, many of everything.
Better go sober up and study so we'll have time to be lighthearted, gay, and un-doddery next time staff makes a visit.

Love and lotsa hugs,
Jim and Me

Chapter 9
Turtle Tushies

Dear Folks,

    The people are still the most impressive subject here, even better than the food, climate, and sigh...the language.

Industry, enthusiasm and smiles abound. Full of energy, people seem to run everywhere for the sheer joy of it, or maybe it's to keep warm in the 40° F mornings?

    Jim and I walk the three miles (four plus kilometers) into town on Sunday to attend Mass at dawn (six a.m.), and we walk briskly, because it's cold and we like to keep the blood circulating.

    But as fast as we walk, Burundians always pass us. The populace strolls by us as if we were turtles. They have this neat way of disjointing at the hips when they walk, an easy flowing movement that soon shifts into a smooth, rolling sort of gait that just eats up the ground. Even the oldest, weakest elder seems to out-pace us. Half the time they run--for the sheer joy of it--after cars--after bicycles--after us and each other-- calling out hello or "Hey, umuzungus!" for greetings. And laugh, they love to laugh, at each other, at us, at nothing at all. Since we can't seem to disjoint at the hips properly to get the correct rhythm and flow, we have dubbed ourselves **The Turtle Tushies** until we learn to walk properly. Daily practice is the key!

* * *

    In church, the women all sit on one side and the men on the other on long narrow board benches with no backs. We haven't arrived early enough to get a seat on either side so we stand at the back with all the other slowpokes.

    And here's another thing that makes us feel like Turtle Tushies. The church benches appear full, as in jam-packed, without so much as a molecule of space left between individuals. Then some new person will come stand in front of the seated ones and start wriggling and 'scooching' ever-so-slightly side-to-side down toward the bench, and before you know it, they are planted in the middle and no one has fallen off either end. They have the tiniest hiney's I've ever seen. If a westerner were to try it, with our big bums, we would have half the occupants on the floor by the time our tushies touched base and probably start a riot!

Almost all of the Mass is sung in Kirundi (good for them, hard for us), and we haven't understood much yet, but it lasts up to three hours per service so we have plenty of time to try to decipher words, or pray on our own. It all seems very somber and the stand-up-sit-down parts aren't the same as ours, so it's hard to tell where we are in the Mass, or unfortunately, get much out of it.

* * *

Shopping and bargaining in the market after church is our entertainment for the week, and we are finally getting a bit of 'feel' for the rhythm of the language, culture and people.

The best artisan products so far are the women's hand-woven grass 'Tupperware®' storage baskets interlaced with colorful purple, blue, yellow and red zigzag designs. They come in two rounded halves, one half slightly smaller than the other. The smaller half fits into the larger, and snaps shut tight against a woven 'lip' on the upper basket, thus the label, 'Tupperware'® (great for protection against insects in the food). They are sturdy and beautifully crafted so we'll be purchasing them as we go along till we have enough to send home.

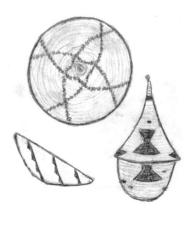

* * *

--Interesting. The outgoing volunteers seem to be leaving disillusioned by the incredible slowness and lack of change they've seen in their two years here (the majority of them were school teachers).

They say they have come to realize that the most they gave or got out of the experience has been in the personal exchanges and relationships, which may or may not equal progress or positive change.

But I think this must be true for teachers anywhere. Tangible results are often difficult to see and not so many students come back to say, "You did good!" or "Thanks Mr. or Mrs.---I learned something".

Jim and I decided before we signed on that we only expected personal growth out of the two years, so we feel we are going to do O.K. Our only expectations right now are in how much we can stretch and grow individually and in our marriage. OF COURSE, we will do our very best for the farmers and the people while we are here, but it's really up to them and the country as a whole as to how they utilize the information. We can only live and work by example and be responsible for our own choices of doing our best when it's all said and done.

                          * * *

--Speaking of French, we have 'beaucoup de Francais' coming out our ears, but mass confusion still reigns with me over the rules and regulations of the language. Jim's doing great now because he understands the structure and only needs to loosen up and unwind his Indiana engineer's tongue.

Me, I speak well enough, just don't know what I'm saying, and tenses are a bear. It makes us both wish that we'd had a liberal arts education or Latin, or even proper English so we'd have some basis for the language, instead of just engineering and biology / chemistry.

                          * * *

Bits and pieces:

--Sports are a big, BIG, **BIG** thing here for the guys of all ages, and the women just keep on working.

--The dry season is still in full swing, which we thought was winter, but our prof's tell us this is the warm season and that when the fall and spring rainy seasons begin it is REALLY cold. I tell you, if the shower water gets any colder, I'm going to order a wet suit. We haven't been able to use our solar shower bag yet because things tend to disappear if we leave them out. Once we have our own abode, with two (required) 'guardiens'--(guard-ee-anz--or a day and night guard), we will be able to use it, maybe.

--The system of day-to-day living here is much like the U.S., and as easy or difficult to work within the boundaries as any bureaucracy, depending on one's attitude and resourcefulness. We're learning yet another language in communicating with both Peace Corps and our local counterparts, the agronomes (ag-ro-nome-zz--the same as our county extension agents--which is sort of what we'll be if we ever graduate language school).

--We traveled to Sunday market in a neighboring village, Kayanza, (Kye-yawn-zah) some 65 kilometers away to help buy vegetables for the school (and also because the driver--a--former Peace Corps Volunteer (ex PCV)--a really cool, sweet guy named Charlie, was looking for a unique kind of hand-knitted stove-pipe hat to take back to the States).

While he was shopping, Jim and I stopped at a vendor's mat laid out on the ground with some very interesting looking 'things' for sale. They were the size of golf balls, a creamy light brown color, compact, hard and some of them were wrapped in dried banana leaves. We asked a wonderfully tiny woman with character written into a sea of weathered lines on her face, in broken French what they were for, but she shook her head, and chattered back rapidly in Kirundi.

We shook our heads, and she picked up a golf ball, tilted her head back and pointed it to her lips, like she was kissing it, indicating, we thought, that it was good to suck on, like candy, maybe? So we haggled over the price for a few minutes (this is expected, as you don't get respect if you don't bargain), finally paid 10 FrBu (Franc Burundian-- about eight cents) and walked away with our prize, all three of us thinking what a good deal we'd made.

We sought out the school secretary later and asked him what it was. Guess what? We'd purchased a hard ball of yeast starter for the sorghum or banana beer. And it comes complete with little insect shells and other good things all wrapped up in a fresh banana leaf. What a neat treasure- -for the Volunteer who has everything!

* * *

--During the dry season (now), farmers and families harvest the grains and legumes (their staples of beans, rice, manioc--same as cassava-- peas, potatoes (both sweet and russet), sorghum and bananas.

This has apparently been a good year so far, with plenty to eat, and there was a good cash flow from the coffee and tea harvests before we arrived (average income of $300 per year per family), so everyone is all smiles.

This is also the season to go visiting and make **lots** of sorghum or banana beer. They carry the jars on top of their heads on two-inch thick circular woven-grass 'ingatas' (in-gah-tas), perfectly balanced, to friends or relatives for a visit. Everyone sits around the jar-pot with long bamboo straws and sips out of it, pulling beer up into the straw, then tilting it and the head back to swallow.

We've been invited to a few sit-downs, though we're still at the Wave and Smile stage, don't know what anyone is saying and haven't quite got the hang of the straw thing yet, with beer flipping and dribbling everywhere. But like the disjointing at the hips while walk-running, we keep practicing.

The sorghum beer tastes sort of like soured coconut milk. Not especially fond of it...yet. Think it must be another one of those 'acquired' tastes--maybe. I like the banana beer better so far.
The bottled Primus and Amstel beer, however, are the best anywhere, warm or cold. With Belgian recipes and clear, crisp Burundian spring water, they are the pride and joy of the country, and both are very smooth and rich.

We are still not used to the foe' (foo-foo), and afraid it will not ever be our favorite. Still smells like upchuck and still swells up in your belly till you think you'll pop--but everything else is near perfect.

The mosquitos (moustiques--moose-teeks) are plentiful in the dry season and are like dive-bombers coming in for a strafing run. We finally installed our mosquito netting over the bed, but they still buzz loudly against it all night. We awaken each morning to see the net covered with a polka-dot rash of hungry little bodies, most on the outside and patiently awaiting our emergence, and well--you can't stay in bed forever.

--Can't get over the natural beauty of this country. It's like something in a magazine from paradise. Each succeeding day tops the one before with spectacular sunrises, even better sunsets, and exotic colors everywhere. Even the air seems to be a different color. We can't wait to send film home for developing and hope it captures even a portion of what we're seeing with our eyes and hearts.

--The one thing we are anxious to receive is our motorcycles (hereafter referred to as 'motos') so we can go exploring a bit and truly get to work.

--We just had our second rabies booster and the moon is full, so better go now. We are off to the dungeon to study.

With love and lotsa hugs,
Hey you and What's-her-face

Chapter 10
Popeye

Dear Bill and Theola,

HEY! Hurrah! We're almost finished! (As in 'done in'). Yep, we can almost speak the language now:

"Parlez vous Francais?"

"Mai oui, madame, monsieur. Je le parle tres bien, maintenant. J'espere a faire le bon travail."

In other words, we can find the 'petite coin' (little corner or toilet or Water Closet or bathroom) now, with almost no problem. It remains to be seen if we can build fish ponds in French or even in clay.

The local language of Kirundi still hasn't progressed much past baby talk. Beautiful, musical, and complex, it has twenty noun classes and everything in a sentence changes with the noun's gender, plus it's tonal like Chinese, so depending on inflection you can say the same word twenty different tiny ways and get into trouble for nineteen of them!

* * *

Speaking of being understood, last week our language-school secretary approached Michael and Dann (two of the fish-volunteers) with a list of American idioms he wanted translated. Imagine trying to explain the following to someone with no knowledge of our culture or humor and just learning American English:

Popeye

The Incredible Hulk

Hells Angels

Gimme a BLT and hold the mayo

Hit the road Jack!

Gimme a break!

Chill out

Put that in your pipe and smoke it

Crazy as a bedbug

Goobers
Rough as a cob
Between a rock and a hard place
Never thump a free watermelon
Gotta' go see a man about a dog

We had more fun trying to explain them to the 'stage (stahh-jeh or language-school) Secretary and the professors in terms of their culture and with our inhibited language skills.

*   *   *

--Thanks for sending the information on raising earthworms! It is just what I wanted. P.C. has a great microfiche library of appropriate technology: solar ovens, solar hot-water heaters, grain mills, oil presses, water wells, construction, and bridges, but I couldn't find anything on earthworms as an alternate source of protein for the fish.

Our P.C. fisheries chauffeur, Girard, fell on the ground laughing when I first told him I wanted to start a worm farm. (Chauffeur, you ask? We are not allowed to drive vehicles until after training, and even then, we'll be limited in general to the motos due to insurance and liability problems, plus, we have no desire to spend any time in a Burundian jail--as the driver always seems to be at fault no matter the circumstances.)

--Back to our story: Realizing I was serious about the worms, Girard was truly bemused. You see, myth and tradition have it that worms cause blindness by squirting a poison at their attacker! The source of the myth appears to originate in a giant snake-like thing that resembles a night crawler, but is a foot long and an inch thick, and its secretions can apparently cause severe eye irritation.

If its smaller cousins prove easy to raise and the cost of building a worm bed low enough, and if they are acceptable to the farmers, I may try to introduce them into our program next year.

Best go for now. In the meantime, think worms!

Love and a hug,

Jim and Me

Chapter 11
Beer and Church

Dear Theola and Bill,

Woe is us, (or is it we?) well, never mind, we are still in language training, and the initial excitement has worn off. It's not only our luggage that's showing some signs of fraying around the edges. One major cross-cultural barrier we've discovered is that Burundians are rarely quiet.

They appear to be mostly extroverts born into large, noisy families in small homes where everyone talks at once and the concept of 'quiet time' is completely foreign and even uncomfortable to them. Thus, they think nothing of carrying on to all hours of the night in the dorms while we're all trying to study or sleep. I believe one of the worst punishments they can think of is to have to be quiet or still for any length of time. And they are so full of life, laughter and questions it's hard to say no, but sometimes we simply have to.

* * *

Thanks so much for the care package with all the goodies! Only one small request? Please don't list the contents and value for the post, and please don't insure. We had to pay $45 U.S. dollars import taxes for the calculators and earthworm pamphlets. If you'll just put educational material and personal items on the outside, we've been assured we'll receive most things without duty charges.

The M&M's® are great and being enjoyed by all, a real treat but we're being selfish and saving the Kool-Aid® till we're on our own up-country.

* * *

We took a fish trip to neighboring Zaire a few weeks ago to discuss fisheries problems with U.S. volunteers, and got to spend two nights at a language center with HOT WATER! Forget the fish--we soaked in a warm tub for an hour (no showers)--then tried their cuisine of rice with termites. Yummm. Does NOT taste like chicken, but we were happy not to see any of it still squirming, and called it protein.

The other two nights we spent in sleeping bags on the ground at volunteer's houses and splash-bathed in streams that were at least as 'fresh' as the showers at our own language school. Brrrrr.

During the day we ate dust in the back of the Landrover, bouncing over bumpy red-dirt roads or climbing up and down steep mountainsides to look at ponds. It's the 'dry season' and everything turns red here after awhile, clothes, hair, skin, food, eyes, lungs. Not sure even the powerful local bleaching soap, OMO will get our stuff clean again.

--Best part? We attended Mass in Swahili at a local baked-mud-brick cathedral with a tin roof. What a beautiful experience. Not the somber, conservative services we've come to expect. Hands and voices lifted up, the congregation here sang and danced for almost an hour before twelve altar boys and the Bishop danced gracefully and slowly up the aisle to the music provided by two electric guitars that sounded like flutes--drums and metal mariachis, with a packed congregation that sang, chanted and swayed to the beat.

The whole service rose and fell in rhythmic beauty, then swelled to the climax of the offering of the gifts and sharing of the bread three hours later. You could see it in their eyes, feel and hear it in their voices, the closest thing to Spirit we've felt in a long time. We were just readying for Communion when our P.C. driver, Mateas, tapped us on the shoulder and said it was time to go--that the truck couldn't wait for us. Oh, me, and au revoir. The service was still beautiful and we will carry it with us forever.

* * *

On our last day in Zaire, we visited three farmers out in the bush, walking past mud brick huts with thatched roofs and drank lots of kasiksi (banana beer), which was the farmer's way of showing appreciation for our visit and even our questionable input (what do WE know, we haven't even started work yet!). At one place we were invited to a local bar, a small mud-brick building with low ceilings and whitewashed walls.

As we ducked into the doorway, the first thing that caught the eye was a four and a half foot tall mural of the George Foreman/ Muhammad Ali fight, with the date, rounds, and the winner. (Guys and their sports!)
On the back wall was a mural of a Mermaid (a symbol of good fortune throughout Africa). Our host proudly informed us that most mermaids wear wristwatches, but that his did not and that made her very special.

Never did hear or figure out why--but interesting, yes?

The final mural was of the battle for independence from the Belgians twenty-five years ago and reminded us of how young the countries are in this region, and still struggling to define themselves and who they are.

* * *

--We crawled back into the Landrover that evening with its two inches of red dust and wound around some heavily rutted twenty kilometers (seemed three times that far) through dense jungle to the exact middle of nowhere, where we arrived at a guardhouse with a divided exit and entrance, a tall wrought-iron security fence and well-groomed grounds beyond. The armed guard indicated that it would be an excellent idea if we chose to sign his guest book, which we did and he allowed us to pass.

We drove past large, mostly deserted scientific research buildings abandoned by the Belgians and occupied now by a handful of Zaireois (Zy-ear-wah) scientists who we discovered are still hanging on in hopes the government will eventually find money for them to continue their agricultural-research. Not likely. Very sad waste of talent and education.

As we pulled up in front of a beautiful European-style 'hunting lodge' a lovely smiling man bounded out to welcome us saying, "Oh, so you've arrived? Good." (Traditional Swahili manners whether you were expected or not, like greeting you in the mornings first thing, with "Oh, so you're awake!" as if they'd been waiting on you to wake up for hours.)

We entered a beautiful deserted place where we were the only guests. The interior was old-world exquisite with fifteen to twenty-foot-high vaulted ceilings, intricate hand-carved oak, cherry and walnut furnishings, polished terrazzo tile floors, crystal, china and eight linen napkins for our party of ten. As an artist, I drank in the fine craftsmanship, but still couldn't help wonder how many 'workers' (either slave labor from here or imported artisans?) had been used to build it? We washed up, sat and ordered from the extensive menu--two steaks, one chicken and seven braised beefs.

What we got were two chickens, five beefs and three steaks, because this is what they had. Very tasty and we didn't have to do the dishes, while an old piano with two young players banged out Auld Lang Syne for our dinner enjoyment. The only reminders that we were even in Africa was the massive stone fireplace which had been painted the Party colors of bright chartreuse-green and white, and the standard servings of beans and rice in place of salad and vegetables.

We also learned there was a German zoological research camp not far away, higher up in the mountains and hope to return on our vacation to view the mountain gorillas, cross-mountain cousins to the ones Dian Fossey is working with in Rwanda.

Rumors also reached our ears of a small herd of wild mountain elephants (smaller versions of their savannah cousins) and a last wild band of chimpanzees close by.

* * *

Dinner and quiet laughter provided a good end to a good five days, but we're back in Burundi again and trying to complete the last requirements in our language courses--will we ever be done?
Hope this finds you both doing well, and thanks for holding down the many details of our lives in Texas.

Love and hugs,
Jim & Anita

Chapter 12
Worms

Dear Carol,

There we were, just the two of us. Me, with my abysmal French and bantu-baby-talk, and our P.C. driver, Girard (who has the patience of Job, but laughs a lot more; thin, wiry, Burundian, very protective), bouncing along rutted backwater roads.

I'd been looking forward to my first excursion 'alone' into the bush (as in no other white folks) for weeks. Girard and I crawled up into the Land Cruiser after classes Saturday and headed for a valley with an old abandoned Belgian lake. We surprised a group of boys skinny-dipping, which sent them racing for their clothes as we drove up. Once dressed, they quickly surrounded us, demanding to know what we wanted and how could they help and how much did it pay?

When I told them I wanted to dig up some worms they went hysterical, till I said I'd pay five Francs-Bu per dozen, a small fortune for them.

Trampling us in their haste to pull out washtub, buckets, and shovels from the Land Cruiser, they were off in a flash. Clods of dirt and mud flew through the air along with not a few worm parts. They only slowed when I told them I had to have the worms alive and whole and wouldn't pay for pieces.

Allowing me the grace to struggle with the language, Girard laughed till tears ran down his face while my newly found crew and I sorted, sized, accepted and rejected.

A group of adults suddenly materialized from thin air and asked what we were doing. The kids explained I was raising worms for fishing, and the elders fell to the ground laughing (guess that's where the kids get it from). Girard added to the merriment by telling them I actually had a home built for the worms in the school garden. This sent them into absolute hysterics, but they kept a close watch to make sure

the insane umuzunga didn't make a sudden move for the shovels. I
suppose none of them wanted to end up as worm fodder.

Mud-splattered and happy, I thanked and paid off my fine workers,
helped Girard load the precious cargo into the truck and bid the kids and
elders a "Turabonanye" (tour-ah-bow-non-yay--a polite good afternoon).

As we drove off, the kids ran alongside demanding to know when
we would be back. Said they could have a whole army of cohorts ready
to dig up the valley.

Girard suddenly slammed on the brakes, jumped out, and plucked
off the six or seven kids clinging to the back fender and roof and angrily
began chasing them off with a stick. I was surprised at his
uncharacteristic violent reaction until he explained that if a child is hurt
by a vehicle, the driver is always at fault and could go to prison--
forever--if he first survives the immediate wrath of the family.
Something for all of us to definitely keep in mind. Can't build many
ponds in jail or from heaven.

* * *

Arriving back at school, I planted my worms in their newly
constructed home, then watered and fed them daily for a week; pleased
so many were still alive.

But one day, I could find no activity. I dug down, and kept digging.
No sign of even a single worm. I dug up the whole bloomin' bed and
still found nary a one. Then I saw the track--just a small path coming in
from the grass and weeds around the garden. A track only an inch wide
where all the grass had been trampled down, or cut--but by what? Down
on hands and knees, I pushed the grass aside and followed the trail for
some fifty feet and finally discovered the marauders. Plunderers.
Pillagers! A band of roving army ants had marched in and carried off
every last worm. Drats.

--We had a short service out there in the garden, Jim and I, for my
poor innocent victims. Those brave, courageous, legless, squirmy
things. Never to have their day in the sun or a fish's mouth. Oh, woe is
me.

Guess I should have followed the bottom-line "Oh, by the way," advice
in the literature and built a bed above ground with the legs planted in
cans half-full of water and a skim of oil to keep the ants out. Live and
die and learn.

Unfortunately, there's not time enough to start another bed here at
the school. I'll think about building one after we are posted up-country
and have the right tools, time, and money to construct a proper home.

Then, once again the battle cry will resound down hallowed halls:
Think Worms! Think Worms! Think Worms!
Gotta go study, Love and lotsa hugs
Jim and Me

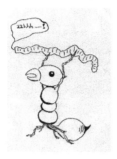

Chapter 13
Almost Done
July/August First Year

Dear Carol,

Not being ones to lay guilt trips, we won't tell you we have been waiting every day for a letter, but alas, alack, my baby sister has fallen off the earth. I've received **three** letters from Mom, all on the same day with news of your trip to Europe (sort of, no details) Dawn's new job and De's trip to California.

Things are still pretty busy here, no slow time. Finding it harder to think and write in English, our heads are so full of French and Kirundi. The result often is Franglais (frawn-glay--a mish-mash of Anglais--English--and Francais--French--with a bit of Kirundi thrown in), which doesn't make sense to anyone.

We are despairing of ever speaking Kirundi well, the more we learn about it. When "Have a good day" can be mistaken for "You stink a lot", there's bound to be trouble. We decided to start with a few simple words (forget about sentences--it's baby-talk for us) that can't be easily misunderstood, like itangi (pond), or kwimba (dig), kwubaka (construct), umugezi (source of water) and ifi or amafi (fish).

The only problem with even these simple words, is that they change (conjugate) with each person (I, you, he, ours, yours, them, etc.) Also, all of the nouns change every time you use a different adjective. Thus, "uwo mwana akunda ifi nini cane'," becomes plural with "abo bana bara kunda ifi nini cane." Huh?

Well, enough already. Suffice it to say, that with two full languages to learn we haven't been into a lot of mischief. In addition, we've each been asked to give short presentations in class to stretch our vocabulary and pronunciations.

Jim gave a great demo on salmon spawning, and a second more animated one on the state of Texas and our problem with armadillos digging up the flower beds for grubs and worms in summer. Had everyone in stitches with his summer score and illustrations, Armadillos-0, Garden Hoses-5. It was a big hit.

I gave one yesterday on the use of solar energy in Burundi with a short demo on how to construct a solar oven with cardboard, tin foil and insulation for about $15.00. It achieves upwards of 325 to 350 degrees F, and you can bake pizza, cakes, bread and casseroles in it. (Though still way too expensive for our farmers, it could work for a volunteer--as electricity and ovens are in short supply).

I also gave diagrams for a solar water heater with an explanation of the principles behind it. (You think it's not difficult to explain the 2nd Law of Thermodynamics in French?) Threw in a lot of cartoons and the French name of the oven design, "Avare comme Harpagon", which translates 'tight like Scrooge', because it gets the most for the least money.

--Good News! We were finally given our posting assignments. Guess they wanted to wait and see if we'd make it. Jim and I will be in a small village called Ngozi (in-go-zee), the farthest volunteers from the capitol of Buja, which suits us just fine. We won't be in P.C.'s hair and they won't have to worry about us often. (Ha! Whom am I kidding? The grapevine of news and gossip moves faster here than the speed of sound, so I doubt we'll be able to even kick-start our motos without it being reported.)

--We had a cross-cultural session yesterday that was supposed to demonstrate how to hire kitchen help and night guards (since everything around the house has to be done from scratch and washed or boiled to keep the critters out of clothes, food and house, and we apparently won't have time to cook, clean or wash once we start work--plus our host country expects us to support the local economy with household help, even on our meager salaries).

But in class, one of the school cooks was so excited to teach us how to interview for kitchen help that he ran away in Kirundi and we couldn't understand a thing he said. The prof who interpreted for us also spoke such rapid French, to keep up with the cook, and so softly that it didn't do us much good either. So, we're back to flying by the seat of our pants and counting with our fingers.

* * *

You asked about the four other 'fishies'?

Dann, from Tennessee, Washington D.C. and parts unknown: mid-thirties, ex-catfish farmer, loves to party, drink beer and have fun. Good sense of humor, hard worker, nervous as a cat, slender, blue eyes and the second-most conservative, though not above a bit of mischief or a practical joke. Spoke no French, like Jim and me, but he's picking up on it faster than us, maybe because he's in the dorm with the prof's? His parents joined Peace Corps at the same time he did and are in the Caribbean teaching, as we speak. Neato.

Mary, from D.C., late twenties, beautiful, tall, slender, dark brown Cleopatra hair cut, city girl who's going to do just fine as a fish farmer. Really sharp and funny wit, smart, hardworking and practical. We like her a lot. She'll be posted in the strawberry, blackberry and vegetable growing region, so we hope we'll be seeing her often. She had four years of French in college, so has no trouble with the language.

Michael, from Tennessee, biologist, mid-twenties, spent two years in France, so also has no trouble with the language and is tackling Kirundi with enthusiasm. Somewhat of an enigma. Blue-eyed, bearded, a rebel against most authority, yet tows the line when he's around elders he respects. Always ready to take the other side of a discussion just for fun. Likes hard rock and sports. Don't know him well yet as he seems to have written us off because of our age or maybe the amount of luggage we brought (temporarily, we hope). Have no doubt though, that he will do exceptionally well as a volunteer. Has the personality and work ethic for it.

Sarah, early twenties, from Minnesota: Younger, smaller and rowdier than the rest of us, cute, punk rock spiky, light-brown hair with a tiny braid in the back. Witty, loveable, likes to watch over everyone, super-smart, picks up on technical things quickly and sees the bright side to everything. Also super-competitive--and very funny, though her laugh could break the sound barrier. It took a while for us to catch up with her speech patterns and realize she doesn't speak in complete sentences (not her problem--just shows our age gap!)--Like, great, man, ya know, that thing? We've since determined her mind is moving so fast that her words can't keep up (again, shows our age gap or maybe just a faster, upper mid-west mind vs. slower Texas?). She was already fluent in Spanish, so is rapidly picking up on the French, and with her boundless passion, ready smile and energy, should be great at her job.

--They are all very tired of us, and each other, and of being cooped up. Everyone is ready to head up-country to their assigned post for work and some 'away-from-each-other-time'.

Well, enough. We are both well, if weary of our total (twenty weeks) five months of fish and language studies and ready to work up some callouses somewhere besides our tushies.

Take care, with love and hugs,
Jim and Anita

Chapter 14
Hogs and Motos Don't Mix

Dear Mom and Pops,

Hello again. Well, our final exciting week of training is in the bustling capitol city of Bujumbura, before we each head up-country to our respective postings. (We packed up and left the language school in Gitega behind to relocate in Buja because the boys' school is starting and they needed their quarters back)

We've had a full schedule that's been revised at least once a day because of the way things 'don't work' (just like home, so no worries). Have had too many 'dead spaces' of hurry-up-and-wait, wait-and-hurry-up, with excess time for the things that don't matter so much and not nearly enough time to cover the things that do. Still feels like 'training' for the real stuff of life. Like yesterday:

We were to have four hours of motorcycle maintenance instruction (instead of the one week originally scheduled), and to become instant experts. I was placed with the other two women for the first session and the three guys got the second session. Both of my gender compatriots are fun, neat people and fast learners, but they are also both city-folk and I think they may never have done anything mechanical--whatsoever.

We're talking basics here, like which direction a nut tightens or loosens. They caught on quickly though, and we did fine with the clutch and brake cables, but popping the chain off to fix a flat tire on the back wheel was like auditioning for a role in The Keystone Cops, as they'd never used pliers and had trouble gripping them at the end of the handles for leverage and strength, made worse as we all three turned 'girly' and got a case of the giggles.

Our poor instructor, Eddie, didn't know what to do as we collectively put three new holes in an old tire tube and two in a new one with the tire tools trying to seat the bead around the rim. Each time we'd approach the finish line and wedged the tool in for one last bite to put the rubber in place, you'd hear this 'SSSSSsssssssssss' sound...and there we were again. One of our intrepid trio lost her grip and balance and pitched forward onto her head into Eddie's lap. I thought he was going to cry.

Then it was the guys' turn. Fortunately, we three were allowed to sit through their session to observe. They learned all the stuff we hadn't had time to 'mess' with. You know, the little, unimportant things, like cleaning the carburetor, checking and changing the oil, pistons, spark plug, brakes, clutch, choke, mysterious wires, etc. All those pesky, nice little what-cha-ma-call-its that make the thing go Vrrooomm.

--Lesson completed, we were all on a high until we learned that we wouldn't have motos for the first month on post. (By that time we'll have forgotten--lots.) Our P.C. Director smiled as she said she wanted to make sure we get 'the feel of the land' on foot first? (Ha! Don't believe it! The grapevine--which travels faster than a speeding bulletin) says our motos, ordered long ago to be here in plenty of time for our arrival, are still stuck in transit somewhere between here and the Ugandan war front.)

Oh, well, walking is probably a good idea, anyway. We're all fattened up from the lack of physical activity, too much food and beer. We'll be happy to embrace life on 'post' with a regimen of steady exercise and a limited diet for a while.

Another news bite: we will also receive a two-thirds **reduction** in pay once we're sworn in as volunteers instead of trainees (stagiaires), and here we hadn't even realized we'd been living high-on-the-hog.

--Speaking of hogs, there aren't many here. (Certainly no Harley's.) They are considered dirty (unclean) (the animal, not the moto), as in trichinosis disease.

That's another lesson we're learning. Change versus tradition can be difficult to accept, or even the idea of change. If they've done without it so far, they may not see the need for anything new, unless it's transportation or funding for projects. That's a big adjustment for us coming from the U.S., where change, movement and the 'latest things' are king.

--All is also not so perfect in our paradise. Because it's such a small country and the populace is very conservative, and ours is the first program allowed out working directly with the people, our directors are protecting the program by imposing several restrictions on us once we get to post (of course, we hear our work position here is tenuous at best, so there may be good reasons for the many rules and we just don't know them yet).

We are not allowed to ride our motos (if they ever arrive) in Buja, or for that matter, out of our own assigned Province (county) to see other volunteers. We are also not allowed weekends away from our posts without permission, and even then it counts as days of vacation.

...Oops, amend that statement; we just returned from a policy session and it turns out we can catch a local bus for a day's visit to other volunteers--once in awhile--with permission. Also, we can travel down to Buja once a month--again on the bus, for sanity, groceries or money from the Bank (which we've discovered is a half to an all-day stand-in-line process with folks who press and push and cut in line and who don't queue the same way we do at all.

And the motos? It turns out Mona (our boss) and her boss, (Chris) had to fight hard for us to get motos at all. There have been too many accidents throughout all of Peace Corps' countries, and Washington is threatening to take them away altogether. One guy was medi-vac'd from here last year with a broken neck after driving through an unexpected road barrier at night. It was set a little high off the ground.

* * *

Speaking of banks and money, we really have to be careful with cash. It takes a half-day of standing in line (a queue) to obtain it at the bank and then it spends like play money because it takes so much of it to buy anything. (The first attempt cost us a full day and the bank closed before we reached the front of the line--others kept squeezing in ahead of us--, but we enjoyed people-watching, practicing our language skills and learned something new.)

We will receive $130 U.S. dollars per month (very high by P.C. standards, but this is an expensive, landlocked country, so it's still on par with other countries). Example: a galvanized bucket is $350 Francs or 3 to 8 large colorful paper bills--which translates to approximately $3.50 U.S.; a small block of cheese (1/4 lb.) is $640 Francs or $6.40 U.S., so we won't be buying much umuzungu (white man) foods.

* * *

--We just heard a fun story from Todd, one of the voc-ed teachers in training with us. Big guy, (6'3", 220 lbs.), young, from the upper Midwest, who was supposed to teach heavy equipment operations, but surprise, no heavy equipment available in-country for another two years, so they placed him teaching auto mechanics, which he claims he knows very little about. As part of his orientation, they sent him up-country by bus to meet the director of the vo-tech school and his fellow teachers.

Now this guy never seems to sleep, talks ninety miles a minute and is wound up like a two-year clock on every subject you can think of (don't get me wrong, he's very bright, absorbs tremendous amounts of information, is well-informed, funny and interesting, just a bit excited and overwhelming for our slow Texas ways).

There also wasn't much room for someone his size on the bus, so he said he climbed to the back and sat down on a huge sack of potatoes. He doesn't speak Kirundi (yet), and the other passengers couldn't understand his French or English, so he got bored and went to sleep on the potato sack. An hour later, he woke up some 30 kilometers past his stop, with the potatoes and half the people on the bus disappeared and gone.

We're still trying to figure out how they lifted him up, took the potatoes, set him back down without waking him and left him with all his belongings intact.

Oh, and his latest favorite French word is 'incroyable' (on-croi-ah-bull), incredible), which so far matches our own impression of the country and its people.

* * *

Bits and pieces:
--Each day seems to bring a new emotional roller coaster ride. Just learned today that there may not be any money for our fish project? The funding agency apparently found other uses for the money allotted to the fish program--a private agency--not Peace Corps, which was another surprising thing we learned. The U.S. government pays to train and send us here, but doesn't support the actual programs we are here to teach?

Not all, but many Peace Corps Directors and APCD's (assistant PCD's) apparently spend much of their time scrambling for private donors Stateside to fund the various projects. What a sad thing. And poor them, having to spend as much time as fundraisers as they do internal administration and volunteer support.

We will be OK for a month or so because our local P.C. office has borrowed enough to keep the program going, hopefully, until they can find alternative funding. Not sure what that means, but keep those cards and letters coming in case we wake up in another country some morning, like the poor group of teachers who were cancelled before they even arrived.

--Just FYI, the White House band currently receives more funding than Peace Corps, and Congress spends more on their magazine subscriptions than on the total Peace Corps budget. Go figure. The things you learn when you are not looking.

--Even after two months in-country, we haven't adjusted to the twelve-hour days on the equator. The sun pops up at six a.m. sharp, bright and shiny, works all day, then goes down at six p.m.--poof, all of a sudden, somebody turned the lights off. And it is instant dark, no twilight, no warning, just braille or a flashlight. Makes for long evenings, especially if you haven't found your way home before then.

--We've discovered we get to cook off these weird charcoal things (sort of like an upside down hibachi), called 'Imbabulas' (im-bah-boo-lahs), which don't look all that friendly, so we're thinking of building a small brick oven for bread, casseroles, etc., and fuel it with local peat. Grand plans, yes?

--We are grateful for the small pressure cooker you sent, Mom, just not sure how we're going to fuel it, yet. And if it hadn't been so heavy, I'd have brought our ancient, hand-crank, table-mounted food grinder. So far, all the meats and some of the veggies from the local markets (not the white-man stores), need processing a bit more to be chewable, except the rice--maybe, even with our great teeth!

--Tomorrow, we journey out on a Greek boat for a night of fishing on Lake Tanganyika. They don't speak French or English and we don't speak Greek or Swahili (yet), so it should be a very interesting trip. Not to worry, they keep telling us it will be okay as long as we can all swim well.

--Remember Jim and fish training back stateside? He was one of three guys who were natural sinkers, and the only way those three passed the one-hour survival 'float test' was to sink to the bottom of the swimming pool and then push off to come up occasionally for air. Well--Lake Tanganyika is verrry, verrry deep at 4,823 ft., so he's been practicing holding his breath.

On that cheery note,
Love and hugs,
Jim and Anita
* * *

P.S. --Remember The African Queen, with Bogart and Bacall? Well, the lake in the movie is this one, right here, Lake Tanganyika, and the German boat they 'blew up' is really a ferryboat, still in use on the lake and looks almost exactly as it did in the movie (pre-blow-up). Neato.

Chapter 15
School's Out!

Dear Folks, alias Mom and Dad,

Yippppeee! We are officially through with training. Life before ten weeks of fisheries and another ten weeks of language training seems an eternity plus two eons ago. At the moment, it is difficult to remember any life before, or fathom there might be something after, the present moment being all we have.

We had our 'Swearing-in Party' to become bona-fide Volunteers this evening (September 20th). Both host-government and American officials attended and it was 'heady', but our French is apparently still abysmal. Didn't think it was so bad until someone from the local Ministry of Waters and Forests visited with us in French for twenty minutes, then said,

"We are so very glad you are here, but I really don't know how you are going to work when you don't speak French."

Our French was so bad, he thought he was speaking English the entire time!

Talk about deflating any semblance of accomplishment! What a bummer. But, what the hey, we can only improve from here, right? (We were surprised to find that the other volunteers met with similar reactions. Since we consider them heads above us in pronunciation and vocabulary and we all passed our FSI--Foreign Service Institute) competency tests, and our professors can understand us, it must just be our slow, harsh, non-musical American accents?)

* * *

We head up-country to our post day after tomorrow! Hurrah! We have a good group of volunteers, but after spending day and night with each other for five unsolicited months, we are all ready to get to work and be apart for a while.

* * *

Shopping with our settling-in allowance at the market took all our time and energy today. Talk about haggle-city. These people love to drive a bargain. It's all a big game involving lots of shouting, laughing, jostling and fist shaking (they count with their hands and fists). Jim is great with it and they loved him. Me, they are not so sure about. I don't haggle enough and I'm way too quiet, so mostly I pointed and Jim haggled. We bought pots, pans, dishes, household supplies, and food staples that we are told we can't get up-country.

rimwe   kabiri   gatatu

kane   gatanu   icumi

Our two biggest 'finds' of the day were the tiny one-burner kerosene stovelet--and the small charcoal brazier (imbabula--im-bah-boo-lah--which most local people use to cook on). The imbabula looks like the kind of thing that could develop a name, a history, and lots of stories really quick if it only half tried, and the kerosene stovelet is for emergency days when we can afford the fuel and don't feel like charcoal.

Good tools were hard to find and we had to settle for a 'finishing saw' with very fine, small teeth, one hammer and a pair of pliers. We brought our own screwdrivers and one good German carving/chopping kitchen knife from our collection, which we guard with lock and key.

* * *

Health/Sante' (sahn-tay): We have learned not to go barefoot anywhere and to wash and check our feet after we've worn sandals or been to the market. 'Jigger' worms infest the soil via animal droppings then burrow up into your feet, toes and nails to lay eggs. There's a special way to dig them out to prevent them from spreading, and does it hurt. One nailed me in language training but we caught it before it grew too big. Poor Michael, one of the other 'fishies', discovered a huge one this morning that nearly took over his entire toe. Watching our APCD's housekeeper dig it out was ghastly and must have hurt like a bear. Yuchhh! Worse than dead grapes!

Local farmers get them all the time because, for the most part, they have no shoes. There are also hookworms in the soil, which I have absolutely no desire to experience, so will continue to wear shoes and socks, I do believe.

Bon, enough lore and gore on the local wildlife. Other than taking weekly pills to guard against malaria, and encountering a few worms, everything here seems quite safe and healthy. Jim's had no problems and I've only had dysentery once, but that was my fault for eating salad from a 'non-approved' moving outdoor cafe.

Live and learn quickly.

With love, lotsa hugs, and no bugs,

Jim and your #3

Chapter 16
Free at Last!

Hey you guys!

We made it! We were driven up the twisty, turny, up-and-down climbing road to Oz, otherwise known as the burgeoning village of Ngozi (In-go-zee), gratefully riding the seventy kilometers up into the clouds to an altitude of six thousand feet and freedom.

The P.C. driver located our house and we found it filled with activity inside and out. Two guys were slapping white paint on the thin cement-veneer-over-mud-brick-on-the-outside with enormous whitewash brushes, while a virtual army of men threw water on the green cement floors inside, splattering blue walls in the process with bright red mud-water. Two guys with brooms-without-bristles swiped irregularly at the mounds of red mud tracked in by the army. The resulting collage of mud, wet feet, wet brooms, and flooded floors did wonders for the fresh paint, like a watercolor-wash painting--quite pretty actually.

We hauled our stuff in, locked them in the only lockable room and promptly accompanied our P.C. Director and her Burundian counterpart to meet our Governor, then were dropped back off at the house filled with strangers with an "Au revoir!"

We pulled our belongings back out in the middle of the least-flooded room, and looked around. There were no locks on the many windows or the back door. The chef (French for head honcho) of the workers was sweet and enthusiastic and spoke non-stop telling us why things weren't finished and what didn't work, guaranteeing us the problem of locks or anything else we could think of, would be remedied within the week.

We finally shooed the workers out--again with thanks, assuring them we'd finish the cleanup job ourselves, sat on our huge bags full of elephants in the middle of the flooded floor, and breathed a sigh of relief. For two full minutes.

Then, what seemed like the whole village began dropping by to check us out. Locals usually go strolling or visiting most evenings and on this particular evening, they all just happened to be in our neighborhood. Our next door neighbor wanted to know if we had a stove, electricity, and/or running water, and strangers asked to look in our bags to see what we had brought them from Europe, and by the way, where was the beer? And how many employees would we hiring? Several hours later, amenities, introductions, and checking out our belongings over with, the crowd finally bid us a friendly adieu and dispersed into the night.

Finally. Free. At last, we have control over our lives again. Well, sort of. We only have to report to our Provincial Governor, four people in the Department of Waters and Forests, and three folks at the P.C. office in Buja, on a regular basis, in French. But at least for today, we are free. Yippppeee!

                    With love and two big hugs,
                    Free to be, Him and Me

Chapter 17
Bicycle Bums

Dear folks,

We've hired a cook and a gardener in the first few days we've been here. The town plot to make sure we are up and moving by 5:30 a.m. continues. If it isn't the gardener, it's the neighbors, or even complete strangers knocking on the doors and peeping in the windows. We are going to learn to ignore them or outwit them, or it will become old hat and they won't tease us anymore (probably the latter).

Cook's son, Odance, (the gardener) pounds on the door at 5:30 to ask for the machete or the hoe (we have no shed for storage--so they stay in the house overnight).

The cook, Sylveste himself, appears bright-eyed and smiling by 6:30, happily banging pots and pans in the kitchen to let us know he's starting the day's chores. They would both like to stay till 6:00 p.m. and have supper with us, but for now, we find we need the privacy more than their happy company, and we send them home early, around 4:30 or 5:00. Although we pay them for a full day's work and send food home with them or have them eat early, they don't feel it's the same. It's a matter of pride to have a twelve hour-a-day job (or maybe they've been asked to keep an eye on us to make sure we don't get into any trouble?)

* * *

Our motorcycles (hereafter referred to as motos) haven't arrived yet, so we haven't done much surveying or actual fish work. Our P.C. assistant Country Director (hereafter referred to as APCD), Mona, did manage to procure us two large chunky (heavy) Chinese bicycles until the motos arrive.

Storms:

While building shelves and worktables for the kitchen and home office, we ran short of lumber and lathing and had to order more. Word came that it was ready several days later and climbing onto our wobbly

Chinese bicycles with the big tires, we pedaled up to the Catholic mission.

We drew quite a crowd ordering, paying for and then tying the 10 ft. long 2 X 6's along the frame of my bicycle. Jim had the biggest job of balancing a whole slew of long lathing strips across the handle bars with his right hand, steering only with his left and with only light string holding them semi-together (no extra bungee cords).

Midway through our purchase, a huge black storm rumbled its stomach in the valley, warning us to hurry home like all the other villagers. First mistake? We took time to put on our ankle-length rain ponchos, just in case we didn't beat the rain. We'd just started home when the freshening wind whipped around us, billowing the ponchos out like sails, giving us extra momentum or brakes at just the wrong times, and making steering nearly impossible. We pumped like crazy for the half-mile home stretch against the wind as the storm laughed and hiccupped hail down to spite us.

With no shelter in sight, icy rocks beat down on our hard heads and bare hands, but letting go of the handlebars to cover craniums didn't seem an intelligent thing to do.

We topped our hill and I applied the brakes to slow for the sharp left turn up over the 3-log bridge into the yard. Jim unexpectedly whizzed by me with the lathing sticking out in all directions, like pins on a pincushion, nearly knocking me off my rusty steed. Fast and faster he sped, past the house and on down into town, until he was swallowed up in a curtain of heavy rain.

"He couldn't have forgotten where we live. No. Must have forgotten something important at the store, to go in this storm." I eased across the bridge and up through the growing mud wallow in the yard to unload the fresh green lumber onto our covered front porch, keeping an eye on the road and the pouring rain for my errant husband. Some five minutes later, he reappeared, trudging out of the watery curtain and back up our hill. Without a word, he threw down the lathing and collapsed onto the porch beside it.

"Uh, Honey, where did you go?" I asked.

"Where do you think I went? Down the hill and into town!" he groused.

Curious, I asked him what he'd bought at the store. He gave me his driest 'dry up' look and enlightened me.

"The lathing got caught between one brake and the handle bar. The other brake was too wet to work. I couldn't stop! I dragged my feet the whole quarter mile to the other side of town before I could slow enough to ease into a turn and head back! Mostly, I was just praying for a soft place to land and not break the lathing, since we can't afford more!"

Now you have to admit, a story like that deserves some dry clothes and hot chocolate made with imported Netherlands-powdered-whole-cream-milk--Nido® brand, and that's just what we did.

With love and a hug,
The Bicycle Bums of Big B.

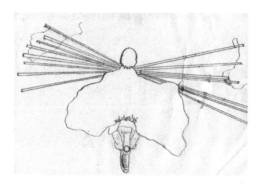

Chapter 18
Obstacles

Dear Folks,

S'cuse the long interruption! We had one and a half weeks in Buja to finish up language, be indoctrinated, sworn in, meet everyone in the Embassy of importance or necessity to us and do all of our shopping for the household items we needed up-country: Dishes, towels, cooking utensils, kitchen supplies, soap, 'imbabulas' (our quaint little cooking 'thingy' that uses homemade charcoal and an open fire, about twelve inches across by twelve inches high of tin or sheet metal), pots, pans, food, etc., etc.

We have been here a week in Ngozi, met lots of people and had our first earthquake (shook us out of bed) but not to worry, it was very mild and everyone says it has been that way for as long as they can remember.

We've scrubbed the layers of mud off the cement floors of our tiny three bedroom house, scrounged around for materials to build shelves and cabinets (the furniture which was supposed to be here when we arrived, has only half arrived and we don't really expect it soon as promises appear to be long in the future for expensive...anything).

We've also given everyone the opportunity for a hee-haw as we pedal around on our trusty, clunky Chinese bicycles (motos are still hung up in Uganda somewhere with the blockade and the problems there--not sure if or when they'll ever arrive, so we're scrounging around to see what secondary projects we might initiate in lieu of fish-farming).

Good news--we have already started to lose some of our weight, trudging up and down steep mountains (think 50-70 degree inclines), and without all the wonderful-but-too-rich food being stuffed down our gullets in language school, our systems and bodies are quickly returning to normal.

So far, there are not many over-processed 'white-man' foods available here (we're posted the farthest from the capitol, (happy with that as we don't need the distractions away from learning the job and the languages), but we've found great fresh foods from the local market three days a week.

We've also met a really terrific and fun Canadian couple (Phil and Trudy) and they've offered to take us or our cook with them to a larger market two hours away every ten days to stock up on fresh veggies and grains. Great!

We met a brilliant German woman (Elke), a 'cooperant' (co-op-per-ahnt), which means she has more responsibilities than a volunteer, more education, heads her own program, and like the Canadians, she has a car. She also speaks 6 languages fluently, is working on her PhD, served in Argentina for three years and is in her third year of a five-year goat project to improve the local goatherds and produce milk and cheese.

The native goats are scrawny, stunted little things (barely a foot tall), while her imports are so big the native nannies may have trouble giving birth. But the native stock is disease resistant to the many maladies here, so it's necessary to use them in the program. (Cattle are the same, but so far, attempts to improve the herds have resulted in weaker cattle--just too many parasites and diseases.)

We have also run into a group of wild Irish rovers (witty, delightful guys) who are just finishing up a two-year Peat assessment project and are ready to report their findings, projections and suggestions to the Government.

There's also a Belgian man, Jan (Yhan), here for twelve years now as the resident coffee expert of the country, and who's already offered to bring us fresh veggies or food from Buja every weekend when he descends to be with his family--and a French agricultural expert, Monsieur Joset, we keep hearing good things about but that we keep missing and have yet to meet.

--Did we tell you we've hired a cook, Sylveste, and his son, Odance, as our daytime guard and yardman? We've also had to hire a night guard, Vyance, so that things don't disappear. And we have been told that sometimes theft is not called such in this culture, but is referred to as 'degrees of providing for oneself' (and the better one provides for oneself, the higher standing in community, as long as one does it well, with grace, and doesn't get caught--a different way of looking at life, and different apparently from region to region. If one gets caught, though, one is not good at providing for oneself and punishment is severe).

We currently bring the bicycles in at night, but I bar the door at smelly 2-cycle motos (should they ever arrive), so our next big project is to construct a secure shed for the motos and bicycles that can be easily guarded by Vyance.

* * *

Two days later. We just heard that our APCD gave up on the motos ever making it through the Ugandan blockade and borders, sought other sources and managed to scrape up motos for three of the other fish-volunteers. She tried to keep it a secret from us so that we wouldn't be upset, but gossip travels faster here than the event itself. One of our Burundian counterparts was only too eager to tell us all about it the very same day the other volunteers got their motos.

--Now a large part of the personal harassment we endured during fish training was that as a couple, we were told every day that we wouldn't make it this far. (Based apparently on problems they'd encountered with a large Catholic group (with older couples like us) in the training just prior to ours, who had rebelled against the style of provocation training.

Their entire group was scrubbed and not accepted into P.C., which is very sad for them--but waaayyy beyond our control.

But, because we were a couple, Catholic, and reminded the head trainer of the other guys, we were hounded daily, discouraged from continuing, and treated as unwanted troublemakers. Assistant trainers spread that attitude of non-acceptance to some of the other trainees and it took us till the end of our ten weeks to discover why we'd become pariahs. And in spite of our best efforts at the time, a report apparently followed us in the formal papers to 'look out for these guys'. (We're getting this all through the notorious grapevine--so not sure how much of it is embellished.)

We made it through fisheries training because we'd committed to do this work. We put our house up for sale, sold our possessions, found homes for our beloved pets (the really hard part), gave up really good incomes, security and success at home in what most friends, family and co-workers considered to have been the height of both our careers--and a really foolish move, and now this. The final straw. But no way were 'the multiple theys' of the world going to stop us before we even got started.

--So we built up a high head of steam, climbed on a bus to Buja and confronted our boss none to gently, laying out all the reasons we needed to have this one tool for our work. Guess we were convincing enough, as she found us two new 125cc mountain bikes the next day, but we're back in Ngozi waiting these past two weeks for all the paperwork and license plates to come through.

--Why don't we walk or take the bicycles, you ask? Good Question. Several answers. We've discovered there are only two directions in our beautiful village of Ngozi: uphill and downhill, and that in either direction it's a long, long, long way to anywhere. If you flattened out all the hills and mountains, the country would be ten times bigger!

North, south, east and west aren't nearly as important as up and down. It is a winding thousand feet down to the first valley, half a mile across, and a thousand feet back up, with a half dozen more valleys over to the first good clay-bearing soil for pond building (that we've found so far). That's probably only five miles (8 kilometers) as the crow flies, but even setting out at sunrise, by the time you've walked the up and down distance to the first viable (maybe) pond site, the day's half over and it's time to turn around and walk back.

And that's if you can find a farmer who will talk to you, or locate the local administrator's office and an administrator who will approve the construction--and the big one--if you can find your way home again, because so far, all the green-covered mountains and valleys look the same when you are down in the narrow bottom looking up through huge banana and Taro leaves, with no roads or signs visible.

We've also been informed by the governor's office (and by many of our new friends) that we are not much good to the community on foot. Though there appears to be plenty of enthusiasm for the idea of the fish-project itself, it also appears we are an embarrassment to the country because we don't have transportation like the other 'cooperants' (development workers who are actually about two steps above us in education, background, pay and language skills). And without respect, we'll receive little cooperation. Credentials are important here, just like home.

* * *

Our generous Governor gave us an office this week in the local Development Projects building, not wanting us to sit around all day in House (even though our office is officially in the house,) and wanting us to report 'somewhere' every day, because like us, he has to report our progress frequently to the Ministry of Agriculture. We haven't found much to do there but read books, plan secondary projects and practice new French vocabulary by grabbing the unsuspecting stranger who occasionally wanders by, though most are out working at their own jobs.

Today was starting out really sad as we faced yet another day of office doldrums trying to get a secondary project off the ground, but the

French agronomy (agricultural) expert we've been trying to catch up with, Monsieur Josett, dropped by to speak with us, (another delightful, cheerful soul) and we discovered a good many mutual interests.

He wants to start Angora rabbits here for a fur export market and for weaving ($3,000 FrBu per Kilo of hair would be a fantastic income for any family); a regular rabbit market for protein and skins (he has a neat tanning procedure using the bark from an indigenous tree, the Blackwater tree, and is going to show us how the tanning works so maybe we can introduce an integrated system here with rabbits, worms and fish.

He also bemoaned the fact he couldn't find anyone interested in designing an oil press for sunflower seeds or a pellet machine for pelleting legumes for feedstock. Jim was excited and pleased to volunteer his engineering and design services for the oil press and pellet machine designs, and has spent the day sketching out possibilities. (He designed and built a successful mustard seed press in Peace Corps India twenty years ago.)

M. Josett also told of us a nearby abandoned Belgian pond system that had raised trout with some success in the past, so we will be visiting that site next week. And he offered all the assistance and money or legume seeds we need to start any of the above projects and also the rabbits from two or three sources. Yippppeee! We may not get around to fish farming, but we now have multiple viable options and funding for other work at least, and work that we can do closer to home, without transportation. May actually feel or be useful to PC and the country in another week or so.

* * *

On a lighter note, I have enjoyed wearing jeans since language training, but it has provided a major source of amusement to the locals to see a woman in pants. They alternately laugh, point or sneer every time I emerge from the house. But we are beginning to be accepted in some parts of the community as we've been invited to several homes and even a wedding--unheard of to be included, so guess we appear harmless enough--just not yet sure of the dates, as the tenses of time and future in Kirundi are still a mystery--I hope we arrive on time and on the right day.

Society and development work here seems to be geared to specialization, everything regimented and parceled out in rigid categories, so two 'generalists' who are supposed to be Fish-folk but who also build cabinets and desks and are talking rabbits and clay and other stuff are causing a lot of talk. Mostly I think they are wondering if we will ever start work.

* * *

We hired a local French tutor to improve our French, but he's only shown up two out of the five scheduled evenings, so we are looking for a replacement (maybe he despaired at our progress). Language is coming along very slowly because we haven't had daily exposure (no transportation--no work-- no contacts--no language practice). And it's way too easy to speak English with one other.

We still wonder almost every other day, after some small crises, disappointment, or cultural difference (a strange emotional roller coaster over things that should be insignificant, but aren't), what the heck we are doing here, and should we just chuck it all and come home, but then our stubborn kicks in, our chins come up and we are here for another week.

* * *

More About House:
Our house is in the middle of a long line of small cement-covered mud brick houses painted in bright pastel colors, all with yards, most with gardens and flowers, and all except us with fences for privacy, and wonder of wonders, electricity and running water for eight to ten hours per day.
Gossip says the former tenants abused our house, were evicted, and are now in court for non-payment of rent, but they could just as easily have been evicted to give us space as a favor to P.C., or if it was politically expedient. We'll probably never know for sure, and it's better we don't ask.

The former tenants did allow the property fence to get run-down or pulled down so when we moved in, half the traffic from the whole town (foot, cars, bikes and motos) were using our driveway and yard as a shortcut to the local market or a place to park.

The traffic is bad enough, but every day, every week, every single one has stopped to peek in our windows, laugh at our carpentry efforts or ask for a job, or ask if we have beer or something to eat, starting in the dark around 5:30 a.m. and lasting till long after dark on the other end of the day.

We've finally learned enough Kirundi to ask Odance-the-gardener, to gather or buy some poles and papyrus reeds to make a barrier across the driveway and mend the broken fence, which he did--in one day!

Cutting off their shortcut only disrupted village life for a millisecond and there seems to be no hard feelings, as a privacy fence is respected. They simply chose another route, but for us it's been a great couple of quiet, stress-free days without the peepers.

* * *

--Our house also faces a miles-long exquisitely beautiful green valley a thousand feet below us with only the narrow paved road that runs through town separating us from the drop-off. It offers a thousand different perfect photo opportunities daily, with sunshine streaming through the clouds to the lush green fields far below (makes me wish I had paints, brushes and a canvas).

But the twenty-foot-long line of short bushes on the valley side of the road are, unfortunately, sometimes used as a public toilet and a portion of everyone going to and from the marche' (mar-shay or market) stops and does his 'business', sometimes hidden, more often openly along our road.

The other day there was a beautiful, ferocious rainstorm rolling up the valley with high black clouds, sunshine streaming down in front of the dark billows and a rainbow in between, tying it up like a ribbon. One of those 'once in a lifetime' shots. Jim ran for his camera and sped across the road before he lost the light. He had to kneel slightly and wait a half-minute to get the best frame. When he finally stood and turned around, he found half a dozen Burundian women pointing and giggling, obviously thinking he'd been in a hurry to 'do his business', and in such a funny way.

* * *

I spent today with our German friend, Elke, rescuing a sick goat buck (ticks carry a rickettsial disease that can cause quick death if not treated in time). All of their improved goats have been raised in protected areas and have not yet acquired gradual immunity from occasional exposure to the ticks. She says they will have to change their system or risk losing lots of goats and three years of hard work. But her new hybrid crosses are giving lots of milk, are sturdier, larger and mostly healthier. She has brought us samples of her first fresh goat cheese over the last few weeks and it's terrific!

We have her over for meals to repay her for the protein and always enjoy her energetic mind, brilliant smile and great stories. Best go now, before anything exciting happens out on the road and we miss it.

Love and lotsa hugs,
Jimani (alias, aaaaahh-nnneeeee-taahhh)

Chapter 19
Ngozi, First Impressions: October

Dear Family, (Please forgive any repetition--can't remember who, what or when we've written.)

Some first impressions of our new home:

Ngozi --Population: approximately 5000. Located in the middle of one of the most densely populated countries in Africa with over 450 people/sq.km. That's equivalent to five million people in an area the size of the Dallas-Ft. Worth metroplex, almost all trying to make a living from the land.

Elevation: 6000 feet and cold. Banks: Three private (none of which we can use, we have to descend to Buja to use the public bank). One cinema (closed for the moment but it has posters of Stallone's *Rambo*, in the window--understand he is very popular here), two paved streets--one coming, one going, depending which way you face, (others are red dust or mud), several small cafes, a government development complex, and a fair produce market in the large town square three days a week (important to remember which days because we buy most of our fresh food there).

The hard-packed red clay of the town square is surrounded on three sides by some thirty small shops of painted mud-brick (sun-dried) or low-fired brick, with tin roofs, all selling small quantities of exactly the same thing: bottled beer, sodas, small cans of Kraft cheese, shampoo, nails, kerosene, Chinese tomato paste in teeny-tiny cans, bolts of dress material for the ladies, sugar, pots, pans, and soaps. Used clothing is sold on dry market days, laid out on hand-woven grass mats and Jim thinks he's recognized things we donated to the Salvation Army.

Meat: (goat and beef) is butchered at the nationally controlled slaughterhouse the day before it's sold (non-refrigerated), then transported to market and displayed in the open-air stalls. And yes, there are flies here. Wealthier people send their cooks to buy meat the day of slaughter, before it sits in the sun. Think we'll eat more veggies and depend on small amounts of meat we can afford from Buja where the standards and quality are a bit more secure, at least till our immune systems catch up. (Most everything is very clean here, but every region has its own intestinal flora and fauna the gut has to get used to--would be the same for them if they visited the U.S. or any country in Europe, or even us when we return home.)

Housing: We 'fishies' are the first volunteers or development workers allowed to work 'en brousse' (on-bruce--in the countryside directly with farmers and not through a local official or agronome (extension agent). The Government still insists we live in town and in a good house, so our living quarters are a cut above the usual P.C. standards. (There goes our vision of a mud hut in the bush!)

Emotionally, we find ourselves defensively building our own private world in response to not understanding much of what's going on around us yet (i.e. language–mostly Kirundi–very little French, culture and customs, etc.) Thus, inanimate objects such as house, yard and furniture have taken on names and living anthropomorphic characteristics. We refer to and talk to them almost as much as to our neighbors, as we seem to understand and be understood equally well by both.

Now, about House: House has green cement floors (a thin layer of cement lathered over mud bricks), and blue everywhere else. Blue walls, blue curtains, blue upholstered furniture (which arrived yesterday, so Yippeee, and we now have chairs and a couch to sit on), blue ceilings, blue, blue, beautiful blue, the color of a Robin's egg. It's a good thing that's our favorite color, yes?

House has a tiny living room with a fireplace which doesn't work, two real porcelain toilets (one works, but neither have seats, just the basin and one's actually a bidet--a flattened toilet with a water spigot to clean the behind, for those of you who don't know already) in one bathroom, three tiny bedrooms, a small dining room, and a tiny kitchen which is really just an empty room. All compact and cozy and just right, as in our own fairy tale.

House also has running water approximately six hours per day; an extraordinary gift, even in this high-altitude rainforest country, as the alternative is to haul it up by hand from the valley a thousand feet below. (Local families--not attached to the government spigot--and with money, hire a kid or kids nonstop to do just that.)

Peace Corps provides us with a small kerosene refrigerator (frigo--free-go) for health reasons and two large porcelain water filters for pouring boiled water through to eliminate bugs and parasites. The landlord provides the furniture.

The best part of House is its spectacular view. House faces the paved road (the one that goes both ways), and across the road the terrain immediately drops off a thousand feet into the long wide valley below.

This is the beginning of the short rainy season and storms race at us from the north at regular intervals up the valley floor, creating a fantasy landscape of lightning bolts and rainbows. They sling swirling wind and rain almost daily up onto our bluff in mile-wide sheets to pound at our door.

Most mornings we look out to find the very tip-tops of clouds at our feet, the valley below filled to overflowing with soft billowing grey pillows of fluff. I do so hope our photos turn out to be as spectacular as the real thing.

Think we told you we officially (or is it ostensibly?) hired a cook. (The government expects us to support the local economy, and we also understand we won't have time to wash, iron, or cook if we ever do our job well.) Cook's name is Sylveste and although we were assured he spoke and understood French, so far it consists of "Oui" or "Non". We spent an hour communicating salary and starting dates, as in we wanted him the next day. It's been a week now and he still hasn't shown up! So much for first communication efforts. Must have used the Kirundi tonal inflection for a bit too far in the future?

Ngozi is one of the national centers for development so there are numerous foreign-sponsored projects on-going in our little mountain village. The Belgians and French are working on coffee and rice production; Irish with a peat project; Germans with goat, cheese, and fodder projects; Italians with road and agricultural development; Chinese with roads, nursing schools, artisan activities, and a porcelain project; Swedish with artisan projects; and lots of priests and sisters who have been here for forty or fifty-plus years working in all areas (population is nominally 95% Catholic). There's even one German and four Russian doctors.

The Russians are not allowed to talk to us or visit socially. They even turn the other way when we pass them on the road so they can't see us wave. Since we've also heard they monitor each other constantly, we haven't tried to compromise their positions or increase their paranoia, which is too bad, as we'd like to get to know them.

And, oh yes, our three favorites thus far, the Canadian couple, Phil and Trudy, the German goat-project head, Elke, and the Flemish coffee expert, Jan. All the others are great too--it's just that we've spent more time with these three.

Canadians Phil and Trudy are working with the secondary schools, which depend on the government for food. That translates into beans or rice, but not both, day after day, two meals a day. Trudy and Phil have a project teaching administrators and students about nutrition, home gardening, and small animal husbandry, and giving a variation to their diet at the same time. It's more than just fortunate for us to find another couple near our age, English and French speaking, and with many of the same interests and likes. We've started a weekly weekend SCRABBLE game and have fun beating each other. They are expecting their first child in November. (More on Elke and Jan later).

The last three weeks have seen us scrubbing and cleaning red dirt from House and checking out the local terrain on foot for possible pond sites. (We look for clay deposits (ibumba, ee-boom-bah), a water source for the pond, and run percolation tests to make sure the clay will hold water (not too much sand)--you dig a hole, fill it with water and time how long it takes to leak out--not high-tech, but very effective and 'appropriate' technology.

We have also planted a vegetable garden, a flower bed, built a long office work desk in the largest bedroom to accommodate the both of us, several storage shelves, and two work tables for the kitchen (I can't see cooking off the floor for two years if we don't have to--guess we're either too old or just 'tourists'--but this macho P.C. stuff is not for us).

Wood: Speaking of wood, if you don't know the answer to a question, any question, the answer is always...Eucalyptus. It's one of the imported reforestation trees introduced by the early missions and not great wood because it's soft, but it does grow fast, and grows back from the roots once harvested, so they have a 'forever' tree. And they do use it for everything.

The local Catholic mission sells Eucalyptus lumber and makes expensive furniture. Because wood is so scarce and in such high demand, it is sold or used almost the same day it's cut. If you want some for a specific project, you have to stand in line to order in advance, then drop everything and get there really fast when word reaches you that it's ready for pick up.

--So fresh and green is it, that tree-juice spurts out when it's sawed or nailed. Remember our fine-toothed finishing saw--the only saw we could find in the Buja market? Well, it would have been difficult enough to use on kiln-dried wood, but you won't believe what happens when you try to saw through a green board.

The space behind the saw swells up as you cut, and puts the saw in a bind. So you push-pull very fast back and forth a little on one side, pry out the blade, then saw a little on the other side, then across the top, then flip it over and hack across the bottom. Then you 'bend' the board at the cut and keep sawing until it bends in two, tree-juice dripping on the floor all the while.

--We bent our fresh wood and made kitchen worktables to fit tight and perfectly at the seams and the joints (you know how my engineer-Jim likes linear things). But after only two weeks in a dry house, they are curing and separating with big cracks between the boards for the flour to fall through when I knead bread. The pots and pans on the shelf beneath are now always covered with flour or other sundry cooking parts and pieces, but infinitely better than cooking off the floor.

* * *

Names: The elementary school kids walk by the house every day on their way to and from school. They quickly found enough courage to step into the front yard and ask me, "Who are you?"

I explained we were volunteers from America, here to teach fish culture. That went over their heads pretty fast, but then they asked me my name. I told them it was Anita, forgetting that in this culture, you give your last name first, then maybe, and only if it is a very good friend, eventually your first name.

They like the sound of aahh-nneeeee-tah, though. Lots of vowels just like their names. They've quickly taken to calling it out every time they come within shouting distance. Unfortunately, they think it is OUR name, so Jim has become aahh-nneeeee-tah also. In fact, word has spread all over town that the umuzungu couple aahh-nneeeee-tah are here to bring fish. Each time we go to market, kids come running from all corners, yelling, "aahh-nneeeee-tah, aahh-nneeeee-tah, where are the fish?" at both of us.

Must say, Jim has been very good-natured about it. Especially since we tried to remedy the mistake, only to find that they have trouble with one-syllable names like Jim. They try to make it into something like ijiima. But either one is preferable to umuzungu (white man, stranger).

--I think we must be the only entertainment in town. Morning and evening, the kids call for us, keeping it up till we come to the window or door and wave, or come out to talk. They are very patient (or is the word persistent?) and will stand in the street for hours till we acknowledge them. This could annoy our neighbors, so the second we hear OUR name, one of us runs to the door or window to wave or yell greetings back, visit a few minutes and send them on their way.

Remarkable how well trained we've become in such a short time! We make good pets.

> Oops! There they go again. Gotta run. Take care.
> With love and lotsa hugs,
> the couple aahh-nneeeee-tah

Chapter 20
Tempests and Toilet Seats

Dear Folks,

Did we ever tell you about our toilet seat? Or should I say the lack of one? Well, we don't have one. On either toilet. Not that it matters on the second one, because it's a bidet and doesn't work anyway. But the first one does. It flushes and everything (we are extremely fortunate for lowly volunteers to have indoor plumbing and it's an immense improvement over the squatters in language school or a regular out-house.)

Only trouble is, for some reason it is an abnormally short-to-the-ground toilet and without a seat, you fall for what seems like forever that last three or four inches, especially in the middle of the night when the noggin isn't awake or working, but the bladder is.

--A note: Toilet seats are imported and hard to come by in this country, though they are not hard. No, they are made of very soft, flexible plastic; so thin and flimsy that the hinges on the back quickly tear off, leaving the seat free to float and slide over the surface of the bowl, fall on the floor, or stick to you when you get up. And should anyone over fifty pounds actually sit on them, they flatten and pop inside out, and if you are not really careful, stray parts of you can get pinched very hard during the popping part. Still, they are infinitely better than no seat at all, as they at least give a reference for your tush and keep you from falling into the hole.

New toilet seats cost an arm and a leg and if you are going to lose them sitting on it, you certainly don't want to lose them paying for it. So we decided to make one with our good green Eucalyptus wood. But first, we needed a model. Now, where to find one?

--It just so happens we were pedaling home from our no-work work at the Governor's free office today on our Chinese bicycles, when what did we spy, lying alone and abandoned by the side of the road? I kid you not. In all truth and honesty--a black, plastic toilet seat.

Now you may think this rather silly, but it was market day and the road was filled with people going home, all oblivious to that little black piece of gold. But they certainly would have noticed if we had stopped to pick it up, and Jim and I have become a little sensitive to being laughed at for every single thing we do or say.

We journeyed on to the house to determine the best course of action. We discussed making a mad dash for it in one low-flying inconspicuous swoop, but decided we'd probably fall. I suggested we stop along side it in the morning on the pretense of checking a spoke or tire, snatch it up quickly, and hide it in the knapsack. Jim quietly agreed...too quietly and too quickly.

Supper finished and cleaned up, I struggled with typing our first monthly report in French on the ancient French manual typewriter the Irish Peat-bog boys had so graciously donated to us as their project ended last month. It had never occurred to me that other languages would have typewriters laid out differently than our English QWERTY system, but of course it makes sense. This French monster has keys in totally different places and presents another learning curve I didn't anticipate, so it's hunt and peck till the fingers and brain patterns learn their way around. Who'd have thought?

--Some time later and deep into the report and proper verb usage, I heard the front door open and close.

"Jim?"

No answer.

"Jim?"

Again, no answer. Now where could that man have gone? Fifteen minutes later, the door opened softly and closed again. Jim appeared in the hallway, grinning from ear to ear.

Then I heard voices calling outside to our night zamu, (zah-moo or guard--we now have three full-time employees!). Vyance (Vee-ahnce) began to laugh uproariously on the front porch.

"What on earth?" I queried.

Jim pulled the toilet seat out from under his jacket and I fell on the floor laughing. Catching my breath, I asked him how Vyance, the zamu had found out?

Jim looked at the floor sheepishly. "Well, it turns out, the seat was laying casually beneath the only street light on the avenue, and for some peculiar reason Ngozi has electricity tonight."

So neighbors sitting out on their front porches had a grandstand view of the crazy umuzungu-who-walked-around-under-cover-of darkness-picking-up-broken-toilet-seats. They passed the info down the line from house to house till it reached our zamu, where it stopped momentarily until he could recover from the absurdity.

Am sure the Governor will have a good chuckle tomorrow (or tonight if he's home), as we are told everything we do or say is reported to him almost before it happens.

--At any rate, we have our model, and we're going to make one humdinger of a toilet seat.

Well, enough for now. Gotta go sit on the porch and watch the road to see who's passing in the dark.

Love and lotsa hugs,
Jim and aahh-nneeeee-tah

Chapter 21
Motos and Marriage

Dear folks,

Four weeks and no motorcycles yet. This place is so mountainous it is almost impossible to do even beginning survey work without motorized transportation. A few weeks ago, the Governor loaned us a vehicle for a day, complete with chauffeur, and we discovered that the first good clay deposits for pond building are more than thirty kilometers out. That's a little farther than we want to stray on foot or bicycle till we learn the territory. Once you're down in a valley and take a few side-valley tours 'a pied' (ah-pee-ay--on foot), everything begins to look the same and it's too easy to get lost. Banana and coffee trees all look alike and they forgot to put up road signs. Since many of these people have never worked with an umuzungu and are suspicious and afraid of us, we would rather make the best professional first impression possible. That precludes wandering around lost for days on end.

But every week spent from here out is approximately 1% of our service, and 4% has already flown by.

* * *

--One week later. Hey, guess what? Our motorcycles arrived today! On my Birthday!

We've since discovered that our Governor had asked P.C. when we were going to start working, so they scraped someone's barrel for funds and bought the motos locally to get us going. And here we thought we'd had something to do with it! Poor Mona and Chris, catching it from all sides.

Neither of us has ever ridden a motorcycle before, and the steep inclines of gravel, sand, and slick red clay are a challenge to maneuver in this beginning of the rainy season. But what a joy compared to sitting in an office or the house staring at the walls or developing secondary projects. Thus far, our metal-mounts are a lot of fun and not nearly as dangerous as driving a car. (You are a smaller, more flexible target for the buses and coffee trucks and they have to go out of their way to hit you, plus you can always slide under many of them if your aim is good.)

* * *

I had a great birthday. We splurged and made pizza (used the Canadian's gas oven and shared with them). Goat cheese is great on taste but not so much on melting. Not quite the same as mozzarella, just sort of sits there in small white lumps, but we're grateful for pizza any day, any way, and it is still very tasty. Trudy made a Boston cream pie for dessert, yummmm, and Jim bought me an expensive Snicker's© candy bar.

Since Friday and Saturday were national holidays, we spent the weekend touring with our new motos and breaking them in to mountain climbing (sure is hard to teach a moto to use ropes and safety harnesses).

Next week we will have real live fish work with the county administrators, agronomes (extension agents) and real, live farmers. Yippppeee!

* * *

--Another week (1%) later. The excitement of finally getting out to do some real work is heady, and chewing up all our energy and time (12 hours per day plus evenings on paperwork).

We have begun surveying the valleys to see where the best pond prospects and interest lie. Our province (state) is divided into nine communes (counties), each filled with dozens of mountains and valleys, and we are averaging 150 kms (75 miles) a day each, on narrow footpaths called pistes--pronounced peests, as in beasts.

We have split the communes equally between us, using the highway that goes both ways as the dividing line, and will work independently to protect the marriage (an artist/biologist and an engineer have totally different approaches--to arrive at the same result), and to keep the farmers from being confused by two different working styles or playing favorites.

--I have started writing a dictionary of technical terms and basic directions for fish-work in the local language of Kirundi for our survival and for success of the program, because as it turns out, not too many folks up-country speak French (as in none of my contacts so far, though one in every group of Jim's contacts has some rudimentary French--they are a few kilometers closer to Buja? Ngozi seems to be the dividing line, with my contacts all North of that line--who speak only Kirundi and a smattering of Ki-Swahili).

Everyone laughs at my baby-bantu, but they are all very patient and kind with my efforts. They seem tickled (literally and figuratively that an umuzungu would take time to learn any part of their language. I've also established some criteria to select farmers and pond sites for pond construction, and have narrowed most of the concepts down to some very basic and simple repetitions (for my benefit in learning the Kirundi, as much as for the farmers) Life is settling into a routine (at last)!

* * *

There are only a few things we are having trouble adjusting to. One is Sylveste's cooking. He came to us knowing how to make four things; soup, cabbage salad, meat patties, and sombe' (sohm-bay is manioc (cassava leaves pounded senseless and cooked lifeless then mixed with ground peanuts, onions, hot peppers, and LOTS and LOTS of palm oil.) Sombe' tastes really good, but I'm not sure how much nutrition is left after the two hours of boiling (though much better than leaving the astringent properties in it, yes?).

Sylveste also puts too much salt (even for Jim) in the soup, too many hot chili peppers (pili-pili, pronounced pee-lee-pee-lee) in the meat, and too much palm oil in...everything. (Palm oil is bright orange, looks like thick axle grease, and when cooked, creates an orange oily slick that permanently stains the dishes--and is probably guaranteed to clog up our insides and arteries.)

But Sylveste is gentle and good-natured, always happily humming or singing and keeps the house in very good order. And most important, he keeps the laundry done up, as it is all done by hand and we get really, really muddy-dirty almost every day in this rainy season. So--we'll work on the menu in time.

We have also had to put Sylveste on a budget. If we give him 500 francs to go to the market for a few items, he comes home with 500 francs worth of whatever we sent him after. Try eating ten pounds of ripe bananas before they go bad, or six huge cabbages at a time, or ten pounds of overripe tomatoes with no way to can, freeze or preserve them. We hope our language skills improve soon--am sure it must be our lack of good instruction.

We've also had to restrict the amount of laundry detergent (a wonderful boxed soap called OMO, guaranteed to dissolve and bleach dirt, thread, cotton, nylon and skin) that he employs to get our clothes clean. Our water access is limited and he uses so much soap that our clothes dry stiffer than the boards we've been using to build desks. Actually, the boards bend easier than our jeans. Can hardly pry them open to climb into them each morning, and are afraid to get caught out in a rainstorm for fear of working up a lather and drowning in the suds.

* * *

--Another week later (1%). I am doing most of the cooking so we can have fresh steamed or stir-fried vegetables and hot, whole-grain breads. I will spend time teaching Sylveste new stuff when work and routines settle down a bit--plus with two of us getting muddy at work, he's busy washing, ironing and cleaning all day anyway.

--We baked bread--whole wheat--the other evening on the imbabula (small charcoal fire contraption) by putting a large Chinese aluminum pot with two inches of water in it on the charcoal fire, then another smaller pot with the bread dough and foil over it into the boiling water and then put a lid on the water pot (like a double boiler). An hour later we had nice hot, fresh yeast bread.

Only problem was, it wouldn't brown or crust-up in our steam bath, so back to the drawing board we went. Next we tried two inches of sand in the big pot and a sheet of metal over the sand raised up on three small rocks. Placed the dough on the baking sheet, covered the pot with a lid and it worked GREAT! Fresh, hot, crusty brown bread. I'm getting the hang of cooking with the charcoal fire, though would still trade it for an oven with real burners and a thermostat most any day of the week.

--Jim fixed the hot water heater today (and you didn't even know we had one or that it was broken) and it looks like we might be able to afford the electric bill, if only for one hot bath a week, especially if we can rig up the solar shower bag as a supplemental source in the meantime.

* * *

We received a fun letter from Carol this week! It was 4-5 weeks in transit, making a detour through Malawi for some reason. Surprisingly, mail from the states is only taking one to two weeks to get here, but mail between African countries is more like two months to a year, so, sadly, we don't expect to hear much from our fellow volunteers from fish-training.

* * *

To answer your questions about our house: It leaks like a sieve and every time it rains, we drag out pots and pans to catch the drips. We've requested through P.C. that our landlord fix the tin roof, but we're not holding our breath as tin is very expensive, and we are lucky to have a roof over our heads.

Our bed is 'almost' a queen-size and 'almost' long enough for Jim, with a wooden frame, wooden slats and a four-inch thick foam mattress, excellent by Peace Corps standards. Our guest bed is more traditional; leftover metal springs stretched between a saggy metal frame--too short for anyone over five feet and no mattress--yet.

The house is on a cement slab with a covered front porch, on a hill (like everything else) and is very upscale compared to the unpainted mud-brick homes on the outer edges of town.

The yard is red and green (the National Party colors)--mostly red dirt with tiny patches of green grass, and we have two banana trees, one avocado tree and yellow Shasta daisies and Coleus in the flowerbeds. I've just planted marigolds and some bulbs--don't know what kind yet, they were just for sale in Buja--and we have a teacup rose bush producing fifteen to twenty blooms per day. Perfect.

--The rainy season has arrived. Some days, it's raining too hard to go out (from one to six hours/day and anywhere from a half to six inches in a day). We work on record keeping or think up secondary projects to plan out in the house office. (We've vacated the Governor's gift office now that we have real work. Yippee!)

--Even in the rain and no-work days, we are keeping busy: Jim is working out how to make lead weights and floats for the fish nets we brought (and no, they didn't come with the nets). I'm designing rabbit pens from appropriate and available native materials (not Eucalyptus), and both of us are looking into making a solar oven from used cooking oil cans, and maybe fabricating low-fired clay water-overflow pipes for the ponds we hope to build as we've not found a reliable source of bamboo yet.

The steeply sloped mud hole with foot paths running through what was our back yard is finally semi-leveled and planted in grass and food grains that are actually beginning to set roots and hold the soil. But the neighbor above and behind us continues to sweep his hard-pack dirt clean every day, and since his yard is three foot higher up the hill, every gully-washer of a rainstorm brings another portion of his yard down into ours.

We had the gardener, Odance, dig a small trench around the perimeter of the property to avert at least some of the flood, but a wall of red mud still rolls in daily over our freshly planted grass, wheat, and rye.

And we finally got around to reading our complimentary Peace Corps Medical Source Book, entitled, "Where There Is No Doctor". Here is some of the sage advice:

"When a person is having a fit, try to keep the person from hurting themselves."

"There is no medicine for varicose veins."

"To prevent a cough, do not smoke. To cure a cough, treat the illness that causes it, and do not smoke. To calm a cough and loosen phlegm, drink lots of water, and do not smoke."

"Eat nothing while vomiting is severe."

"Do not let flies or other insects land or crawl on food."

"Do not spit on the floor."

Since these are pretty easy instructions to follow, we should be very healthy during our tour and can show others how to do the same.

* * *

--Did I tell you that House has a tin roof? Well, it does, and every day, dozens of crows, bored with riding the thermals rising up off the bluff, come to roost on House's tin top, recognizing us as umuzungus as readily as the local human population. They are noisy, raucous things, (the crows) and they have developed a game to drive us crazy. They land on opposite ends of the roof, then clank, claw, and screech along the pitch toward each other in mock battle, their talons clopping along the roof peak--chunk--clonk--chunk--clonk--scronch--screeeaakkk--claws sliding down the pitched tin like chalk screaming off a blackboard. Then they're off with a flap and a caw to pick up stones and rocks to drop on the heads of their still-perched brethren. WHAAP! Cling--clonk--chunk.

Then it's off for another one in a never ending battle of sound effects and escalating war. And thieves they are, one and all. Nothing portable is safe outside. Sylveste has to tie our socks and underwear to the clothesline, lest, in a moment of madness, they end up in the Governor's yard via our feathered friends. Must say though, the crows have provided hours of entertainment. Better than TV.

In a land so hungry, we've wondered why crows are the only bird left in significant numbers in populated areas. Our neighbor explained that it is against the law to kill crows because they are scavengers, and therefore unsafe to eat--or there wouldn't be nearly so many of them. Well, gotta go. I see one trying to pluck a sock off the line.

With love and lotsa hugs, The OCWSN
(Official Crow-Watchers Society of Ngozi)

Chapter 22
Kamikaze Banana Bikers

Dear Folks,

A bit about our motos: We were called down to Buja two weeks ago for 'official' motorcycle training, which consisted of reading the manual and a show-and-tell how-to-ride, a short trial run on back streets, then delivered to us in Ngozi in the back of the P.C. truck. Now we are to climb on and ride them slowly for five hundred kilometers to break them in and become experts by trial and error--hopefully without too many errors.

--Jim's is a new blue and yellow Yamaha 125 mountain bike we've named Delilah, and mine is a new blue Suzuki 125 mountain bike, named Samson. We figured the driver's test was to survive two days in Buja with buses, trucks and cars tearing at you in excess of sixty to seventy kilometers per hour--between stop signs.

Driving anything in Buja can be dangerous, with rules we haven't picked up on yet. We're glad to be back in Ngozi on the back dirt roads where life and traffic are slower and more reasonable until we get a few kilometers behind us.

Moto riding is much easier than falling off a horse and you will be glad to hear neither of us has, or is planning to fall off as we are told it hurts considerably. Speaking of hurt, the only volunteer who has had even a minor problem so far is one of the women who has never driven anything with a clutch. P.C. found her a used, local, clutch 90cc, which tipped over with her aboard while she was shifting and she had to have five stitches in her knee. Ouch.

P.C. scrounged around (bless them), found her a 110 automatic and she's doing great, even having fun and starting real fish business with real ponds and farmers. Very exciting!

* * *

Did we forget to tell you about our first bus ride?

Buses:

Now buses are an interesting subject--one to bring laughter to the joyful, nightmares to the sane, and tears to the eyes of all. But I get ahead of my story.

Our first non-P.C. driven ride came a few weeks ago when we descended to Buja to request motorcycles from P.C. We walked to the Ngozi central market (also the bus stop), knapsacks in hand and looked around. Then came the hard part, how to select a bus?

You see, buses here come in many varieties. There is the extra-large, new, shiny, rectangular, un-scratched, un-crunched government variety with lots of large clean windows for viewing--called a large Coaster--of which there was one, but with no one on it. But as I said, it was very nice and clean, so we got on. Eventually someone was kind enough to come aboard and tell us it didn't leave until tomorrow.

First lesson: pick a bus that is leaving the same day as you.

Then there's the medium-sized, privately owned Toyota 'Coaster' with the front windshield spider-webbed from people's heads whacking it due to sudden stops. But it's only half filled and doesn't look like it's going to leave any time soon either.

Last are the small, privately-owned Toyota minivans with the eight double rows of homemade wooden bench seats bolted in so closely together you have to disjoint at the knees and hips to fit in, but several of them seemed more than half full.

Now, all the buses have 'barkers' (paid help who hang out the door, yelling and banging on the side of the vehicle, barking out their destinations). Barkers grab poor innocent bystanders, yank them inside and try to convince them they need to take a trip that day. Barkers also handle the money, leaving the chauffeur free to worry about the little things: like cattle and kids jumping out in front of him or trucks and cars that take their half out of the middle. You know--the little things.

Once the assembled realized we weren't there just to check out the scenery, but actually needed a ride to Buja, the fun began. We were accosted on all sides by barkers pulling and tugging at us and our backpacks--yelling, shouting, pushing and shoving each other as well as us. Each told us they were going to be the first to leave Ngozi and the fastest to reach Buja. We panicked, pulled free and withdrew to a safe distance to reassess the situation.

Now let's see. Maroon Van over there had been rolled, the engine and frame rocking in time to the beat of the 90dB Zairois (Zye-ear-wah) music. Nope, not that one, at least not if we wanted to retain our hearing.

Green had only been rammed in the side once and the windows were in good shape, but it didn't have many people inside.

Orange Van appeared to have been through a rock crusher. You know, superficial, cosmetic damage. But it was practically full up with people. Only problem, the reggae music blasted our ears from twenty feet away.

So, brave souls that we are, we opted for Green. An immediate blockade formed from the Orange and Maroon barkers, but when we pointed at Green, its barkers made a corridor of strong arms borrowed from the crowd and we climbed aboard and collapsed into the fifth row seat, thinking we didn't want a front row seat to see any up-close crashes or sudden stops. We asked the chauffeur when we might be leaving and he grinned back at us and said, "Right Now!"

With that, he slammed it into gear and peeled out of the market, throwing everyone else back into our seat with us. Tires squealing, he headed the wrong way out of town, and we had just long enough to think, "Oh, Noooo!"

Second lesson, pick a bus going the right direction."

But at the last second, just before we began the descent down the mountain on the road that goes both ways, he slammed on the brakes and slid around the corner of the last street in Swahili Village (edge of town) and began to lean on the horn; beep, beeeeeep, beeeeeeep! The barkers swung and swayed from the windows and doors, banging on the sides, yelling, "Buja--Buja--Buuu Jaaaa. Buja--Buja--Buuu Jaaaaa!"

One tiny older, wiry, grey-haired lady emerged from her house yelling and shaking her fist at us. As one, the barkers catapulted off and out toward her, legs and arms pumping to stay upright as the bus screeched to a halt. Bodily, they picked her up and deposited her unceremoniously into the front seat, then disappeared down the alley as she chattered away in a mixture of KiSwahili and Kirundi and shook her fist at them. Minutes later they reappeared with two huge sacks of charcoal (eighty pounds each), two large regimes of green bananas (fifty pounds each) and two screaming, kicking kids (weight unknown).

"Oya! Oya! Oya!" (oh-ee-yah, means no). "No! No! No!" the old woman shouted, "The children stay here!" Bang--Whap--Crunch--and all her belongings (minus the kids) were hoisted up and strapped down to the roof rack with thin strips of tire inner tube (hereafter known as bungee cords).

Bouncing up the rutted, washed-out dirt road we drew within sight of the market square once again. Orange and Maroon suddenly raced in from the opposite direction, their horns honking like geese on the wing.

Green gunned it, and in a cloud of dust we screeched around the square in a small circular parade matching beeeep for beeeeep with Orange and Maroon, stirring up dust into tall red clouds.

We all ground suddenly to a halt in front of a large, newly arrived Coaster from the Eastern hinterlands. The Coaster burped passengers from its dark recesses like living sardines from a can. A tug-of-war ensued between the disembarking passengers with their belongings and the barkers of Green, Orange, and Maroon.

Some of the passengers began beating barkers off with their belongings and fists, and a small riot developed. All of us fresh sardines, safely ensconced inside, laughed merrily at the fracas.

A momentary calm befell the mob when a serene, beautiful little nun emerged cautiously from the coaster, the last victim. Barkers immediately descended upon her, pulling in three distinct directions. She maintained her composure until someone wrenched her cardboard suitcase away and tossed it up to be strapped onto Orange.

Gripping her umbrella, she lashed out un-serenely at the barkers, beating on them until they relinquished the suitcase back to her.

Indignantly stalking past our bus, her chin held high, we heard her muttering under her breath, "I'm not going to Buja! I LIVE HERE!"

We were suddenly inundated with passengers, and thought, "At last, we are on our way." But such was not to be.

Third lesson: Buses get 'fake passengers' to fill up the seats so they can tell people they are almost full and ready to go, if they can just fill one more seat. Real passengers get on and the 'fake ones' are kicked off. It's all in fun and everyone has a good time guessing which bus has the most real passengers on it.

This went on for two hours, with vans and buses squealing and screeching up and down back streets and alleys, raising dust clouds, sending people running for cover, beeping, honking, whacking, until we suddenly hushed to a halt. Word came that Orange had filled up and left town.

We were off in a flash, twenty passengers strong (and I use that word in many senses); in an eight-double-row-seat van, with drop down wooden jump seats between each row, speeding up and down hills, taking corners on two wheels, and reaching speeds in excess of 100 km/hr.

Without warning, Green would suddenly slide to a halt and one or two people would appear from the banana groves and jump on. (We never did figure out the signals or how he knew they were there, our visibility limited by the press of bodies.) Before being seated, they would haggle over the price with the barker and impart the news that Orange had passed by not five minutes earlier (so we figured the second and third buses like our in the downhill duel must offer better ticket prices). Then, the race was on again and we couldn't decide whether to abandon ship, close our eyes and pray, or just hang on to enjoy our last minutes on earth.

Concern for life was soon overshadowed by another, more pressing matter. Every two or three kilometers we stopped to take on another body. At twenty-six passengers, not including the driver or barkers, all the seats were more than full, and the jump seats had been pulled down into the aisles and also filled.

As we approached thirty sardines, it began to get a little tight. I thought it couldn't get any worse until a tiny elderly lady and her husband squeezed on and proceeded to crawl over the bodies of those in front of us to plop down in our laps. She'd had a little too much kasiksi (kuh-seek-see or banana beer)--strength and courage for the voyage no doubt--and her breath would have pickled cucumbers. With the added weight of the last ten people and three more sacks of charcoal, the van began sliding around all corners, its back end spinning out at every turn. The sheer drop-offs down the steep sides of mountains added just the right amount of tension to keep things interesting.

Her eyes bright with joy, my lap-partner leaned across me and out the window around the curves just to see how close we came to the edge each time. Exuberant cackles filled my ears and she tugged and pulled at me to look with her, laughing in the face of death.

Legs and arms, asleep in their cramped positions, became agony itself, and we were almost relieved when a young mother with a baby, seated just behind us, yelled in our ears to stop the bus. The driver screeched to a halt and she crawled out a back window with her child and disappeared off in the bushes for five full minutes to answer nature's call, which gave us time to un-tense our muscles and breathe in and out. Twenty kilometers later we caught up with Orange and passed him on the wrong side of the road on a blind curve. Our side cheered and hooted out the windows to Orange that we were going to beat him.

Of that I had no doubt. The question was, where? Visions of twisted wreckage and broken bodies swam before my eyes when we narrowly missed a large flatbed truck roaring down the hill straight at us from the opposite direction on the wrong side of the road.

Back and forth. Up and down. Careening around hairpin curves, passing blind, sending pedestrians and bicyclers leaping and sprawling into the ditches as our own driver checked out all parts of the roadway.

This is it, I thought. We are going to die. This is what we came here for. They'll plant a banana-beer tree over the crash sight for our minerals and not even shed a tear.

By now the body count was up to thirty-four adults and two babies, and the body odor was overwhelming (our own included), the fresh air from the open windows not finding it's way through the press of humanity.

It was neck and neck with Orange when we reached the highest point on the road (6500 feet) before descending the last thirty kilometers down to Buja.

--Have you ever seen those road signs with pictures of trucks on them on a steep grade that say: DANGER SLOW STEEP GRADE? Well, they wouldn't have done a bit of good here. We took that last downhill stretch like it was a straightaway, our complement of hardened travelers leaning into the wind and urging the driver ever faster and faster to beat Orange.

The only ones brave or foolish enough to be on the road at the same time with us were the kamikaze banana bikers.

Banana Bikers:

These guys take their heavy Chinese bicycles, push them up the steep thirty kilometers from Buja, and load up with regimes (ray-jeems) of bananas to sell back in town at high prices. But, because it's an all-morning job coming up the hill, and because they are crazy, they strap on as many regimes to the bike as possible to go down the hill. (The most bundles we've counted on one bike was ten, with an average of eight, at forty-fifty pounds to each regime. Let's see, that's almost four hundred pounds!)

Then the kamikaze wedges himself onto the seat between regimes and takes off! For the first time that entire day I was glad to be in the bus and not anywhere outside, as biker after biker whizzed past us, doing faster than our sixty km/hr. Most had no brakes and at the speeds they were going, brakes wouldn't have been good for them anyway. If they miss a curve, hit gravel, or have a blowout, it's goodbye banana-Joe!

Just before Buja and the police security stops--where they check travel documents-- people began to abandon ship; out the windows, through the door (including our lap partners), and suddenly we could breathe. With only twenty people left on board, we raced through stoplights and suburbs and headed toward the Central Market. Green arrived in a cloud of dust and squealed to a halt just seconds ahead of Orange. Our driver leaned back, lit a cigarette and nonchalantly grinned our way, "I told you I would arrive first."

To think, he'd done all of this just for us!

This is where we get off and out, but our legs won't move. They've lost all feeling and life. If you don't hear from us again, it's because we're on a bus, still riding forever through the beautiful hills of Burundi.

Love n' hugs n' please send BenGay...and deodorant,

Jim and your #3

Chapter 23
Ditches and Tin Lips

October, 1st year
Dear Bill and Theola,

    Sad news. We had to let the cook's son go (Odance, our gardener, day guard and grass whacker). He was too enthusiastic! We would give him a specific work list of a morning, only to come home and find him digging trenches and canals ever deeper to help the water drain during heavy rains. He also cleaned all the 'bad weeds' out of my flowerbeds-- marigolds I had just planted from seed which were coming up well--and 'repaired' our new papyrus fence until it fell down from the added weight and strain.

    Hate to curb such industriousness, but we couldn't handle the constant change in environment he produced with the fences, weeding and the trenches running through the middle of the yard. Besides, they were beginning to undermine the house. Can see the headlines now: Volunteers Swept Away as House Takes Roller Coaster Ride Down Mountain!

    Also, he didn't like cutting grass, which was supposed to be his main job. The grass grew taller as the trenches got deeper.

    --In his defense, we have since learned that grass whacking here is a real art but not a respected job, and one apparently reserved for elderly men or for those who can't do anything else. They use a short-bladed scythe, which for some reason is always about three inches too short in the handle for the user.

    The short handle forces them to bend over to do a good job, and it's a killer on the back. Jim is having one made the proper length, in case we end up with a new yard-guy or doing it ourselves.

* * *

    One week later: We hired a new yard-man-gardener this week to protect the motos (if we are home during the day) and the wash when it's on the line. But he arrives an hour late and goes home an hour early, and has started out his service by digging more and deeper trenches where we don't want them and pulling up more of the flowers and newly planted grass. He also sings to and gossips with everyone within hearing distance all day long. Most of the gossip is about us and what we have, or how we live, and how silly we are. He has only been here three days and is already driving us crazy. If we can't quiet and slow him down, we will try again with someone else.

Theft:

We lost another pair of britches off the line today. Don't get the wrong idea, thievery is not that bad here, it's just that we are the new kids on the block and haven't learned the rules or been totally accepted yet, so we are fair game, as are all the other volunteers. When we asked several different sources, local and ex-pat, we discovered that the local culture also mandates a different perspective on possessions than does ours. If someone has an excess of 'things', it is often considered providing for oneself if you help relieve them of some of the heaviness of their responsibilities, and the finesse with which one relieves others is semi-respected. It's a game of skill, and similar I think, in a way to the ancient Native American concept of 'making coup'.

Kids:

We draw a daily crowd of kids to the house who have decided we are just funny-looking albinos. (Surprisingly there is quite a high percentage of albinos in the population.) The kids come peeking in the windows, calling out "aahh-nneeeee-tah, aaahh-nneeeee-tah! Where are you?"

They play a neat game of "Donnez moi," (don-aim-wah) (give me-- give me--this or that or everything) with all our possessions. And then there's the game of ten thousand questions, typical of kids everywhere, till we are worn out and shoo them off home.

* * *

Our new back door lock broke this morning in the closed position, forcing us to leave the front door key with Sylveste. We were both late arriving home from work, so he locked up and left our one key with one of the neighbor's kids.

We drove up minutes later, and finding Sylveste gone, walked next door to see if the kids had our key. They did. But Mama wasn't home from work yet, and the kids weren't about to let us have it. In fact, the littlest one started screaming bloody murder the moment he saw us. (We've heard that parents sometimes threaten their kids with throwing them to the white man to be eaten if they don't behave and I guess we looked hungry!) To keep him quiet, we quick-hurried back home and sat quietly on the porch breathing in and out unthreateningly till Mama arrived home and delivered our key.

* * *

After three months in country, one on post (only four months, but it seems half a life-time already), it is not too soon to see that people are the same the world over. Not necessarily all the same values, but definitely the same problems and everyone is pushing, pushing, pushing to 'get ahead', wherever ahead is.

Whenever I hear someone say, 'just trying to get ahead', I'm tempted to ask where I can get one, too, because mine isn't working so well these days!

* * *

During our first month here the back yard was just hard-packed rutted red dirt with hundreds of teeny-tiny empty Chinese tomato paste cans that all turned to sharp tin lips and mud when it rained. Now our newly planted grass is taking hold, the drainage ditches are working fine, the tiny tin lips are stacked neatly in a corner waiting for a use to present itself, and we should soon have a yard the neighborhood goats will love. All in all, life is grand. Miss you. Love you. Do good things and take care.

Down in the trenches, the ditches, and the tomato can holes.

Jim and Anita

Chapter 24
One Week after November-something

Dear Mum and Dad,

Have had such a hectic, bone-wracking week (weak?), that I can't remember when or what we wrote last. Think the motos have dislodged our brains or at least severed some vital connections. We are thinking seriously about making some kidney belts for the lower organs, but can't think of anything short of straight jackets for the upper!

What was terrific, exciting, and novel the first week has settled into bone-jarring reality in the second, third and fourth, and if we survive two years of torture on these roads (and I use the term loosely), it will be wondrous indeed.

Rest assured, Dad, we will not be buying motos when we return home. Oh, for anything with four doors and a roof! More and more we realize why so many more younger people do this fish thing than older. It's crazy! We're having lots of fun, but it definitely also involves a bucket-full of 'learning experiences'.

We find ourselves fluctuating from the heights of ecstasy over minor successes when our farmers understand another step in the process, to the depths of despair over the smallest problems; like when a packet of mail lost itself in transit from Buja to House last week and no sign of it anywhere. It was such a downer, we could have cried. The mail mix-up was a simple thing and not life-threatening or the end of the world, but it has become our lifeline to familiar things and home in this strange new place.

--After a bit of boo-hooing, we realized we'd lost perspective and had allowed ourselves to get worked up over things far beyond our control--so we tried to take a lesson from our farmers, sat down, had a good laugh, and reassessed our reactions. I think it stems from coping with a totally foreign environment where familiar rules and concepts no longer apply. Also, though our language skills are slowly improving, it doesn't seem to help in fully understanding the culture, or why people do things, and I think that's a bigger part of the problem. Anyway, if our letters sound like we're on an emotional roller coaster, it's because we are. But not to worry, it's just another part of the experience and I'm sure it will get better from day-to-day as we adapt.

* * *

Just when we thought we were safe, Jim ran into a herd of wild chiggers **and** an intestinal infestation of Giardia. Between scratching bites, running fever and running to the toilet, he's had a full two days of misery. The P.C. nurse gave him something for the Giardia, and calamine lotion is keeping the itching chiggers from taking over entirely.

* * *

Dear folks,

Just wanted to add a few lines to Anita's letter. After an intensive two-week study, I have definite proof that wearing motorcycle helmets is dangerous to your health--your hair's health specifically. The friction between my head and helmet is systematically taking what little hair I have, and removing it with every bump in the road. Wouldn't dream of riding a moto without a helmet, (too many trucks out there ready to not see you) but am afraid the tradeoff will be a bald pate. In French, helmets are called 'casques' (pronounced casks), which sounds an awful lot like casket--which is what's left of my hair will be ready for before this two years is up.

With love and two dozen hugs,
Two baldies in Burundi

Chapter 25
Falling Down
Mid-November

Dear Folks,

Had my first moto fall today, and was it a dilly. Well, more like silly. More like the old TV show, <u>Laugh In</u>, where the tricycle is toodling along and just topples over? Yep, that's me.

Remember my 125cc Suzuki motorcycle named Samson? Well, I've since discovered her true name and gender. Jezebel had acted up all day, missing, coughing–and stalling every few kilometers. Cleaning the spark plug multiple times and fiddling with the carburetor hadn't done a thing for her.

It had rained off and on and the red dirt roads were slick enough, but our short steep clay driveway is especially so in the rain, and you get to the yard by crossing a narrow three-log bridge, over a four-foot deep and wide drainage ditch. And before you say, "Three logs? That sounds wide enough," but they are not placed cross-wise, but length-wise across the ditch, as in the same direction you are going, which makes them about thirteen inches wide---including the cracks.

I was looking forward to dry clothes and a quiet evening after a long cold day in the rain, but just as I downshifted and turned up onto our 3-log bridge, Jezebel coughed, sputtered and expired--again. Right on the bridge. I came to an abrupt stop, no glide. My feet automatically came off the pedals and went down to support the weight of the moto. But they touched only air, and as gravity applied itself, I slowly tipped over and fell off the bridge, wondering how this could be happening. Crash, plunk, head plant. Ouch. Jezebel immediately followed, straddling me and the ditch.

Gasoline dripped onto my visor and into my helmet as Sylveste ran out of the house and up to the disaster. A crowd of sightseers sprang from nowhere in the rain, grew, and all fell on the ground laughing at the dumb-umuzungu-woman-who-thinks-she-can-ride-a-machine!

Mortified that I would embarrass him in such a public manner, Sylveste ignored me completely and busied himself enlisting on-lookers to help extricate the precious moto. He spent the next two hours fussing over it, washing, cleaning, and polishing. Fine with me. It gave me time to fix my wounded pride in private!

With love and a hug,

Hey you and what's-her-face

* * *

P.S.--a few days later--per his request, I met up with the administrator in a commune (county), which, so far, has had the friendliest people to work with, but the worst rutted mud roads and moto-paths of any we've encountered, with pits, holes and deep wash-board stretches that rattle the teeth and bones.

To show the gathering villagers it was O.K. for him to work with a woman, we stood and talked fish business for about twenty minutes. He asked me how it was going, and didn't I find it difficult driving the moto being a woman, and how could my husband allow me out by myself, and how could I work since I didn't speak the language? Trying to be culturally sensitive, I kept my response to, "No, I don't have any trouble with the moto, but I could use some help finding good clay soil and farmers interested in fish-culture."

Then we walked over to his house to meet his wife (I think also to reassure her I was O.K. for him to disappear with that day). We visited another twenty minutes while his niece finished an omelet and steamed bananas for him, me and herself, but not his wife (guess she'd already eaten, but was afraid to ask, in case in their generosity, I was eating her portion)--and a Fanta (soda of any sort). I was honored to be included in a meal and we had an amiable conversation about life here, where I was from, what I hoped to do in the commune--normal stuff.

But amenities over, it came time to start work and a look of glee lit up his face like a pure beam of sunshine. Administrator 'Glee' (easier than his 17 letter-multi-syllable name for writing purposes--and a reflection of his happy personality) informed me he just happened to have time that day to show me some possible pond sites. He climbed on his motorcycle. I climbed on mine, but before I could even kick start Jezebel, he was off in a cloud of dust and mud. (Yeah, takes only a few hours of sun to dry things out to dust, with mud puddles left in the deepest ruts. Interesting.)

It didn't take long to see he was trying to see if I could keep up, so I gunned it and kept right on his license plate. Up, down, hurtling over cliffs and around blind corners, over hill and dale we went, beeping wildly to scatter chickens, children, goats, mamas with babies, everyone having a great time waving and laughing--eating dust in the high dry parts and sending mud to the skies in the low.

Everything was fine until he disappeared over the top of a steep hill. I roared up and over the crest myself, going too fast. To my horror, I saw a tightrope of another three-log bridge over a wide and fast-running stream lying in wait for me at the bottom.

I know, I know. "Horror? At a bridge?" you say. But wait--just wait--the populace places big logs lengthwise across the river or stream, running the same direction as traffic and with huge cracks in between. Then they chink up the cracks with mud.

During the dry season, the mud eventually dries and falls out, leaving the cracks exposed.

During the rainy season--like now--torrential rains wash the mud out, and again, the big cracks appear.

Now these cracks pose no problem for the usual foot traffic. People just balance and walk across on the logs. Nor does it pose a problem for the occasional small car or truck (if they're careful and there are at least six or seven logs wide). But a motorcycle tire is just wide enough to fall perfectly into one of the crevices. This brings the moto and the rider to an abrupt halt, catapulting the rider up and over to slam into the opposing bank. Or sometimes, one can just lose balance and nerve and fall off into the river of one's own accord.

-- Back to our story. Life flashed before me and I thought--"This is it. The Big Ticket. I'm going to die."

It was too late to use the brakes or change my mind as Jezebel and I plummeted down the slope, plus it was the only way across. The cracks seemed to yawn open wider in anticipation of their next meal. An instant before I hit the bridge, the solution arose and I jerked the handles and went across lickety-split at a 45° diagonal. Great strategy, huh? Two years of strategy could give a person grey hair, or in Jim's and my case--no hair at all!

It took a few moments to catch up with the administrator, but when I told him at the first potential pond site, that he drove very fast, he beamed with pride and we spent the next several hours looking at possible sites and talking to people about fish. It was actually the best day I've had here for fish culture. All too soon, I found myself bidding my helpful colleague adieu.

It was only later I found I'd made a convert that day. In a positive light, the Administrator has told everyone about the new umuzungu woman who kept up with him all day at work on a moto.

Never thought becoming a Macho-Motorcycle-Mama would help me, or the program! Only trouble is, now I have a reputation to maintain.

With love and a hug,
MMM

Chapter 26
Mad Dogs and Englishmen (alias Bits and Pieces)

Dear Folks,

Lots of itty-bitty news bites:

--Speaking of bites, I was bitten by my first African dog today. We were visiting friends and one of their two dogs was sick. I crouched down to examine the sick one when the healthy one charged up and bit me--didn't want me messing with his friend. Glad they've had their rabies shots (the dogs, not our friends), and us our rabies boosters and tetanus. Mushed my right hand, but only broke the skin in a few places, mostly just bruised--a warning.

---We have been invited to a Burundian wedding next month and are so looking forward to it, a real honor, and they are a neat young couple, full of smiles, promise and the future.

---We visited a Catholic Mission Hospital (Italian-sponsored) today, out in the middle of nowhere on the worst road we've been on so far, and discovered a fully equipped modern facility with over one hundred fifty beds and a two hundred-patient per day out-clinic. It has a surgery unit, pharmacy, obstetrics ward and a pre-natal care unit. It has been staffed for the past twenty years with Italian doctors, but the last one is leaving in two weeks, and there will be only a German (Michael) physician and one Burundian doctor left to run the entire place. We haven't heard why the Italian charity is withdrawing its support.

* * *

--Interesting. It appears to be a vocational hazard the first few months for new volunteers to go from the heights of ecstasy over small successes to the depths of despair over the tiniest things with emotions running the full gamut in the space of minutes or hours. As a couple with our own built-in support system, I had thought we would be immune, but no, we are experiencing the same thing as the other volunteers.

Though descriptive, culture shock is a mild word for being constantly under a microscope and surrounded by thousands every day, and though they are mostly happy and full of questions, it can be overwhelming. As we don't like losing our tempers or being out of sorts, we have taken to re-claiming our Sundays instead of socializing. We spend those hours mostly inside the house, reading, talking, planning new projects, and just securing quiet time for ourselves for re-balancing. Even though the town persists in knocking on the door, pestering us to come 'play', laugh and be rowdy along with them, we've drawn the curtains and don't answer. Sanity is slowly returning, and we are feeling more grounded again.

* * *

---Oh, almost forgot something terrific. We finally located a source of cucumbers--the ones we planted never came up and we've discovered that most U.S. seeds don't germinate here--has something to do with a different soil, pH, aluminum and the equator?

The Belgian coffee expert, Jan, brought us some fresh cucumbers from a market two provinces (counties) away, on his way back from visiting his family in Buja over the weekend. (He's a really great guy and is always offering to pick things up or take things down to Buja for us--like mail and reports). The dill seeds the Canadians gave us are growing like weeds in our garden, so I made icebox pickles yesterday (they almost cure in a day). Yummm. And the alum we brought with us keeps the cucumbers crunchy.

Jim has also been craving potato chips, so we have taken to making that an occasional weekend pleasure, splurging on a little oil and heat, a little time, two or three thin-sliced potatoes and voila! Potato chips. We stand over the skillet, saltshaker in hand, scarfing them up as soon as they come out of the hot oil--crisp and salty.

---We took a Sunday afternoon trip with Elke (German friend) to meet another couple at a tea factory higher in the mountains some thirty-five kilometers away. Our first sight was of eight hundred acres of tea, solid on the sides, tops and valleys of mountains, in the most exquisite varieties of intense greens, as if light were shining from inside the plants like the highest quality emeralds.

Our host and the tea plantation manager, an British ex-pat from Kenya (Robin), explained that he could tell by leaf color which tea came from each original stock or bush imported into the country.
And we could see it too, on closer inspection, that they really were different, some strips a deep dark, forest green, while others were more of a lime color, and still others a bright iridescent chartreuse.

--The plantation starts new bushes out as buds a half inch long in tea nurseries from parent stock, covering the fresh buds with plastic like miniature green houses until they root, then cultivates them to around six to eight inches high before transplanting to the hillsides. The bushes grow to around three feet tall before harvesting begins (Robin says they would grow to twenty feet if unchecked). Only the new tender shoots are handpicked off the outer edges (called a two-in-a-bud) for making tea.

As the bush grows too tall (four feet), it is pruned completely back down to the stump and the process starts over again. There are tea plantations in Kenya with seventy-year-old stock, and in India one-hundred-year-old stock is not uncommon.

In season, this factory processes 88,000 pounds per day of AAA tea leaves. We are shipping a basket of tea and the equally high grade AAA Arabica coffee home via friends and hope you enjoy and share. (It is the best tea we've ever tasted, sweet, mild and no bitter after-taste, and our coffee-drinking friends say the same about the coffee.)

Robin and his wife, Gayle, were nineteen years in Kenya working with tea until the political climate made it expedient to leave. They are into their third year of a five-year contract in Burundi. Really a delightful couple and though thoroughly British in their demeanor and global alliances, they love Africa, especially Kenya and its people, and consider it their true home.

Another good part, they love books and reading as much as us, so we have another library source when we get desperate, and have already traded dozens. We've an invitation to come back soon as they also are very isolated from white, English-speaking colleagues, and like us, enjoy a good visit with other couples from time to time.

Robin and Jim hit it off as they discussed politics, farming, machines and mechanics. Gayle entertained Elke and me with her art projects (she does paintings on T-shirts to raise funds for World Aid) and shared talk about books, dogs, art and kids. It was a wonderful mental break we all seemed to need.

--We stopped on the way home from the tea plantation to see the German hydroelectric project due to finish in February of next year and hopefully supply 24-hour electricity to over half the country by next August. It's really an impressive project, with an imported wild Austrian team tunneling through an entire mountain to create the water drop for the turbines. (Rumor has it that they party so hearty on the weekends they are not allowed to make any stops between work and Buja, but must drive straight through to the capitol where the government can keep an eye on them.)

--We also got our first glimpse of the last high-altitude tropical rain forest in the country, which extends down to the reservoir site, and where Peter, an ex-Peace Corps volunteer, is now doing Chimpanzee studies (with a promise we can come visit once they are acclimated to humans).

* * *

--Speaking of hills, I was riding up one today and saw a kid coming down the opposite side on a bicycle. He paid too much attention to me as we passed each other and went down into the ditch, up the other side and tumped over into a thorn bush of some kind! Ouch!

It's sad and bemusing at the same time. On these back dirt roads (called pistes, pronounced peest's or pissed if you like) many locals are not accustomed to seeing

1. motos or
2. white people riding them, or
3. two-wheeled gas-powered vehicles of almost any kind.

So here you are, driving along at a moderate to slow speed and you can see in the distance ahead, a group of older women standing there watching you coming for 10-15 seconds with mild curiosity. Then, they suddenly realize they don't know what or who you are and arms and legs akimbo, they scream, scramble and flail up the mountain to the safety of a banana or manioc grove.

Little kids are the same. They scream (in delight at first) and wave hello and jump up and down until you get close, then their eyes get big and they turn on a dime and run screaming (in terror) up the hill as fast as their stubby little legs will take them. Not sure if it's the white skin, a stranger of any kind, the huge black helmet with a one-way visor or the moto.

--A medical question? Most farmers and their families are barefoot, and when you look at the toes of young and old alike, many don't have any toenails, except for scarfy, gnarled remnants--and many of the toes even seem to be stunted, not completely formed. Have seen several with only stumps. Could it be just long-term fungus and exposure to soil organisms?

I was wondering if the toenail problem could be 'fixed' with something as simple as shoes or a local herbal astringent? (Though shoes are another step up the economic ladder, I'm afraid, and years away.)

Also, I saw a man with apparent elephantiasis and have forgotten what causes it? Or if there is any cure?

--One other thing we've wondered about, till today. We occasionally see older women walking along the paths with long, pointed homemade clothespins over their noses. Couldn't figure out what kind of medical-magical practice this was until our Belgian friend enlightened us, explaining they push tobacco snuff up their nostrils and pin it shut. Hmm, I wonder what that does for you?

Well, enough about snuff. Hope this finds you both well.

Love and a hug,

jimani

Chapter 27
Imbabulas and Wretched Things

Dear Mom and Dad, alias Dottie and Dick,

Guess I told you I'm doing all the cooking now. Sylveste has all he can handle with the laundry, groceries, housecleaning, and washing the motos in this season of mud.

But have I told you about the thing we cook on? Remember the letter about our buying spree when we were first assigned to Ngozi? You remember, the one that described all the 'stuff' we bought, and the charcoal brazier that looked like something that might acquire a NAME without half trying?

Well, its official name is imbabula (im-bah-boo-lah) and it looks like an inverted flying saucer with a top hat on the bottom, breathing holes on the side where the windows should be, and with a wire handle for holding on to.

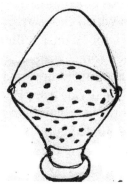

It has since earned the name of "The Wretched Thing", and we cook almost everything on it.

The procedure is quite simple; first you dig some charcoal out of the four foot tall burlap 'gunny' sack on the back porch, being sure to get all the grimy black stuff you can under your fingernails, along with a few well-placed splinters.

Now, this is not your every-day-sure-fire-light-every-time-American-brand-with-nice-little-briquettes-all-the-same-size-type-charcoal.

Oh, no. This is your handmade-all-different-sizes-from-logs-to-powder-eucalyptus-type-African charcoal, no starter added. And to start it, you place it in The Wretched Thing, pour a small amount of kerosene on it, light it, and stand back.

After it burns (not always guaranteed) for a few minutes and the flames die down, you grasp the wire handle and swing the imbabula gently back and forth by your side for ten to fifteen minutes for the slow method, or in a wild, alley-oop-over-the-head-round-the-world-and-back-again-swing-over-and-over for the fast method. This fans the flames, spreads the fire among the coals and gets them going glowing red.

Then you set The Wretched Thing down and presto, zippo--another thirty instant minutes later you have a charcoal fire ready to go.

For cooking, you just squat down level with The Wretched Thing, add skillet, food, and cook.

But baking takes a little more effort.

First, you start out with the big Chinese-made aluminum pot fifteen inches across and seven inches deep. Then you locate some nice fine sand, dry it out, and put a two-inch layer in the bottom of the pot. Then, when your Wretched Thing is red hot and glowing, you put the pot with sand with lid on the red, hot glowing part. Another twenty minutes or so, and you have an oven which cooks at an unsteady 325 degrees, plus or minus 50 degrees or so, for an unspecified length of time.

--Well, today I wanted some cornbread in the worst way, so I fired up The Wretched Thing and mixed up some corn batter (and yes, all the ingredients are available locally or from Buja).

But a rain shower flew over, blew into the back porch and put the fire out. Cornbread still sounded good, so I decided to light The Wretched Thing indoors. I swung the window open (inward) to let the fumes out, and started swinging T.W.T. to fan the charcoal. Well, Wretched Thing hit the open window frame and freshly lit charcoal sailed and scattered across the kitchen floor.

Poo. Really wanted that cornbread, so cleaned up the mess, scrubbed greasy black scuffs off the bright green cement floor, put all charcoal back in The Wretched Thing and started over.

The rain had let up a little, so I went outside and did the hurry-up-quick-please-fire-alley-oop-overhead-swing.

This works fine if you swing at a fast steady pace and away from your body, but on the third circle, the hook and handle on the wretched thing shifted and bumped my leg, and charcoal went flying all over the yard, where the rain and the wet grass quickly put it out.

By now, it was beginning to be an issue. Didn't give a damn about the cornbread, but I wasn't about to let that Thing beat me. Meanwhile, the baking powder was busy expending itself making gas bubbles in the batter.

And where was Jim during all this? Struggling on the front porch with cleaning the chains on our moto's, and making his own variety of bumps, thumps, curses and crashes.

On the fourth and final try, the charcoal glowed hot and red, the sand oven heated, and the pan of stiff, dry batter was carefully nestled into hot sand to begin its baking and browning.
One hour later, we had hot steaming, crusty cornbread with locally made strawberry jam and hot tea!

I know, I know, strawberry jam and cornbread for supper? Sounds awful, but believe me, you ought to try it on a long, cold rainy evening! Utterly and truly delicious.

Licking our fingers in Ngozi,

with love and a hug,

Your two red smackers

Chapter 28
Thanksgiving

Dear Mom and Dad,

We had a great Thanksgiving and hope you did as well?
All the volunteers and many from the American community (former
volunteers) rendezvoused at Mary's house (another fishie) halfway
between Ngozi and Buja, in the teeny tiny fruit and vegetable metropolis
of Bugarama, where we utterly stuffed ourselves silly.
English-speaking again was wonderful, and we laughed, joked, picked
on each other (just like home), and sat around sharing funny 'work
stories' till the wee hours. Only details missing were the football games
and pitter-patter of little nephews' feet.
Sated and satisfied, we rolled out sleeping bags at two in the morning on
the nice, soft, cement floor and didn't sleep a wink.

* * *

--My first work after Turkey Day was to visit the long-long-long-
long-distance commune (seventy-five km. one-way) over really rough,
rutted, rogue pistes. I arrived bruised and battered, only to find my local
counterpart was in Buja on business. Then the sky opened up and let
loose with a gully-washer. Reaching into my pack, I found I'd forgotten
to retrieve my rain poncho from Jim's pack after the Thanksgiving trip.
Not wanting to be stuck there overnight or risk a washout on a log
bridge, I struck for home. Motos, water, clay and mud don't make good
traveling partners. Like trying to climb Flattop Hill on a bicycle in an
ice storm. I slipped every way but straight up and finally resorted to
using legs and feet splayed out on either side as training wheels to push
my way forward.

But I hit a stretch of road overflowing in knee-deep sticky, gooey,
red clay. Jezebel ploughed into it, bogged down, and quit. Took two
guys and me to push her out, and my boots picked up an extra thirty
pounds of goo. (It is amazing how well tuned peoples' ears are to a

moto stopping on the path, and they appear from nowhere and everywhere, usually in great numbers to watch the show or to help.)

My rescuers took the last of my soggy cigarettes in payment. No, don't worry, I haven't taken up smoking, (remember the Health-book advice--DO NOT SMOKE) but everyone here has and does, from five years old on up, and store-bought cigarettes make great rescue payments. I don't like contributing to their health problems, but it's safer than carrying money, and goes a lot farther.

Word went out there was an umuzunga stuck in the mud. A large crowd quickly gathered as the rain temporarily let up, all bellowing with laughter when my helpers told them I was a female. Some of the braver ones dared approach and peer up into my mud-spattered visor. But they scurried out of the way when I finally got Jezebel to kick-start and waved goodbye, then slipped and skidded down the path, my monstrous training-wheel-feet picking up more clay each time I touched down.

Some of the log bridges are only one or two logs wide, too narrow to take at a diagonal, and with the mud pack gone from the crevices, before long I was so tense I couldn't have let go of the handles if I'd wanted to.

But the final blow came with another big stretch of water and muck flowing over the road--and a hole with no bottom and no way around. Jezebel sank rapidly and I came up sputtering and spitting, feeling like a bog monster from Willow Creek. Nearly broke myself breaking the suction-cup grip of the muck on the moto, but finally got everything upright, pushed out, scraped down, and carburetor cleaned--again-- enough to move on.

Struggling up the driveway of Home-Sweet-Home hours later, I spent the last part of the afternoon cleaning Jezebel, taking everything removable on her apart, washing, dousing parts in kerosene, then oiling and replacing. If only I could do the same for me! Not sure my leather hiking boots will ever be the same. I'm glad we brought saddle soap and mink oil, but it is fast running out.

We've talked seriously of retiring our leather footwear and sticking to the rubber wellingtons we picked up on our fish-farm tour through Mississippi in fish training. At least if the rubbers wear out, we've heard rumors we can buy Chinese replacements in Buja.

In spite of the falling-down-and-mud-stories, work is going well, with interested and interesting farmers, and we usually come in tired, beat, or beaten as the case may be, and happy. French is beginning to make sense and even some of the Kirundi is recognizable from one day to the next.

Think of us when you light the first flame in the fireplace and thanks for being there for us.

Love and a tired hug,
Hey you and What's-Her-Face
* * *

P.S.

Jim is over his Giardia now and feeling better.

And thanks ever so much again for the Popular Science and Omni magazines! They prevent our brains dying from lack of being tickled by new ideas.

Also, p.s.--weariness has prevented us from finishing our wooden toilet seat, so we are still falling into the hole. Hope to have the seat and the falling remedied by this weekend. Will let you know how the trial run and christening work out.

Do hope this finds all of you well and happy and eating the first snow-ice-cream of the season in preparation for the coming Noel.

P.P.S.--Kirundi has a word for "Hey You!" that believe it or not almost sounds the same.

It's Hewe (hay-way). Neat, huh? Haven't found a translation for What's-her-face, however. May have to settle for aahh-nneeeee-tah.

Love and hugs all around.

Chapter 29
Weddings

Dear Mum and Dad,

Burundian Dictionary term: Weddings: a word synonymous with marathons.

--Had another bout with the flu this week. Poo. I'd just returned from a hard day in the far commune late Friday, weary from climbing into and out of valleys on foot to check out pond sites; from being drenched by four rain storms; cold, tired and covered with mud, and was looking forward to sunset and a quiet evening at home under the covers.

But a man pulled up to House in a jeep and said there had been a slight change in plans for Leonard's wedding (a neighbor and friend–he's a judge and she's a nurse). All prominent town officials had been unexpectedly called to Buja for the weekend, and none would be there to perform the civil ceremony on Saturday as planned, so it was right now or never. Could we be ready in thirty minutes to take the promised pictures?

Panic! I am not a good photographer under the best of conditions, but dark-skinned people with no extra lighting inside a dark building are especially difficult to take. Relief arrived in the form of Jim ten minutes later. But he was tired, cold, and dirty also, and definitely not pleased at the change of venue. It took a few minutes of convincing him that we simply couldn't let Leonard and his bride down.

Excess mud swiped off and clothes changed, we jumped on the motos to hurry to the equivalent of our county court house--to sit and wait, while everyone else was thirty minutes late. (Being late seems to be a form of making coup or establishing status--or maybe even just culturally expected. To be on time is to admit you're not in a high position of authority. One always tries to arrive a little later than those socially or politically less important, and just before those ranked higher than you. We were merely happy to have the quiet time to breathe in and breathe out.)

* * *

A simple one-hour ceremony for the secular fulfillment of the bonding saw us back at Leonard's house to celebrate and take photos. After such a long day, even half a beer did us in, and we tumbled home to bed without supper.

We worked our usual half-day Saturday, and I was still digging mud from under my fingernails on the way to the wedding Mass (the religious fulfillment of Leonard's joining) that afternoon. I felt more than a little dowdy in my traditional American costume of a soap-faded brown cotton skirt and white cotton blouse, with brown plastic sandals from the Buja market.

Wealthy women's formal attire here involves rich silky fabrics draped in layers to the floor in vibrant, wonderful colors, much like Indian saris, and they are as beautiful as the women who wear them. The artist in me actually drools for a palette, paints and canvas every time I see them.

After the two-hour Mass, we filed outside to join an entourage of owned, rented and borrowed vehicles behind the bride and groom, and began a slow parade around town, honking horns, singing, and cheering--honk--honk-honk-honk--honk--in rhythm and cadence for another hour. The reception (the fun, people-part of the marriage) came and went (another two hours), and then the wedding dinner, which endured, yep, you guessed it, two hours.

The military dance hall was the final stop, and surprised us with the variety of western music from rock-and-roll and disco, to country-western and reggae. Jim and I danced with half the assembled until one a.m., when our bodies reached total collapse and shutdown and we began a slow exit toward the door. Friends informed us politely that it would be rude to leave before the wedding couple departed.

So we sat and yawned our way through to two o'clock, and exited three seconds after Leonard and his lovely bride. We heard later that the wedding party found their second wind about that time and continued on into the dawn.

Even moderate amounts of the Primus and banana beer on Saturday left us ripe for a sleep-in hangover on Sunday. I roused just in time to see the bride's family passing House with huge pots of banana and sorghum beer balanced on their heads, in route to the groom's home. In long-ago times, this was the moment for the bride's family to see if the marriage night had been successful and the bride truly acceptable.

Today, it seems just another reason to celebrate and dress up again. Several women left the entourage to ask us to join in, but we begged off the extra revelry and good times, and spent the day recovering from the Primus and banana-beer-blues. I tell you, one really has to be burly and hardy to survive a wedding here.

* * *

---Oh, me, the governor's admin was just here, tap, tappy, tapping at our door, and guess what now? Just when our garden is coming on for harvest and we are enjoying and getting to know our neighbors and make friends, he says we can't stay here, that they have another house ready for us and would we please move today!

Flabbergasted, we explained we would have to notify our director and make some arrangements first. Maybe it's all a bad dream, or an illusion, or maybe we can just say we did--and not do it. We wonder if we have done something terribly wrong, or offended someone? To be continued...

With love and a hug,
Jim and Me

P.S.

--Did we tell you our Canadian friends had their first baby last week, but there were complications and after two days of labor, Trudy ended up with the German doctor (Michael) helping with delivery, out east at the Italian hospital. Mom and beautiful baby Daniel are doing fine, just worn out.

--This weekend, Germans, Dr. Michael and Elke were coming back from a weekend trip when they had a flat some 10 km outside of Ngozi. No tools, no flashlight. So Michael stayed with his car and Elke walked the 10 km into town in the dark to pick up her car and us (in case we had tools and could help, which we did).

Dr. Michael was the one who fixed my broken crown (saving a trip to Kenya to a dentist) and also gave us some medicine for Jim's Giardia, so it felt good to be able to repay him even in a small way so soon. Within the hour, we had him home safe and sound. It was a good reminder to us that we haven't built toolboxes for our motos yet, and must do so soon.

We are looking forward to the rest of a quiet Sunday so I can shave some more on the toilet seat and maybe finally get it installed, and Jim can build moto-tool-boxes.

And in a few hours, off to bed with us for an early evening, and let tomorrow take care of itself.

Chapter 30
Termites
December 20

Dear Carol,

Thousands and gazillions of huge winged things inundated our house during dinner last night. They fluttered suddenly into our food and faces and streamed in through every crack, open window and door, seeking out our light.

We, and our dinner-guest--the Belgian coffee expert, Jan--quickly covered food, closed all the windows and doors, and quick-turned off the lights. The bi-annual flight of winged termites had arrived. Jan explained that it occurs at the beginning of each rainy season, and there's not much to be done but wait for it to end.

Millions and Gazillions of them hatch, fly for perhaps thirty minutes, have an hour to mate and lay eggs, then their wings fall off and they die. An amazing sight.

But their hour was during our hour to eat and they won. Our two newly acquired cats (questionable gifts from our otherwise very cool P.C. Director, Chris) went crazy batting down the winged creatures, then caught and ate the intruders until their little cat-stomachs distended in a definite state of over-fill. No wonder they were sick all night, retching on the floor every ten minutes or so. They must have eaten three to four hundred apiece! Yechhh!

In some African countries, termites are considered a stir-fry delicacy because of their high fat content, and the bi-annual flight is awaited with great anticipation. We've been told they also fry up well and taste just like bacon bits. Mmmmm. Yummy!

Just fyi. Buildings and houses are made primarily from sunbaked or low-fired mud brick or mud covered with cement rather than wood planks. But even the brick and cement require some kind of framework, and the wood framing they do use is riddled with termite workings within months of initial construction.

Example: You can shove the end of a stick in the dirt, come back in two weeks, and find there's nothing left below ground. It's all been munched away by fat little white bodies. I'm glad we're not on their menu. We could wake up some morning and find ourselves missing a limb or two.

* * *

--Walking around town with our Canadian friends and their new baby this afternoon was an experience. Everyone wanted to see what an umuzungu baby looked like: "Oh, look! It's white, too--blue umuzungu eyes--but it has hands and feet just like us!"

Each day we feel a little more settled and accepted in the community and at the same time as if we'll never understand or be fully a part of their lives. Interesting paradox.

Hope this finds all well, warm, and happy in the wintertime. Caught some sunshine today to enclose with the letter. Hope it lasts to the USA. Also ate two delicious, tree-ripened, four-cent avocados in your names for supper.

With love and a hug,
Jim and Anita

Chapter 31
Sylveste

Dear Mum and Pop,

Sylveste is doing great since he doesn't have to cook, though he still puts too much soap in the clothes. They hardly need ironing they come out so stiff, but he does such a great job of keeping us clean and clothed, and attacks every article with a full frontal assault, putting all his weight behind the blistering charcoal iron. (Clothes must be ironed to destroy the eggs deposited by bot flies while they are drying on the line. These lovely creatures hatch in your clothes, burrow into your skin, and make wonderful tracks and sores all over your body unless you kill the eggs with heat before they invade. Neat, huh?)

But the charcoal iron has Jim's briefs looking like boxer shorts and it has melted the elastic out of most of my underwear. In fact, all of our apparel, including underwear, knit socks and knit shirts are gradually becoming bigger and looser. It's works magic on plastic buttons too, and Friday night has become Replace-The-Buttons-Night (glad I brought extras and thanks for suggesting it!) The baggy underwear and socks make us feel like we're losing weight by leaps and bounds even though we're not.

Between being washed in the acidic water with too much and too strong a soap, blistered by the iron, and rolled around in the mud at work every day, our threads are wearing out much too fast. We will be in tatters and see-throughs by the six-month mark.

* * *

--We have the same night guard, but another new day guard / gardener now, both of whom we continue to be told are necessary to protect against thieves. We can't get used to having someone around all the time, especially doing work we've always done ourselves.

--Our night guard, Vyance, (Vee-ahnce) shows up an hour early each evening (by agreement and in time to have left-overs from supper--

and we especially don't mind because we know it may be his one full
meal for the day). He always carries a big iron poker around with him to
fight off intruders, thieves, wild dogs, cats, and the bogie-man in
general.

Only thing is, once our lights go off and sometimes before, he's asleep
on the front porch, innocent as a babe. But he's funny, protective, is a
really light sleeper, and I like him. If we forget and leave a window
open at night, he worries about it enough to show it to us the next
morning. He speaks no French and we don't speak much Kirundi yet,
but he really gives us heck for making his job harder; lets us know we
should be more careful. We occasionally have these wildly animated
point-and-say conversations, with Jim and I usually reduced to properly
chastised umuzungus before it's over.

     We may learn to speak adequate Kirundi in time--probably just
before we come home.

Trying to stay out of the rain,
Jim and Me2

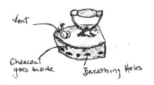

Chapter 32
Feline Fever

Dear Mom and Dad, alias hey you guys,

Not speaking of kitties, we've inherited two wild cats from our P.C. director, Chris, that I don't think will last long. They're not very House-i-fied, and drive us crazy racing from tabletop to bedroom, pulling towels and clothes off the shelves, dishes off the table and causing general pandemonium.

Yesterday, the big one pulled the little one off the table by sinking his claws into the tablecloth and yanking hard. Of course the salt and pepper shakers, breadbasket and clean laundry came tumbling down at the same time.

They only leave the house long enough to get into fights or get muddy, or both, and return to track muddy red paw prints everywhere! Sheets, blankets, furniture or legs--nothing is safe or sacred. They have this neat game of bouncing off the walls in their hourly races around House, and we have paw prints four and five feet up and down the sides of all the blue walls.

They also have this endearing little habit of catching mice, not quite killing them, and dragging them inside to play with--batting them about and tossing them into the air till we take notice and praise them. Then without warning, down the hatch, whole and unchewed, and five minutes later chuck them back up on the floor in not such good condition. Nice, huh?

Have fallen totally out of love with cats. Guess the worst part is their regular food.

Think I've told you before that Lake Tanganyika produces a small fresh-water fish similar to a smelt or sardine, called ndagala (in-dah-gah-lah). These yummy little morsels are sun dried whole (too tiny to fillet) and sold in small quantities in markets throughout the country. You can follow your nose to the fish stands anywhere.

Unfortunately, the cats are addicted to them, so the lovely aroma of rehydrated ndagala and rice permeates the air twice daily. Can hardly bear it first thing in the mornings when the cats are the hungriest.

Norman, the younger kitty, has developed a bad habit of lying in wait in the dark passages of the hallway, then leaping out at us with claws unsheathed and on the attack, attaching to pants or skin or both with great tenacity. We've unintentionally punted him into the kitchen several times in a reflex action.

And lately, he's taken to attacking Jim's feet if they poke out from under the covers at night. This does not endear him to the man of the house at three a.m. It happened again last night and Jim shot up from the bed like a cannonball, bouncing me out on the rebound.

The older one just goes around spraying the furniture. I always thought the comic strip *Garfield*© was a bit exaggerated, but our frame of reference has broadened, and we find he's right on target for certain particular cats in this world! We are still trying to figure out how they got paw prints on the ceiling of our bedroom!

Love and 2 hugs,
Foundering in felines
(alias Jim and Me)

P.S.

Had an interesting thing happen today. We work under the Ministry of Eaux et Forets (Oh-A-four-A, or, Waters and Forests). One of their gentle hierarchy showed up with an Englishman in tow, a PhD in biology who's here for the FAO/UNDP (Food-Agricultural Organization/United Nations Development Project) to give the Burundian government an assessment of our program and the future of inland fisheries here (a bit early in the program since we've no ponds built yet, but, there you go--guess you can't start assessing any too soon).

Now that we're actually here and beginning to establish ponds, people want to know if we could possibly be any good or if they should continue to support us. Had an interesting talk with Dr. D. and then he offered us a job when we graduate from Peace Corps--with only one stipulation--Jim has to grow a beard! (Much to my delight)

"Because," he said, grinning widely, "all AID/FAO people are considered strange and are expected to have beards".

Well, food for thought. Just as long as I don't have to grow one, yes? We liked him a lot, and Dr. D. and our host-country Ministry counterpart brought us a well-deserved smile and break from the routine.

But the duo also delivered a letter from our director saying she'd received notice from the Minister of Agriculture (pretty high up the ladder--as in the top rung) that we actually are going to have to move to a new house. Major sad.

We've just got this place set up, desks and work tables built, hot water heater working, garden up and growing well, fence and landscaping repaired, flower beds blooming, and best of all, we are getting to know and enjoy our immediate neighbors...as in making friends. Poo. Guess nothing is permanent, yes?

Rumor has it that our P.C. Director rented this house (the least expensive one available per month--good business, right?) Maybe. The house owner is a friend of our Number Two boss in Eaux et Forets (thus the good deal), but not an especial friend of our governor (a very nice man, too), but who, it turns out, had promised us to someone else. There's apparently been a back and forth tug and pull, with us in the middle all this time, and so glad we didn't know till after the fact. Our poor P.C. boss.

* * *

Today, we inspected the New House we're being moved to and it is an ENORMOUS homely thing with no view, no privacy, no fence and right across the street from the big agricultural/coffee complex with lots of dusty/muddy, noisy traffic all day long. Plus, it's not on the route for the school kids, so we will miss the daily calls for aaaaannneeetah and ijima!

Also, no electricity, no running water, and we have to start all over on the tables and shelves, as we won't be able to take the ones we made from House One. Oh, well, just need to learn to let go and not cling to things or even expectations so much, I guess--.

Oh, and forgot to tell you about the guest bed in our first house. We've waited two months on it, right? It finally arrived yesterday, just prior to our having to move. Jim was taking French lessons, so I put it together that evening with only half as many screws and bolts supplied as were called for. Lovely wood, though, and it went together OK. Next came the mattress foam, a full four inches thick, which was great and unexpected. But put the two together and guess what? It's a regular full size bed with only a three-quarter-size mattress. Now that we're moving, guess the landlord is stuck with it. Too bad for him as he seems like a nice guy and we will really miss his just-right-for-us tiny blue and white house.

* * *

P.S.p.s.

We are having some trouble convincing farmers of what we thought was a well-known fact--water runs downhill. You can't build a pond ABOVE the source of water (unless you have a pump or windmill, which we don't, at least not yet).

Jim is thinking of designing some kind of simple water-powered lift for raising water to some excellent pond sites, but implementation will depend if the technology is 'appropriate' (simple and uses local materials which are affordable, readily available and fits in with the culture and the land needs--land is at a premium here, so we are very careful not to site ponds if they interfere with agriculture of any kind--fortunately ponds grow best in dense clay and agriculture does not).

We spend many of our evenings trying to see problems through the eyes of our farmers and how we would like to have things explained to us, batting around ideas, inventing, rejecting, building our knowledge base-and-understanding basket-of-tools. Who knows, maybe wisdom will eventually show up?

--Thanks so much for the care packages! Love the letters, the dried fruit, popcorn, Tang, popcorn, beef sticks, M & M's, the letters and the popcorn. We're feeling especially 'loved', not just because of the gifts, but because we know someone is thinking about us as much as we are of them in this far-away place.

--Before I forget, you have asked about fertilizer in several letters. There's really not much to be done for the soil here (so far), until they figure out the aluminum toxicity problem. USDA experts have found that many fertilizers put on or added to the soil are immediately tied up by the high aluminum oxide content (very reactive, and thus making pretty much everything not available to the plants for uptake). Wish I had access to more research and resource links to better understand the problem. But in the meantime, I am working on rabbit poop from rabbit hutches as our small contribution.

Love and a hug,
Hewe and Hewe II
(hay-way and hay-way also)

Chapter 33
Almost Christmas!

Dear Laura and Bill, Steven, L.T. and Little-B,

Merry Christmas! And Happy Birthday! I don't think of myself as getting older until I remember how many birthdays my younger sisters are having.

Work is a puzzle. Each day, we head out to our respective communes to do survey work. If we are lucky, and find deposits of clay, or in Kirundi--'ibumba' (ee-boom-bah) or argile (ahr-jeel) in French, in the right location; if it doesn't interfere with current agriculture; and if we can obtain permission from the local communal administrator; then and only then can we ask a farmer or group if they are interested in raising fish.

Since none of the people I've talked to speak French, they're stuck with my baby-Bantu. I give the traditional greeting of "Hi, How are you", ("Namahoro. Amakura maki?")--To which they respond in kind. Then I introduce myself and I ask, "Do you want fish? ("Urashaka amafi?")

They answer, "Yes, of course! ("Ego cane"--Ay-go chan-ee) and look around to see if I have brought some for them.

I say, "It is necessary to build a pond first, then I will bring you fish." ("Gutegerezwa kwubaka itangi rimwe, na hariyo, ndazogenda gereza amafi.") At least, I think that's what I say.

They smile and say, "Yes, white man, O.K." ("Ego, umuzungu, nivyiza.")

I say, "I am not called umuzungu. I am called Anita. I will meet you here next week to start a pond. What day will be best for you?" ("Sinitwa umuzungu. Nitwa Anita. Nzodwi bibiri? Batatu? Ushaka iki munsi mundwiza?")

Once I think I have the day and week settled, we shake hands all around and Jezebel and I ride off into the sunset. The next week Jezebel and I arrive, on time, to find no farmers. Not one in sight. If someone actually does show up, it's out of curiosity only and not the folks I talked to the week before.

Out of seventy-five contacts, I have only one pond actually started. Jim has two. He found someone who could speak French.

The biggest problem occurs when we tell them we won't pay them for their work. The minimal contact or knowledge they've had of other umuzungus or even other Burundians has been in a paid laborer capacity or in mandatory monthly volunteer communal labor projects to support the country's infrastructure.

We are having difficulty imparting the idea that this is their project, their pond, and their fish. Once built and stocked, they get to keep it all. All they can see right now is that we're asking them to donate their time and labor for no pay and they think we are crazy. I mean we're not even important enough to drive cars! Just who do we think we are?

* * *

--Did I hear someone mention PIZZA? Yes, Pizza. We splurged on expensive Buja-bought groceries to celebrate the birth of Trudy and Phil's baby boy! Our new friend (German goat project) Elke brought some GREAT goat cheese from her project. It doesn't melt--just sort of sits there in lumps and gets hot--but it adds terrific flavor and stays white, so we close our eyes and pretend mozzarella, and we are very grateful to have any cheese at all!

Yummm....

We checked out our proposed new house again today and it's much too big for two impoverished volunteers; a grand colonial leave-over that's been stripped of almost everything. The former tenant appropriated the kitchen sink when he left, and the house has no water source that we can find.

Also, it's on a much busier thoroughfare; a dusty/muddy speedway for the dozens of coffee trucks during coffee season, no view to speak of, and no bunch of neat kids to talk to on their way to school. We are feeling deprived.

PLUS, the acre of yard has foot-high grass and no garden. None of this is tragic or unfixable, but we'd already settled in, built a secure nest in our cozy little blue home, and were enjoying our good neighbors and the routine. Relocating will just take more time away from work, now that we actually have some.

* * *

As to things we could use here? Not much actually, unless you find some spare popcorn lying around and looking for a home. We know two folks in Africa that would be glad to offer sanctuary.

Better go now. Have been struggling with the flu and a cold the last two weeks and haven't had the energy to do much except go to work and come home to collapse.

It's funny--one's energy level seems to drop at the equator and even though we are becoming somewhat acclimated to the latitude we never feel quite on top of things, more like slow-motion 3-toed sloths.

* * *

My workday was cancelled for reasons unknown this morning (I know this because my farmers simply didn't show up), so I will spend the day tearing down Jezebel, cleaning and oiling parts, and putting everything (hopefully) back in the right places.

--2 days later--I have a pond site some 30 km away that needs to have one of its water sources (springs) 'elevated and capped' (using cement, rocks and a pipe) to prevent constant contamination and sickness among those using it as a fresh-water source.

Anyway, to make a long story longer, I tried calling Buja to various aid organizations to see if they could help. No luck. Luckily, Phil--our Canadian friend, was headed to Buja and I caught a ride with him, but due to unexpected delays, we didn't arrive at Peace Corps until after hours.

With Congress not signing off on the national budget in August when they were supposed to, we haven't been paid in awhile and all of us are having to stretch one month's salary into three. I left our last big bill with Jim in Ngozi for food and emergencies and was down to my last 300 FrBu ($3), and a bunch of moto gas tickets for reimbursement (we are required to pay for gas out of our salary, keep the tickets and have them reimbursed periodically).

But I was still in luck! P.C. staff was working late (sorry for them, glad for me) and our boss gave me $10,000 FrBu refund on the gas tickets ($100).

Not knowing when we would be paid again and not wanting to spend it all on an expensive hotel room, I headed to an American couple's apartment close by to see if I could bunk in for the night. I caught them just pulling out of the driveway on their way to watch a video of a Vikings/Bears football game at the American Club on a big screen. (She works with CRS and he runs the American Club, so he has access to the facilities 24/7.)

I pulled out a round of fresh goat cheese as payment for my night's stay, they rounded up some crackers and beer and we settled back to enjoy a reportedly spectacular game. But just as I was thinking of how jealous Jim would be, the machine ate the tape. Rick went into immediate shock then began to cry and beg the machine to please-please-please give him back the borrowed tape.

We spent the better part of the next hour coaxing out pieces of a twisted, shredded brown mess that used to be a football game. They invited me back to their house to enjoy an 'old-movie marathon', but the flu symptoms were returning and not wanting to contaminate friends, I decided to catch a late bus back to Ngozi, where I could at least be miserable in my own bed.

* * *

We received notice today that our P.C. director has scheduled a four-day Kirundi training over the holidays, two weeks hence in Buja, since lack of communication seems to be the most common complaint and problem for all of us. Can hardly wait to hear the misadventures of the other volunteers and compare notes.

Merry Christmas and Happy New Year,
Love and lotsa hugs,
Jim and Anita, alias Hewe and aahh-nneeeee-tah

Chapter 34
Frapped!
Dec. 1st year

Frapped: combination of French (Francais) and English (Anglais) or 'franglais'. Frappe' in French (pronounced frah-pay) means to hit or beat. Anglicize it with an -ed ending and you have frapped.

Dear Mum and Dad,

Jim saw his first Burundian snake Friday--at least he thinks it was a snake, or used to be a snake. It had been frapped lifeless with sticks until it was a long, thin, formless blob of skin that used to have something inside it.

What they do to snakes here! I'm not much for having snakes underfoot, but when you see a mob frapping the foo out of some poor garter snake, it almost puts you on his side. Till you remember there are some fifteen deadly species of vipers listed as indigenous to the country. Then you look around for a frapper-stick to carry with you.

The worst one (we've been told) is the Gabon Viper--short, fat, ugly black-brown, deadly--as in you're a goner 30-40 seconds after a bite, with no antidote.

--Working down in the valleys on the ponds, sometimes you'll hear a woman or a man shriek, see them throw everything up in the air, then run like the dickens. You can pretty much bet on what it is, but it doesn't take long to know for certain. All of their neighbors come running with frapper sticks, and it's look out toes and ankles, because something is going to get frapped that's close to the ground.

We always have our rubber wellingtons on and are very careful where we sit, so I don't think there's any danger from actual bites, or even frapped ankles or toes. Mostly, it's the imagination that bites and gets us all nervous wading through tall grass or papyrus swamps to get to a remote site.

But not to worry. Our main danger will be from running out of oxygen in the race up the hill, should we ever spy a real live, unfrapped, venomous version, and I don't think that's terminal.

Watching out for forked tongues, with frapper sticks handy,
Hewe and aahh-nneeeee-taah

Chapter 35
A Three-Clutch Day
December something

Dear Folks,

At last, a few minutes to sit down and write. When we divided territory, we didn't realize I would have the two furthermost communes and the worst roads (all roads and paths north of the highway that runs both ways--east to west). As the crow flies, some appear closer to home, but the road system doesn't fly like a crow or cooperate, winding around an extra sixty kilometers of rough terrain.

Jim went with me this week to see if we could split things up differently when we calculated I was driving twice as many kilometers as he just to get to my ponds.

One particular stretch winds around in circles, descending and ascending through steep hills with hairpin turns, switchbacks and blind curves. Cruising around an easy curve I'd just been on three days before, I hit some freshly laid ball bearings masquerading as gravel and began to slide.

In my panic to avoid going over the cliff, I locked the brakes and went sliding sideways across the road. Into and out of a ditch on the other side, twice, Jezebel hit a bank and tumped me over into a head plant over the handlebars. The fall whacked both my knees, popped my jaw, and put an apple-sized bruise on my hip.

But the worst part? The adventure broke the clutch-handle completely off.

Once I caught my breath, it occurred to me that one can't go very far on a clutch-driven vehicle if there is no way to operate the clutch. Trust Jim to save the day. He thought we could steal the brake handle, flip it over and substitute it into the clutch slot.

Well...it didn't fit exactly and got stuck in the open position every time I downshifted, but it was definitely better than pushing the bloomin' machine fifty kilometers home. And so we pushed on.

* * *

I introduced Jim to some of my farmers and we looked at pond sites for two hours before it clouded up and began to rain, blotting out the landscape. Forced to take refuge in a small beer and shish-ka-bob canteen, we stayed and talked with farmers and folks caught out in the storm, listening to and discussing some of the differences between our two cultures.

They gave Jim an unexpectedly hard time about letting me ride the moto such a great distance to work by myself. (He swallowed his temper and took it in stride, but it didn't improve the atmosphere any that day.)

The deluge showed no sign of letting up and though we knew the trip home would be a wooly-booger *(an-extraordinary-example-of-a-thing)*, sometimes it is better to ride the roads while it's raining and while you still have some traction. Once the water has had a chance to soak in or the roads flood or bridges wash out, the situation gets downright gooey. It was get moving or spend the night on the canteen porch, so we bid our farewells, donned our rain ponchos and headed out.

The first twenty kilometers weren't so bad, but then we hit mud city. Legs splayed out for training wheels, we still managed to each fall once more, coming up sputtering and spitting mud and goo.

The brake-turned-clutch-handle began to jamb up and not release at all when I shifted, adding to my anxiety and lack of control. Three kilometers from the highway, we hit a freshly churned kilometer-long winding mud wallow, all uphill.

That's when it happened. We rounded a curve and there, straddled-- and very stuck across and diagonal to the road--was a large dump truck with no driver. Some forty locals laughed and cavorted around it in the rain, discussing how to push it out or whether or not it would continue to slide until it fell off the mountain and whom or what it might squash on the way down.

After a few moments of private discussion, we opted to move quietly around the melee before things got worse. There was just enough room to squeeze by the truck cab between the edge of the road and the sheer eight-foot wall of the uphill side, but just as I cleared the narrow opening and angled for mid-road, a man jumped down off the hill, right in front of me, wild-eyed and waving his hands, yelling for me to stop, right NOW!

Of course, to avoid hitting him, over I went, skinning and bruising the length of my shin, with my poor moto stuck down in foot-deep muck.

It took the man, me, and two of his cohorts to pry it out... kkktthhhuuuuck...pop!

When it finally stood upright again, I almost cried. The brake-turned-clutch-handle was broken off in exactly the same spot as its predecessor. To top it off, the jumper responsible for breaking it, and me, asked to be paid for prying Jezebel out of the muck! You do not want to know what I said. Not sure it translates well anyway.

And where was Jim during all of this? Not sluffing off his husbandly duties, I assure you. Sucked into a mud hole dug by the truck, he was surrounded by laughing screaming kids, his chain and tires so clogged that Hardly (his bike's re-Christened name) couldn't move.

We clawed, scraped and cleaned until his tires were clear of mud, then cannibalized his Yamaha brake handle to see if it could become my Suzuki clutch handle. At that very moment, the truck driver emerged from the roadside canteen. Full of bravado and good cheer, he ignored us and fired up the engine as everyone began yelling and pushing from all sides.

The truck began slip-sliding immediately and diagonally up the road--straight toward my parked bike. Visions of crushed and battered moto bits swam into my brain, and in alarm I tore around the mob, tears clouding my eyes and judgment.

My new friend, the jumper, joined me and ran along side, grinning and chattering happily, "Not to worry, Whiteman," (or the equivalent in Kirundi) "it won't even come close, do you think?"

Just about that time, the nose of the truck passed us up and the back end came barreling straight for me and my precious moto. The last thing I saw before I jerked Jezebel over into the ditch and the downhill slide was the grinning face of the jumper as he leapt nimbly out of harm's way. The rear wheels of the truck passed over the exact spot where Jezebel and I had stood.

--We grunted, cursed, cried, and pulled, till Jim, I, and the moto were back up on the road, then sat down to wait for the circus to end. Twenty minutes later, the truck found semi-solid, unchurned ground uphill, and we could hear it slowly groaning and straining around the corners ahead.

I transferred Jim's brake handle to my clutch and mounted up, dreaming of gallons of hot cocoa and tea.

But Hardly doesn't have the rear tire clearance of Jezebel, and it took only ten feet of that fresh-churned goo to clog him up and bog him down. For the next half-mile, we rode ten feet, stopped, cleaned, rode, stopped, cleaned.

People thronged around us from hillside homes, laughing, poking fun, asking if we wanted to hire them to carry us home, or clean our tires, in all sincerity trying to be helpful, but also laughing at the dumb-umuzungus-who-get-stuck-in-the-mud-and-think-they-can-ride-in-the-rain.

* * *

We finally hit pavement, and the driving rain on the ride home semi-washed the muck and grime off the motos and us. At last, we lugged weary bodies up onto our porch, grateful Sylveste was still there to assist in a more thorough cleaning of the machines, then sent him off home with a bonus of food and funds for his family, tucked ourselves into bed with a fried egg on pan-warmed cornbread, and drank cups and cups of hot tea and cocoa.

That day will, without doubt, go down as the very worst workday in our life here, and will not, I repeat, will not be repeated.

Love and 2 tender hugs,
Your everlovin' muddy morons

Chapter 36
Manioc, the Wonder Flour

Dear Mom and Dad,

Great news. We found a good home for the two cats, and life is much quieter without their added chaos!

We're in Buja for the holidays and a refresher course in Kirundi. We've had class by day, fun by night and catching up with the adventures of the other volunteers at all hours.

--Midnight Mass in French was like coming home, with a small intimate chapel at the Papal Nuncio (Papal Envoy) with the Latin responses and songs (having come into the Church after Vatican II, but long before Jim and I met, it was the first time I'd heard the Latin), and the neatest Christmas present we could have had.

Afterward, the priest invited everyone downstairs for cake, sodas, and whiskey. Whiskey? Yep. We've discovered another American reputation abroad. The priest had heard we were coming (the famous grapevine) and was just certain we would take whiskey with our cake and wanted to be sure to offer it! Very considerate of him and too bad we don't drink the hard stuff. It looked like a quality whiskey.

--We spent Christmas Eve at the American Ambassador's house and Christmas day at P.C. Director Chris' house (though sad news, she's leaving for another job and will be replaced in January--we're finding we just get used to and enjoying ex-pats and poof, they're gone--and Chris will be missed). Pitching in to help cook at her house, we drank beer, sodas and all the filtered water, talked, laughed and ate ourselves silly with too much dindon (dan-don or turkey), and gravy.
Christmas carols, work stories, and way too many gingerbread cookies later, we had fun with some minor gift exchanges:

--Mary and Sarah had worked hard the week before Christmas to make and bake hand painted decorations of flour-water-salt-dough for each of us. However, a national shortage of imported wheat flour forced them to settle for manioc flour; yellowish white, powdery, looks like flour.

But when you mix manioc flour with water, and bake it, it smells and smells and continues to smell, like upchuck. Even the paint couldn't seal it up. So after everyone sincerely 'oohed' and 'aahed', we put our lovely ornaments on the other side of the room with the air. In a few days the odor should go away and we can display them proudly.

--Jim has always wanted to make two things (minor ambitions): a perfect coat hangar and a paper clip. We don't need many paper clips here, but at two to three dollars each, volunteers cannot afford coat hangars and don't have any.

He found a great deal on a roll of galvanized wire from our favorite outdoor hardware market and it gave him a perfect idea for Noel-gifts. A quick jig from nails and a board, and VOILA! Enough coat hangars for everyone. What a hit! You'd have thought they were made of gold.

--I drew up personalized cartoons from the shared work stories, using ducks, chickens, monkeys and zebras as a medium for each volunteer and the staff. Except for Dann. He's the volunteer in charge of the fish station and responsible for all the brooder fish and raising fingerlings (fry) ready for distribution.

Because he doesn't have to travel to pond sites and lives close to Buja, he's the only one of us who doesn't have a motorcycle yet, and the lack of transportation (re freedom) is beginning to get to him (can really empathize with that). So his cartoon was a letter to Santa asking for a motorcycle and some gas...

Dear Santa...

"...I will find some cookiez and milk to leave like always. love, Dann..."

* * *

--The funniest part of the evening was the story told from a friend (ex-P.C. volunteer-turned USDA expert), Suzanne. She has a droll way of telling a story that makes you hang on every word, and we did, as she described a summer job as an egg-cracker and smeller on an egg-line moving assembly for a local farm co-op. There was an incident involving a break in the egg delivery pipe...

We all fell on the floor laughing at her story-telling ability, and again as she demonstrated her excellent talent for cracking two eggs in each hand across a knife, sniffing the shells on the fly as Jim moved the bowl by her to catch the eggs (no shells), then tossing the shells and remnant egg parts to rain over us.

--Laughter to heal the soul and hot showers any time we wanted them had to be another two 'best' gifts of the week.

* * *

Had thought at one time we could rig up a solar water heater for warm showers and a solar oven for cooking at our post, but alas, alack, Ngozi hasn't had enough warm, sunny days in the rainy season to warm water for a cricket. Overcast and cloudy most of the time, it has rained nearly every day of the four months we've been there. So we donated our solar shower to Sarah, who's now posted out in Cibitoke, (chee-bee-tow-kay) on the hot sunny plains northwest of Buja.

The other volunteers will be staying in the capital over New Year's for R&R, but with our move to the New House imminent, Jim and I have decided to return home a little early. Work is picking up, farmers are accepting us, and we are really enjoying the job, so don't like to miss even a few days away. Off to pack now so we can catch an early bus tomorrow morning.

Thanks a hundred million times for all the cards, letters and magazines. They make the frustrations and hard work worthwhile. If we accomplish anything here, it will be due in part to the moral support we get from home.

Take care.
With love and lotsa hugs
Jim and Anita

* * *

P.S.   Some very sad and disturbing news. Primatologist Dian Fossey was found slain in Rwanda yesterday. She was working to protect the last mountain gorillas in the wild. No news on why, who or how yet, and no danger for us, just very sad for the community and puts in question the ultimate survival of the gorillas (and chimpanzees), as poaching is rampant.

* * *

p.s.2   We are not raising fish yet. As of today there are only thirty known nilotica in the country, but arrangements are being made to import some two hundred from Rwanda in a few weeks for the fish station. Dann will be responsible for raising the fingerlings from these brooder fish for the rest of us, and he's hoping to turn out 2000-3000 fingerlings per month. Assuming our ponds are finished by June or July, we'll need five thousand or so just for starters. Yeah!

Chapter 37
New House
Jan.8, 1st Year

Dear Mom and Dad,

It's New Year's week. Unlike Christmas, which is a quiet day of celebration at home with family, New Years is one of the three biggest holidays of the year, the others being May Day (like our Labor Day) and Independence Day in July.

Not only is New Year's the time for revelry and celebrating, it is also the time of year to buy household furnishings (because the coffee money is coming in), exchange gifts and give to others. Our neighbors tell us it is a tradition to give whatever is asked of you these few days.

Fortunately, tradition also dictates that the one asking be reasonable in his or her demands. So, every half hour or so, there's someone else at the door asking for a gift of food or clothes. We've made up extra food packets, since we need to keep the few threadbare clothes we have. We weren't aware of it until it was too late to stay in Buja, but most normal work stopped days ago to prepare for the New Year celebrations. But we have truly enjoyed being here to experience the local culture. Music, dancing, sports events and an abundance of food highlight the festivities.

People pour off the mountains and out of the banana groves in droves to roam the streets, hills, and valleys. They visit, laugh, party, and consume unbelievable amounts of beer. Our village even splurges and runs the generator for the duration of festivities, so there is electricity and water.

But twelve inches of rain on New Year's Day and more on into the night made it a good day to stay inside. We moved pots and pans under the various drips from our very holey tin roof and settled in to transport our belongings and set up House number 2.

New House is way too big, with three large bedrooms, a huge salon, two empty kitchen areas, a pantry with no sink or running water, and again, a toilet, but no toilet seat and no running water.

It has turned suddenly colder with the change of seasons, especially at night, and we need two blankets as well as spooning to stay warm. Everybody, locals and ex-pats seems to get sick during this time of year--malaria, diarrhea, dysentery, colds, flu--just like home.

We left the one nice long comfortable bed at House I for two beds in this one that are ten inches narrower and three inches shorter. That's about three inches too short for Jim's six foot one inch frame. So far, the only comfortable way to sleep is at a diagonal, as the large headboards and footboards prevent him dangling over.

The first thing we installed was the mosquito netting over the bed. This house has even more air-leaks than the last and hundreds of no-see-um mosquitos invade during the day to lie in wait for us as soon as the sun goes down. (This would be a great country to raise Chrysanthemums in for the Pyrethrum anti-mosquito coils like we had in Canada. Might even cut down on the Malaria?)

We have a huge yard (180 ft. x 80 ft.) with lots of trees, including a fifteen-foot tall poinsettia tree out front (think Christmas flowers fifteen foot tall with an eight inch thick trunk), and plenty of space out back for a new garden. Our cook's son, Odance, is back with us and is digging up the garden space now for tilling and composting so it will be ready to plant next month. We also have an avocado tree loaded with avocados that will be ripe in three to four weeks, and three large stands of bamboo in the back where a fence should be.

* * *

A week later and none of our farmers is in the mood to work, so we have had plenty of time to move into House II without taking away from our fish work. Next year we will participate more with the P.C. crew, but we enjoyed the local celebrations and our farmers dropping by for visits and a beer this year.

--House II: Still not much water where it's supposed to be (in the pipes), but the plumber is valiantly trying to locate new pipe to bring water into the kitchen, as the last tenant took not only the sink, but the piping that went along with it. The existing remaining lines are so corroded, that to get any water into the toilet, the bathtub, or the bathroom sink, Jim or I get up at 6 a.m.--the one hour per day when the electricity to pump the water turns on--go outside, beat on the pipe with a hammer (the part that's not buried), and jump up and down over the part that is buried. Makes a real show for the early birds walking to work.

If we are successful, a big bunch of orange-brown crud with lots of scary air shoots out of the faucets in the bathroom for four or five minutes. When it clears (sort of), we semi-fill the bathtub--drivel by dribble--for the day's supply. Result? Cold rusty spit-baths again this week because we can't afford to waste even a drop.

The landlord (through Peace Corps negotiations) has promised to install all new plumbing and two water barrels for storage. How soon is the question? We could do it ourselves, but it's expensive and it would take all of our saved vacation money, so we want to give him every opportunity to follow through.

We are also considering a rain catchment system using expensive guttering, but again, we have to locate our landlord for permission first and so far we've not met him.

--The plumber found a used aluminum kitchen sink today with side arms too long for the space available, so his crew took a sledge hammer and knocked out the two-foot square concrete post interfering with the new size sink, brought in fresh brick and mortar, and installed a new one. Impressive and must say they did very good work on the whacking-out part.

But the old drain had been plugged off with a cap sticking out of the floor, and apparently not knowing what it was for, they cut it off even with the floor and were sealing it up as I came in the door from work. I explained to them it wouldn't do much good to have a sink if the water went all over the floor. They agreed to break a new hole in the concrete and replace the drain to the septic tank (didn't even know we had one-- one of those automatic things you don't think about much in the States). Very exciting! Lots of noise, yakking, and brouhaha. Maybe we will actually have water by Friday!

Have we said? The new house is bigger, the tin roof is bigger and the ceilings higher (approximately fifteen feet), and everything is a little noisier, a little draftier, a lot colder, and a lot leakier when it rains.

Tracking down leaks in the attic with a tube of **Goop, Shoe-Goo**® (we brought with us), Jim has found a quantity of fresh bat guano, but the fruit bats exit the moment he enters. Though the bats are huge with foot and a half wingspans, they are not nearly as intimidating as the rats that have taken up full-time residence. These lovely beasties hold a nightly demolition derby upstairs in the rafters after the kerosene lights are out. And red, beady eyes glaring from the shadows have Jim looking over his shoulder at each shuffle-noise when he's up there checking out leaks.

Man, I'm glad it's guys that are good at these things!

* * *

We purchased a bed for our night zamu, Vyance, so he can sleep in comfort now, instead of scooched up in a huddle on the cement floor of the garage (yes, House II comes with a ready-made open, attached garage). We chain the motos up at night to two cement posts Peace Corps kindly installed for us, and he beds down in front of them with his poker stick handy, nice and comfy under his blanket.

There is an actual zamu room attached to the rear of the house, but since Vyance prefers to stay with the motos in the garage, we will probably build a rabbit hutch in the zamu room and install bunnies instead.

--Sad news. Gone the lovely sky blue from House I. House II boasts bilious chartreuse-green curtains, rock-hard maroon plastic furniture, and dark red cement floors. The gloomy interior had dark grey, black and green-checkered walls, which are now painted white, but there's not much to be done for the fourteen-hued Technicolor mixed-up painted rock exterior. Think the painter did it on purpose to designate an umuzungu house, or maybe he likes patchwork quilts.

* * *

--We have been negligent in describing clothes. Most farm-women wear knit pullover shirts with a traditional long, bright-colored length of cloth wrapped around and round at the chest and draping to the ankles. Babies travel strapped to women's (or children's) backs with another short length of cloth, and--or supported by a stiff goat-hide sling strapped to the woman. That, we expected and it looks 'African'.

But the farmers mostly wear European or American style clothing with a vest or jacket over the shirt, double-knit or cotton slacks, and often a hat. Even when clothes become stained or threadbare, they are always as clean as possible.

It still startles me to see someone ankle deep in mud or dirt, hoeing in a business suit. How things look is very important and the better-dressed one is, generally the higher position and esteem they command...not so different from the rest of the world.

That puts us right down at the bottom in our threadbare blue jeans and T-shirts. Jim looks pretty Peace Corps classic in his jeans, shirt, vest, and baseball cap. Me, they're not so sure about. I get so wet and cold on the moto (it's around 40 degrees in the a.m. with an even lower wind-chill factor), that I usually wear three or four layers of clothing, plus my new extra-big rain jacket (thanks Laura!)

And during this cold rainy season, I don't shed more than one or two layers even after arriving at the ponds. Apparently, this has caused some confusion among the farmers. One group finally persuaded the pond-chef's Mom to clarify things.

--So Clarisse walked up one morning with a big smile and gave me the traditional Burundian hug, with the light embrace (barely touching) and the gentle pats on the back with both hands. Then she turned to the side and patted me firmly on both breasts (not traditional), then turned to the farmers and gave them a solemn nod, saying,

"Ego, ava umugori." ("Yes, we have a woman.")

Apparently, there was some question as to my gender, since I wear men's clothing, ride a motorcycle, and give instructions like a man. They'd been discussing for weeks how to find out without asking or insulting, and whether or not I was a new type of white hybrid human being. They seemed very much relieved to find out I was just a crazy woman, confused about proper dress.

The farmers seem to be accepting both of us now, and acceptance is all that matters in the long run, I think. But they also think we're some kind of hybrid Europeans, as each new group asks, "Where in Europe is America?"

Love and lotsa hugs.
(not) Calvin or Anne Klein

Chapter 38
Our Status in Community

Dear Uncle Con and Aunt Dorothy,

We've been unable to find bamboo large enough in diameter for the job, so I've started a secondary project to make clay pipes for the farmers to use as overflow pipes in their ponds. But first, I have to purify the abundant natural clay, removing the organics and most of the sand. To do this, I've collected and dried out some porcelain cannon-ball-sized clay and chunks of other various clay samples in our garage. (The cannon balls are from the kaolin or porcelain-clay 'cannon-ball' factory just down the road, used in the manufacture of cement in Buja).

And today I was to begin mushing it all to bits and pieces and powder for the separation process. Now pulverizing dried clay cannon balls into powder in a fifty-five gallon metal drum in the front yard was guaranteed to draw a large crowd. Sure enough, a crowd formed within minutes after I'd begun--all of them pointing--shouting--laughing.

I hired one of the laughers to continue for me (beats putting an ad in the paper), while I filled two barrels in the back yard with water to receive the powdered mess (we have electricity and water so far for the weekend, must be a dignitary in town--and having electricity is the reason I started the project today while we have water.)

The conglomeration of dried clay mixed into the water will settle out into its respective densities, then 'age' and grow bacterially (bacteria help give clay its plasticity) for a few weeks, then I'll siphon off the water and take the clay off the top, leaving the organics and sand behind on the bottom.

But right now, my hire-ee has a long chunk of tree trunk, a large barrel, the clay balls, and he's pounding the foo out of all of them. Can't believe the vibration is shaking the house.

* * *

Because of projects like the above and the way in which we go about them, we're rapidly gaining the reputation of being the craziest umuzungus in town.

Word travels fast. Especially after some of them saw me talking to the ceiling in the garage last week. (Jim was in the attic tracing down a bad electrical line (for the very rare times we have electricity-- sometimes one hour in the morning for the water lines or when a dignitary comes through town) and he was also looking for water leaks.

I was supposed to be guiding him to the leaky spots and light fixtures by shouting up to him through the ceiling tile. People had gathered in the road behind me and watched me talk to first the garage, then the living room ceiling before I turned and noticed there was someone watching. I thought it strange that they were keeping such a safe distance away instead of crowding up to peer in the windows as they normally do. Guess they understood that sometimes, crazy people can be dangerous.

Oft-times we'll be describing a new enterprise to our coffee-expert-friend Jan, and he'll smile that funny sort of way and say "Yes, I heard already", as if he can hardly restrain himself from laughing at us too, and we know the famous grapevine is alive and well. Nice to know we're always good fodder for a smile or the gossip mill.

* * *

Pond Construction:

Pond construction is progressing in wonderfully fun fashion and we learn something new every time we leave House II for a day's work. We need good tight ponds with no leaks to keep the plankton bloom going for our filter-feeding-plankton-eating fish and to keep the temperatures as warm as possible in this high altitude.

But explaining to our farmers the importance of compacting the dirt every five to ten inches in height during dike construction has been difficult. They don't understand why they can't just pile it all up then 'tamp' or smooth the top layer a bit.

As construction goes along, I run up and down the length of the dike stomping and tromping to show them how loose the soil is unless it's compacted. My guys think this is hilarious, but it's somewhat like dancing, and since they know by now that I'm crazy and harmless, they've made a joke out of it and dance on the dikes with me, even dragging along wonderful handmade instruments and drums for musical celebrations.

Dancing works just as well, we all have fun, and they are beginning to understand the importance of it. When I show them tamped versus un-tamped after a heavy rain, there's nothing left of the un-tamped part. It's all washed away down into the river, while the tamped part barely shows any erosion.

After closely inspecting one of my sketches again, they surprised me this week by creating new T-shaped tamping tools hacked from tree branches and logs with their machetes, and have begun to have competitions to see who can tamp the hardest.

It's a wonderful breakthrough in communications and to see that they're beginning to understand. Any response or enthusiasm is encouraging and I'm grateful they are so willing to put up with my lack of proper Kirundi.

* * *

--Motorcycles continue to be a source of bumps, bruises, near misses and close calls, but we're enjoying the freedom they provide with the work. We're not allowed to take them out of the province or use them for pleasure, and to be honest our PC staff needn't worry. After spending six days a week beating ourselves to death on the back of one, the last thing we think about is going for joy rides on Sundays.

Sound like childish rules for mature adults? Well, sort of. But two reasons give it credence. The biggest cause of volunteer casualties across the whole of Peace Corps is motorcycle accidents. Also, volunteers are supposed to become a part of community and live at the level of their host counterparts. That means staying home on weekends and becoming involved in the local community instead of gallivanting around the countryside or partying in Buja with other umuzungus.
I think our particular group would have been ultra-conservative without the rules, but those coming after us may be wild and woolly instead of dull and doddery, so better to have them in place and a part of history.

Gotta go.
Take care, with love and two hugs,
Jim and Me2

Chapter 39
Four Fou's, or Four's, fou's, and feuille's
January something

Dear Mom and Dad,

First, to answer some of your questions in lots of bits and bites:

--It alternates between hot and humid to cold and rainy every two to three days. The short dry season lasts six or seven weeks, and it is also the season of hunger. Fresh vegetables like carrots, peas, corn, squash, tomatoes, and cabbage are almost gone, and it's two months or longer before the new crops will be ready. So it's back to manioc (cassava, the leaves are boiled senseless to a cooked-spinach consistency; the roots are pounded and boiled thrice to remove the cyanide compounds--then dried to a flour that smells like upchuck), bananas, and dried beans with a bit of rice for most people. Oh, and almost forgot, Taro leaves--same as our Elephant Ears from southern flower beds–they harvest the leaf just before it begins to 'unroll' and steam it to eat as 'greens', and steam the roots to mash up like a potato. Pretty tasty.

--They are hungry a lot of the time. Just too many people and not high enough crop yields. Guess I've already mentioned the problem with aluminum toxicity in already acid soil that causes low productivity and low nutrition in what they do harvest.

--Soccer is the king of sports, and enthusiasm for favorite teams borders on mania and unbridled frenzy. Stadiums and playing fields are packed on Saturdays and Sundays. A throng of people just went by on their way to the game, chanting and shouting. We'll catch the last half of the game after while.

--Jim's gaining quite the reputation as a nifty 'fix-it' man in both the umuzungu and the local community. Hardly a week goes by that something doesn't show up at our door for repair. He's used the volt-ohm-meter you sent with him to diagnose and cure everything from radios and tape recorders to electric stoves and generators. Tickles him to be able to help somebody and gives him a hobby aside from the fish work. He even diagnosed a bad transistor on our P.C. director's Apple computer so she could order parts! Today he's out rescuing the goat project's generator by re-wiring it after it burned up.

--Our German friend, Elke, purchased a used electric stove that didn't work well and told Jim if he could fix it, we could have it. Well, it took some doing and it only has one oven element and one temperature--hot, like our Wretched Thing--but it works, and you don't have to swing it over your head to make it go--yet. Electricity is expensive and infrequent, so will continue using The Wretched Thing, but on days the electrons are flowing and I need my spirits lifted or we have company, I can turn on the stove and laugh.

--We opt not to eat the local favorite of foo-foo (boiled, swelled-up-smelly-manioc flour-dough), though we do enjoy the 'sombe' which is manioc leaves beaten and boiled lifeless with chopped peanuts, salt, chili peppers and palm oil–yummm–tastes a bit like spinach.

--But speaking of foo, there are some very difficult French pronunciations of words beginning with 'F'. There's:

four (fu)--kiln or oven (barely pronounce the 'r' in four)

feu (fu) --fire, to light or make a fire

fut (fu) --large barrel, though I can't find the plural for it in our dictionaries and not even certain it's the right word!

fou (foo) --crazy person

feuille (fuee-ya) --leaf

there's also deux (dyu) --two

Anyway, they all sound a lot alike to the untrained American ear, especially if you try to sound like a local and drop your voice below hearing level for the last half of each sentence and run all your words together with no space in between. The softer-spoken one is, the more sophisticated one is presumed to be. It is a wonderful game of one-up-man-ship, especially in a crowd. We've become semi-adept at lip-reading and guessing games, but if we guess wrong and get lost entirely upon the wrong track, we are in trouble. Conversations frequently take on an absurd quality, what with us mis-understanding or misinterpreting the last half of every sentence.

--I was at the Governor's office the other day to drop off our monthly reports with the bureau secretary, when the Governor beckoned me into his office to 'chat'. This terrified me because my poor vocabulary in both French and Kirundi is alas, limited to fisheries, and inaccurate baby talk at that, so I immediately suffered brain-freeze.

I think he started off by saying he'd heard we were doing good work, but he could have been saying he was sorry our hair was falling out. I did understand him when he asked what I intended to do with all the clay balls piled up in our garage (so he had already heard the stories!)

I explained it was for a clay pipe experiment to regulate the water level into and out of the ponds. The clay was to be made into pipes-- then baked by a 'feu' (fire) in a 'four' (oven or kiln), but that I'd needed the deux grandes 'fut' (two big barrels--or so I thought) to begin the process of purification of the clay.

He looked puzzled then dared to ask what I needed "deux grandes feuilles" (two big leaves) for?

"I'm sorry, monsieur-le-Gouverneur, deux grandes fut," I repeated (I thought, but messing up with the plural).

"Deux folle (plural of fou)?" (Two crazy persons?), he asked, correcting me. "But why?"

"Ummm, No, deux fut", (two barrels) I said.

"Oh, I see," he smiled brightly, "deux fours!" (Two ovens)

I was really beginning to sweat. "Uhh, Not exactly. The fours come after the deux fut. I bake the pipe with a feu in the four after it's been in the fut," I explained.

"Oh," he sighed. "I see. Well, good luck."

He was so nice about it, but I could tell he didn't understand a word of my abysmal French. By now, I think he must think I'm utterly fou! (Crazy) I'd have been better off grabbing his pen and paper and drawing pictures--I know how to speak Art, but he might have considered that an attack.

The biggest problem is that we rarely have opportunity to practice French, except down in Buja, so we are not 'getting' or 'keeping' much vocabulary in our brains or on our tongues, and we are still at the 'translation' stage, having to think about every word in English, translate it to French, put it in proper tense and gender, then try to let it roll off the tongue like we knew what we were doing, all in the space of a milli-second. Oh, Me. I don't think we've fooled anyone yet.

--The Kirundi is also a struggle--coming slowly, and one word at a time. Since it is primarily an aural language and we haven't seen much written down, vocabulary comes down to hearing it properly--and to a good memory. Uh-oh.

Kirundi pronunciation is simple and phonetic, but all the combinations of correct time, space, and gender are killers. Even so, with much pointing, shouting, sign language, picture drawing, laughter and more important, actual demonstrations, we feel we are making progress.

--We've both developed big calluses from handling a hoe--their favorite and only tool besides the machete--and have begun to establish some of our best work and our best relationships in the Kirundi-only places.

They have so much fun laughing at our efforts it takes all the wind out of our egos and forces us to join in with their never-ceasing antics. They really love to laugh. Have begun to believe it cures or heals almost everything.

--Out working at one of my all-Kirundi places the other day (well, actually, all of my places are all-Kirundi--Jim has a French-speaking guy at two pond sites), I couldn't get them to dig the drainage ditch next to the pond as deep as I wanted it. They like to dig wide, not deep, and it is difficult to get them to stop with the wide once they start.

"Why?" you ask. Read on. I grabbed a hoe and jumped down into the ditch. All went well for the first three or four whacks until I struck an underground river, and water and mud came back in a dead-zero splat over my face, hair and the rest of me. Quiet prevailed for all of three seconds until I grinned. Then they fell on the ground howling hysterically, and I was officially initiated and accepted.

I got my ditch. They learned something about drainage. And I learned another thing about their culture. They weren't going to tell me I was wrong, they were just going to do it their way. When they discovered I wasn't concerned with ground water coming into the ditch (since it was a drainage ditch to begin with) or with getting dirty myself, it left them free to make the choice of digging deeper.

--Jim had a similar experience when he strode out across a prospective pond bottom his guys wouldn't dig deeper, and sank up to his knees in boue (boo) or mud. His rubber boots filled up and he almost lost them pulling his legs free. His guy's loved it. Took them thirty minutes to stand up again and catch their breath. It also caused him to move the pond to a spot a bit higher up the hill, one with clay clear to the center, not mud. An Oops, yes, but better to discover it early on than to have a pond that won't hold water or temperature.

--Just got word, the town generator is still out; waiting on parts from...somewhere not close, and we've no water in the house even for our one-hour in the morning for at least another two weeks, maybe a month, maybe ever.

We're getting old waiting to take a bath or even a mini-shower, but with Sylveste or Odance having to haul every drop we use either from the distant community spigot or the valley below, we try not to use more than just the minimal for cleanliness and health.

We did splurge with two pots of hot water on Friday night, firing them up on The Wretched Things to heat (and yes, we are now a two-wretched-thing family--really uptown). The bathtub is still our reservoir for water, so bathing resembles the old #3 washtub nights in Canada before we got indoor plumbing and a shower. Except that the wash pan is about one third the size, almost big enough for the feet to stand flat if you curl your toes. We took turns pouring cups of water over each other and flooded the floor, but clean we got, and scrubbed the floors after, so accomplished two things at the same time!

After our bath, Jim took me out on the town for dinner to the local shish kebab and beer place where we met some of the town-folk and chatted a bit before our order arrived, learning some new vocabulary, which was great, and I didn't have to do the dishes.

The grilled beef has a great flavor but is so tough and served in such big chunks, that masticating the big wads of it makes you feel like a cud-chewing cow. Sometimes you just give up and swallow it whole with a chaser of beer. Sometimes it swells up so big you can't swallow it, whole or otherwise, so you cover your mouth with your hand, cough politely, and slip it under the table to the ever-present hungry dogs. We figure that this finally is the true reason P.C. insists on all volunteers having great teeth.

* * *

--We planted four trees yesterday in our back yard; two orange and two mandarin oranges. Don't expect to see anything from them in our time here, but maybe the next tenants will.

--Speaking of planting, it's rice-planting season. The valleys, overgrown with weeds, grass, and eight-foot high bright green papyrus swamps are cleared--overnight it seems--by thousands of people working communal labor from dawn to dusk. Grains planted two months ago in nurseries are now seedlings ready for transplanting. Valleys transition from papyrus swamps to rich black peat-bog soil, to the soft glowing iridescent green of rice paddies in a matter of days. The 2200 hectares (5500 acres) planted this year is projected to double to 10,000 acres in the next few years. Man, these people work hard! Really makes us feel like Turtle-Tushies deluxe.

--Remember, Think Worms? Well, it's Think Rabbits now. I've decided to build a hutch in the Zamu hut out back and work out the problems of raising rabbits on a shoestring budget, then introduce them to our farmers for integration with the fish culture. We were told by persons un-named, that men won't eat rabbit because the meat is too soft and it is considered women's food. But a brief survey showed our farmers are excited at the prospect.

  I will eventually try another worm bed underneath the hutch if we can keep the ants out. Found some nice big fat ones in our front yard (worms, not ants)--best ones we've seen so far, so there's still hope.

  --The PC microfiche has yielded several methods to tan hides and skins. The best one (one that's appropriate for Burundi, i.e. cheap, safe, easy and doesn't deplete the Blackwater tree), looks like salt water combined with used battery acid (sulfuric). The only application we've seen for leather so far is the dried stiff goat hides utilized as a waterproof sling to tie babies to their mother's backs. Introducing tanned leather for use in arts, crafts or clothing could be a great job for another volunteer.

    Best go get some work done. Lots to do.

     Love and lotsa hugs to all,

     Jim and ME (alias les deux folle)

     (plural of fou--or--the two crazies)

Chapter 40
Leaky Boots

Dear Friends, alias Bill and Theola,

Thanks so much for the box of clothes and the extra goodies you sent! And especially for the Star Telegram. We are now clothed in garments without holes and have gobbled up and reread every word of the literature twice. Mail and news are so important to our mental health it would be difficult to do without it.

Guess we are wimps, though, or would adjust, maybe-- as we talked to some former volunteers from the country-next-door who were so isolated that they went six to eight months without letters or mail and whose description of how to get to their post was: go to Kinshasa, find the middle of town, then turn south three hundred miles. We are way better off than that, and suspect the volunteers ten years after us will have tons of electronics!

Jim discovered the outside brown wrapping on your package and was as excited about that as what it contained.

"Hey, look at this!" he said, "A real live SAFEWAY® paper sack!" I think we are both becoming simple-minded, what with no stimulating public television, Scientific American's, or engineering journals--or maybe we're just learning to appreciate simpler things. At the least, we'll have a paper bag to put over our heads for the hiccups--or is that panic attacks--or maybe just some anonymity to cover our muddy faces.

--Speaking of Jim, he is subject to lapses of memory from time to time. Like every time it rains and he's on the moto with his rain poncho. When he straddles the beast, there is a small depression formed in the poncho between the legs and the moto saddle. This depression slowly fills up with trapped water. Not too critical a problem if you remember to lift up the edge of the poncho and dump it before you get off. But if you forget to dump it before you get off, it has this annoying habit of chuting directly down into the top of your left rubber boot. Which is what happens to him almost every time.

Well, he did it again today, delivering our monthly reports to the governor's office in the rain. Up the steps, clomp squish--clomp squish--clomp squish. The noise brought all the office personnel out into the corridor as he passed, and the Governor now thinks we're both a little touched, what with my deux fou's and Jim's perennial soggy left boot. Sylveste can't figure out why Jim's left sock is always muddy and wet in the laundry. He keeps checking the boot for the hole he can't find. I haven't the heart to tell him it's the big round one at the top.

Another lapse of memory must come from living out in the Texas countryside with no close neighbors for so long. Jim forgets the curtains are open, and is constantly mooning the neighbors, stripping off his wet dirty britches in the living room to avoid tracking up the rest of the house. By now, half the neighborhood knows what a white hiney looks like.

Got to run now.

Love and a hug,

Four Leaky Boots in Burundi

Chapter 41
Questions
Sunday Feb. 2, 1st year

Dear Mom and Dad, (alias Ed and Lu)

To answer some of your questions about why we are here and what's it all about: We're enjoying our work more each day. Yes, it's frustrating sometimes, but no more so than jobs back in the States--just different--and working outdoors (rain and mud aside) makes us feel healthy and alive. There's nothing like manual labor to help you sleep well at night.

--Are we suffering? Actually, about the only thing I can think of that we suffer from is that American desire to 'fix' everything. There are so many needs here--we just can't answer to all of them without burning ourselves out. Guess it's the same back home, just at a different level. But it's also easier to ignore needs at home through entertainment or escape through activities, or acquiring more stuff we don't need.
Or maybe it's because TV and communications are hyped so non-stop, that one feels overwhelmed, intimidated, or unable to make a difference?

--The choices here are difficult and more immediate. For example, women pass by the house every day with empty five gallon jerry-cans, asking for water to do their cooking and washing. Their alternatives of standing in line for several hours at the community water spigot are heartbreaking--or, on days the water doesn't come--walking the three kilometers down into the valley to the river and back up again. It hurts to turn them away.

We struggle constantly between a good dose of Catholic guilt, and wanting to do the right thing. But there is the knowledge that with a population of five million people in the country, when we open our own very limited water system to ten or fifteen individuals, it's only a matter of hours before hundreds surround the house, asking for everything from food and clothing to radios and money. And that type of charity only creates more problems, encouraging people to beg rather than search for their own solutions. We've had to take a stand of 'tough love' and believe we are already doing the most we can for them and the country in teaching our farmers how to raise fish and a few other things.

--As for appreciation from the people or knowledge that we're actually doing some good rather than harm, who ever knows for any of us with the daily choices we make--in any country? Only time will tell, and we may not be the ones to see the results or help with the harvest. Our purpose here is not to change the people or 'gift' them a better life, but to plant a few seeds, and try to live the kind of life by example that encourages them to change for themselves and seek for themselves a better way to live with the information, experience, innovations and the demonstrations we can provide using the tools at hand.

It is a real tight rope, as we Americans tend to think giving is always the answer, whether it be in technology, money, food, etc., when what really seems to be needed is acceptance, encouragement, seed money, information or education, and pointing the way to the resources for them to work out their own solutions.

It's hard to not jump in and do it ourselves, but if there is anything we are learning here, it is that cultures cannot skip steps. They cannot jump from subsistence (survival) agriculture and tribal differences to rocket ships and the stars.

The entire culture has to go through the same education and experiential learning process of agriculture, industry, and technology as did we--though hopefully at a more accelerated rate, with fewer mistakes--and not leave anyone behind.

But we cannot give them--and I emphasize GIVE--roads, money, food, or clothing, and expect them to adapt to the high-tech, 21st century without problems. They have no experience at it. They need the opportunity to work for it and create it for themselves, in their way--not ours--and to decide the direction of their future for themselves, just as we have. Patience and perseverance are two key words in development work.

--As for "is God watching us"? We have never felt more separated from our church community (we especially miss the security and support of weekly or daily Mass in our own language), and yet in a strange way, never closer to God and the community as a whole church. Don't know if that makes sense, but it's the best I can do. Please just know that we feel and appreciate your prayers and support.

* * *

Water:

--On a lighter note, we're almost settled into House II and getting things organized and found again. Jim has plugged some of the more significant leaks in the tin roof himself rather than wait on the landlord as they were located in some very strategic places: right over the bed, the dining table, the couch, the stove, and the kerosene refrigerator.

--But great news! We came home from work earlier in the week to find that the water barrel system had been installed in our absence and we now have reserve water! Sometimes. They even included a drainpipe for the new kitchen sink. Hooray! Can stop doing the dishes in the bathroom sink or on the lawn, and last but not least, they fixed the back door so that it doesn't lift out by the frame (lock, hinges, frame, and all) to open or close.

--Two days later. The water system will be nice if it ever works. The barrels are mounted on a short tower to get enough 'head' (pressure) to deliver water to the house. But we are the last house on the line and there must be a lot of line leaks or blockages, because there isn't enough pressure to pump water up the extra four feet into our barrels.

Back to the drawing board. One alternative is to have Sylveste (or Odance) stand at the valve filling buckets with water, carry them up the ladder, and fill the barrels by hand. But that takes half a day and even if the water flowed for that long--which it doesn't--Sylveste already needs that time just for our laundry. Jim will talk to the Water Department again tomorrow to see if there is a remedy.

* * *

Other Umuzungus:

Of all the development projects we've seen, the Chinese have the most impressive and practical. They address immediate local needs and talents using the resources at hand on a shoestring budget instead of depending on large influxes of foreign monies.

The four Chinese guys associated with the porcelain project dropped in to see us last night. We had a great visit even though only one speaks French and we spent most of our time working on multiple translations.

They were very generous and gave me excellent advice on making better and stronger clay pipes, donating half a dozen cotton sacks to aid in the clay purification process. (How did they know? The grapevine!) Then they asked us where our VCR was and could they exchange tapes, as they had some English-dubbed movies. They were shocked when we told them we didn't have one, either here or back home. They couldn't understand what we did for entertainment!

Feeling sorry for us poor deprived Americans, they invited us over to see their Kung Fu movies with English subtitles, so we took them up on it. The slapstick melodramas were wonderful and hilarious in a true heroic and comic sense, and all followed the same theme of innocent, pure and good, versus dastardly, despicable and evil--except that the good guys didn't always win (in fact, almost never). The hero and heroine ended up dying tragically for the cause as often as not. Perhaps more in line with reality, but not quite as emotionally satisfying to our Western yearn for a happy ending. Still, we had a great time and really appreciate them taking us under their wing.

Really tired now. Too much fun. Gotta get some sleep.

Turabonanye, (Too-rah-bow-non-yay is polite for, "so long")

With love and a hug,

Jim and Anita

Chapter 42
Thoughts, Soap Boxes, and Learning Curves
Some Philosophy and Observations after Six Months

Dear Zants, (alias friends)

Just received your 'the world has gone crazy' letter. Even in our protected, isolated little part of creation it all seems a mess and crazy. But doing work like this has given us a chance to find a different perspective at least on our own lives, if not the world.

Don't know if you've read Toffler's, *The Third Wave*, but from here, it looks like a good assessment of the present chaos: first-world technology clashing with a majority of the impoverished developing-world scrambling to survive. In the States I understood it as a principle. Here I can see it happening. African countries struggling to claim the new and better at forfeit of the old; yet at the same time, needing to throw off the yoke and cloud of colonialism to find their own unique African answer.

But in trying to move and change traditions and cultures too rapidly without resolving internal, territorial and tribal conflicts in the aftermath of Colonialism, even greater problems have been created in societies that are fragile and easily disrupted at best.

* * *

Appropriate technology: Technology that uses the resources at hand, not things that have to be imported, are unaffordable, or unavailable to the average citizen or community.

Appropriate technology helps assure the continuance of a program once the development agency is gone, and avoids long-term dependence on International, national or local governments, or development funds and agencies.

For example: one of the greatest long-term needs in Africa is water: both potable water for survival and water management for agriculture. Of the millions of dollars invested in providing wells, capped springs, and irrigation systems during the past twenty-five years, over 75% have failed once the developing agency left. Why? Often, the communities were not involved in installation of the projects, or (sometimes) the development agency or mission did not take into account the significance of cultural change potable water would bring in local life-styles, and the changes were rejected.

In teaching and encouraging them to select, build, repair and maintain the systems themselves, using materials available and at hand, program continuance is possible.

But if an imported pump-handle or electric motor breaks and cannot be replaced easily or locally, the community is forced to abandon the project or remain dependent upon outside charities. When the community is not involved with the decisions of where, when, and how, the projects have shown to have a high rate of failure.

* * *

The sub-Saharan countries have many problems, from disease and drought to lack of cash flow (economy), lack of infrastructure (roads and transportation), and insufficient food and clean water. The recent 'green' revolution was intended to help many developing countries produce crops grown for export, thus creating cash flow and a growing economy that could pay for their own infrastructure.

Infrastructure allows them to transport and store their own food to feed their own people, build their own schools and hospitals and educate their children. Independent and viable societies, yes? Except that it's not happening, or happening too slowly. The problem is complex, ranging from drought and internal issues, to industrial-world price-control.

* * *

Price Control: Often, in order to protect long-established markets or boost their own economies, industrial or even neighboring countries have imposed trade restrictions or flooded foreign markets with below cost surpluses. This prevents emerging countries from entering the marketplace. When there is no market, their natural resources go untapped or abused. They can't even distribute it or sell it to themselves, as without cash flow, there is no money for infrastructure, education, schools, small businesses.

Our own country's freedoms were hard won and based on the principle of a free and open economy and vast (seemingly unlimited) natural resources. We say we want this kind of freedom for everyone else; that every human being should have the right to choose, work for, and create his/her own future.

But do we really want it? Or do we only want freedom for others as long as it poses no threat to our own way of life, to our own economy? Do we want it only if they are not too successful, too competitive with us? And what do we do when they can produce goods for less than we can because of lower wages and production costs, effectively shutting us out of markets we've dominated. Do we move on to higher technology, always one step ahead of the countries racing to catch up to us? Or do we create wars or control subsidized markets and embargos to keep them impoverished, to disenfranchise them? As a country, I know what our heart says. But our actions often say otherwise. It is a complex and difficult problem.

Where we have been lax, protectionistic or unsympathetic, we've given other powers, other doctrines and ideologies the chance to step in and throw stones at us, and say, "Come---listen to us. Follow us. We have the answer. Our doctrine, our religion, our ideology will change all of that. Everyone will soon have enough to eat and drink. Your children will go to school. Your life will be better."

This scenario is a bit simplistic, but it IS happening, all over the world. And, when people don't have enough to feed their children and can't see any way out of poverty, misery or war, they are willing to believe others who tell them that their way is an improvement. They are ready and willing to believe the villain is the rich American, European, tribe, religion or political machine, and, if they are just not like them, everything will be better.

If any doctrine or power structure did resolve the problems of poverty, hunger, and disease, I would be willing to embrace it. But like so many of our own claims about capitalism, the others are also incomplete panaceas. People still fall down and go boom. What I am trying to say is that any doctrine or ideology, in and of itself has not proven to provide lasting answers. It is people themselves who provide the answers, given the opportunity to create and make them work.

We see the beginnings of change here and in surrounding countries. Of Africans struggling to find their own unique answers, provide for their people while preserving their culture and traditions, with the help of 'proper' development aid and work.

Our main responsibility does not lie in gifts or giving food aid and clothes except in emergencies or as relief from catastrophic events. It does not lie in constantly donating money or things that don't teach or create lasting answers. And it does not lie in destabilizing duly elected governments, benevolent dictatorships or harsh regimes. As one of the leading nations of the world, our main responsibility lies in assuring every other country the opportunity to decide for themselves; through education and appropriate technology; through dialogue with leaders and common citizens of a country; asking them, not telling them, what direction they would go to best serve their people.

Education by example is the most productive and lasting gift we can give; showing them our small-town main-street side, with concerns and feelings very much the same as their own: providing security and safety for our children, sufficient food, clothing and education for our communities, homes, and families.

We have discovered concretely in this tiny little slice of the world that the big enemy in the world is not Communism, Socialism, Tribalism, Nationalism, or Capitalism, or even an opposing organized religion, as people in power would have us believe--but the poverty, fear, and ignorance that all ideologies take advantage of.

I do not advocate anarchy, but I do advocate not taking advantage of the disadvantaged. Every ideology has been guilty at some point of using the poor and disenfranchising them to further their own personal or political agendas.

By ignoring the developing world, we create lasting enemies, while we thrive in our ignorance and are not even aware of the harm we cause. If we REALLY care, we will give the greatest gifts: ourselves, our skills and our time--and make 'space' for them to create their own opportunities. And that doesn't come with guns and napalm or blackmail, but with time and talents shared, so others might have a chance at the freedoms we enjoy.

In a small way, we hope the fish program we're establishing provides some of the above, because it relates directly to the farmer, builds small business enterprise, doesn't involve a lot of money or machinery, and is a program which 'should' continue without our support (once a minimum of three successive groups of volunteers have come and gone to insure program stability). We are currently trying to prove it will provide a low-cost protein that is compatible with other agricultural systems in the region and be of benefit to the nation.

Hard work and economics are two things the people understand very well here. Supply and demand. They are eager for information and technology appropriate to their situation, and are enthusiastic when they can see something that will work for them. The people themselves make us feel like we're doing some lasting good and they are helping us to find some creative ways to resolve problems.

--Well, 'nuff of that. I promise to dismantle the soapbox before our next missives. Suffice it to say we are having our minds stretched and expanded, and it has been good for us thus far.

Thanks for listening.
Love and 2 hugs,
Us

Chapter 43
Kids, Valleys, and Holes

Dear Laura, Bill and boys,

We are still enjoying the work immensely, but the six-month honeymoon is over, and both our hosts and we are realizing the huge cultural gap that exists between us. We've learned so much about ourselves, the American ideal versus worldviews in relation to who we are.

We've also been surprised by the amount of anti-American sentiment simmering in the rest of the world (magnified in our little microcosm of a small country with samplings of ex-pats from around the globe), and we've begun to see how isolated, protected, and naive we are as a country. Still, it is difficult to accept someone disliking or hating you just because of where you're from, never mind who or what you are, believe in or do.

* * *

--Now on to more immediate matters. It rains almost every day--not all day--but enough to make the dirt roads a sea of goo. We try to get out early (by seven a.m.) to drive the hour to our respective work sites, usually in a drizzly fog. Four to five hours of directing, demonstrating, and explaining sees us heading home again, just ahead of or behind some huge afternoon thunderhead full of walls of water.

* * *

--The kids are still the greatest part about being here. They begin to recognize and accept us after the second or third trip to a site. As soon as they hear the moto, they rush out to the road from all directions to wave and shout "Umuzungu! Umuzungu!" Or "aahh-nneeeee-tah! Or ijimma! Yambu!" (Hello).

Their faces light up like Christmas trees when you slow down to wave back and yell "Yambu, abahna" (Hi, kids!). After only a short time working in the countryside, you find yourself no longer seeing the torn or stained dirt-brown clothing; only their shining faces, bright eyes, and big smiles.

--Coming back from a work site the other day in the far--far--far away commune, I passed a half dozen kids, stair-step in size, with the littlest one about three or four years old. They were all yelling and waving hello as I drove by, but the little one was the charmer.

She had on a big, loose, ragged shirt-of-a-dress the dull color of the red clay. And she was in a world of her own with her eyes closed, hearing some special music and dancing to its beat; little hips slowly swinging back and forth, her right index finger high in the air directing some unseen band, sweet face lifted up to the sunshine.

She was so beautiful--filled with grace, and light shining from her like an angel, and I will never forget the smile of delight on her face or the scene of joy and simple happiness it painted in my mind.

* * *

--The farmers at one of my work sites have captured my heart. They've formed a small private co-op to help each other in a number of small business projects, including building fish ponds, and are happy, mischievous and generally full of heart.

Their seven-man team also plays in a band in their spare time and they sing (in perfect harmony, no less)--so we have some great work sessions, making up songs to help get through the hard parts of the day. The chef, Antoine, has a son twelve to fourteen months old. Frederico is always there to dance when the group sings. He often totters over to me when he thinks I'm not looking and grabs hold of my pant leg. The second I look down, he screams with glee and stubby-runs back to Grandma (Clarisse) to crawl under her skirt. All you see of him are two bare little baby-feet planted between hers, sticking out from under folds of material.

And it's so endearing to see him pick up a hand-made hoe much
heavier than he is and scrape dirt up to the dike for Daddy.
There comes a point in acculturation when you see past the kid's runny
noses or bare bottoms, knowing that at this point in time you can't
change it all or all at once, and only see their universal humanity,
knowing you want to be a part of bettering their lives.

* * *

Surveying: One thing I never get used to here is the drainage
systems in the fields. Tradition and heavy rainfalls have forged
murderous methods of cultivating the valleys. The backbreaking work of
pulling up long, high and wide mounds of peat-bog soil leaves three-foot
deep and wide irrigation and/or drainage ditches running parallel to the
mounds.

In itself, this is not too bad. But if families don't weed every week,
which they can't, the mounded-up rows and the ditches are soon overgrown together, with weeds, crops, and grasses covering everything at
nearly the same height.

So you're out scouting the up-slope edges of this valley, right?
Looking for a reported deposit of clay and a good site for a pond. The
only warning you have that the next step under foot is not solid, is
SOMETIMES a slightly darker shadow under the tangled mass of
vegetation.

You take your next step into nothingness and crash through the
overgrowth into three feet of water, mud, and goo. Your chin and chest
hit the opposite bank, knocking the wind out of you. Trying to look
calm as if it's all in a day's work, you gasp quietly for breath and
struggle to break the suction-cup grip and the 45 degree-angle-twist on
your boot, which coincidently, contains your foot inside at that same
angle. With a big squuulomp, the boot, foot, and five pounds of goo
release from the bog.

You crawl dementedly to higher ground and promptly topple over
into the next ditch. You are now covered with water, mud, and hundreds
of maddening, slender little 'stick-tights' that have tiny, hooked barbs on
them. The Burundians call them facher (fah-shay, a French word for
angry or mad--very appropriate, huh?)

There is no longer any way to appear cool, calm, or collected, so
you laugh out loud (cultural sensitivity), curse under your breath
(American reality), and hobble on to the next hole (physical durability),
only to find that the clay deposit is on the other side of the valley, close
to the road, and that all the mud baths were unnecessary (directions here

are almost always a bit iffy--it's the distance-thing in descriptions, maybe).

Guess it's good for the skin tone though, because it's all pulled tighter than a drumhead by the time you get home to wash it off. Don't know how much more 'toning' my legs can take.
P.S.

--Thanks for the audiocassette from you and the boys. Know how hard it is to talk to a dead box and pretend there's someone there, but we've enjoyed listening to it...over and over. Can't believe the boys are learning computer already. Makes us feel old and illiterate on one hand and on the other, gives us something to look forward to trying when we get back. Maybe they can teach us? The songs and news about school and 'Honey' were great.

And thanks again for keeping in touch. We appreciate your calling Jim's folks from time to time, and are grateful to have family like you.

Take care, work hard, and laugh a lot.

Love and hugs all around,

Uncle Jim and Aunt Nita (to the boys)

Chapter 44
Tire Tracks on a B Cup And Little Nubbins
Wed. Feb. 5

Dear Moms and Pops,

We were beginning to think our adventures were over and we were finally settling into a nice, pleasantly boring routine, as nothing especially exciting or funny has happened these past two weeks--when, WHAM--everything happened at once.

We've been taking Flagyl® for a week for what we thought was a case of Giardia. The cure for Giardia and Amoebas are the same but they give a smaller, lighter dose for Giardia.

Apparently we took just enough Flagyl® to make the Amoebas madder-'n-hell because we completed the dose of medication Sunday, and yesterday we both were attacked doubly hard with gas, diarrhea and abdominal cramps. Will descend to Buja tomorrow and pick up the double dose necessary to kill the little nubbins.

* * *

We thought we'd brought a good radio, but with our huge tin roof interfering with reception, we have trouble getting even the VOA or the Armed Forces. About the only thing that comes in half-way clear is sometimes the BBC or the Voice of Russia.

So Jim's been experimenting with the roll of copper wire I bought to make wire sculptures, and he has been setting up some bizarre looking antennas. The radio sits on his side of the eight-foot-long desk, <u>far away</u> from the windows (he likes that side). The wire attaches to the antenna via an alligator clip. At least it started out as one wire, running and looping up, over and across the world map, over my side of the desk and head, around the chartreuse green curtains, out through the window, across the yard and up a tree. When that didn't work, the wire multiplied, had babies and became two, three, now four wires stretched between two trees with a tall bamboo support in the middle.

Friends drop by every couple of days to see what's new. The best reception so far is half of Paul Harvey out of Chicago every night (half means every other word), but still no Armed Forces or VOA, so it's back to stringing more wire--or Jim's wondering now, how he can maybe use the whole roof as an antenna! With all the lightning and thunderstorms ongoing, if you see a bright flash of light shooting up from our region, you'll know something's happened.

* * *

This is supposed to be the short dry season, though it has rained enough every day the past two weeks to stop construction on our ponds. Sunday was only nice for an hour after sunrise then rained off and on the rest of the day, maybe an inch. Monday, more of the same. Tuesday was downright miserable with a cold fog and drizzle that moved right into the bones. But Tuesday night it got serious and rained all night (our home-made rain gauge overflowed at four inches). Today was a steady downpour and we've emptied the gauge twice, so that makes another twelve inches.

We are starting to dread the approach of the BIG rainy season. Maybe we should abandon our other projects and start building an Ark? If we only knew what a cubit was.

--Jim couldn't stand the inactivity any longer and went to work this morning. Lo and behold, when he got to his site, he found some of his farmers willing to venture out in the rain and get soaked with him. But when the skies opened up and laughed on them till they couldn't see the pond, they gave up and he was back home by noon looking like an extra in a Hollywood mud wrestling scene.

Being more prudent, I'd determined to stay home, until I remembered I was supposed to call Buja today for information on funding for some collateral projects. Reluctantly, I donned my rain poncho, helmet, rubber boots and climbed on good 'ol Jezebel for the trip to the P.T.T. (Postal-Telegraph-Telephone, the only public phone in town).

Now House II has a big circle drive in front of it, and one exit of the drive is blind due to our neighbor's tall papyrus fence coming right up to the edge of our own, so you sort of have to ease out slowly onto the dirt road (mud today) to see if anyone's coming.

Which I did and there was. The nose of the moto was half way onto the road and I could just see around the fence, when here came this guy on a bicycle, pedaling ninety-to-nothing directly at me in the rain, right along the fence line with his eyes closed!

You know those slow-motion movie scenes where you almost have time to think? Two choices. Let him hit me broadside and hurt both of us, or lay the bike down and hurt me.

I took too long to blink or think and neither worked out, because when I saw him, I'd automatically slammed on the brakes, which is the wrong thing to do on a moto in a mud fight. The back end fish-tailed out from under me while I was thinking and over I went, right into a big mud wallow.

Just then he opened his eyes and I've never seen anybody so surprised. He veered right for me like a moth to a flame then ran smack-dab over me and the moto lengthwise and fell on top of us.

I was pushing the bicycle up and off when it suddenly disappeared and I rose up out of my puddle just in time to see him hop back on his bicycle and head ninety-to-nothing back in the direction he'd just come from without so much as a howdy-do.

Thank goodness the moto was unharmed and the big mud wallow at the end of our circle drive is about the softest place I've fallen in a long time. You can still see bicycle tracks on my poncho and helmet, though. This red mud is tough stuff.

Made my phone call at the P.T.T., dripping water and muddy goo everywhere. Just let someone try and tell me we don't work hard! Or at least that's what they--the crowd at the P.T.T.--were all thinking--I could see it in their eyes: "Wow, she's really been through hell this morning." They parted to let me by like I was Moses at the Red Sea (or maybe so they wouldn't be contaminated with mud and the crazies). More likely, it's one more story they can take to the Governor.

* * *

Hi, Just a quick note from Jim, here. Wish I'd been here to see Anita get run over by a bicycle. Made for a good story on a dreary, rainy day. You can still see the tire tracks on her poncho and helmet. And best news, (besides her not getting hurt) she still has both the new brake and clutch handles, unharmed!

Well, it's getting late, I'm out of news and it's cold and raining again. Think I'll go fumigate the bedroom. (One thing about dysentery, the effusive odor of the volumes of gas produced keep the mosquitoes away, so I guess every 'cloud' has it's lining--just don't light a match.)
We love you, thanks for being there and keep those cards and letters coming!
Love and a hug,
Jimani

Chapter 45
Buttons and Fish

Dear Mom and Dad,

It's been forever since I've written. I have the best of intentions, but something always seems to come up when I'm in the mood to write. In the meantime, I know Anita has been keeping you informed.

* * *

Laundry:

--We've been battling it out with Sylveste over the laundry again. Finally got him to stop using so much Omo (soap), but he's taken a different tack now. I know doing laundry can't be the most interesting job in the world, especially as dirty and muddy as our stuff always is. But he's taken to folding each shirt a different way so that they don't stack well together OR fit on the shelves. They're always just a little bit wider or longer than the shelf they have to go on. Have been over and over it with him, but he forgets from day to day.

The other thing that drives me crazy is his habit of buttoning all the buttons on a shirt. I'm not the brightest button in the world come mornings, and in the morning when I stumble out of bed and fumble around for a shirt, I have to unbutton every button before I can put it on. Every morning. Sometimes I forget to undo the sleeves and I'm stuck inside with my head trapped at the neck and my hands balled up in the sleeves till Anita can rescue me.

She's tried to get me to undo them the night before or just slip it over my head all buttoned up except for the top, but I get trapped and can't get in or out.

Work:

--Work is going better every week and we're making more contacts now. The language is progressing slowly. It gets so frustrating not being able to communicate as well as we would like. They say when you can 'joke' in a language you've really got it down. So far, the joke's on us!

--I attended a fish conference last week in the country next door with our APCD, Mona, and the fish-station volunteer, Dann, and we transported 562 pure-strain, adult <u>Tilapia nilotica</u> (our native African fish) across the border and long after dark. They were stressed and gulping air from overcrowding so we poured as many as we could into our bathtub overnight to give them a breather, leaving Anita to pump air for them and fix supper, while we took the remainder out to one of my almost-finished ponds (it has a leak that needs to be re-worked)--to 'store' until Dann can return for them. He should have fingerlings grown and ready to transfer to us and the other volunteers by August! Our ponds will have to make it now.

* * *

--We still don't have water to the house very often. Bless his heart, Sylveste spends half his day hauling it from the community spigot and up into the barrels for the washing. Well, it's getting late, I'm out of news and it's cold and raining again.

Love and a hug and best go.
Have a report to write in French. Fooey!
Jim

Hi Mom and Dad, Anita here,

I was out last week getting some good work done. Finished my last pond visit for the day and dropped by a new agronome's (ag-extension agent's) office to give a status report. He decided he wanted to talk to some people about starting a pond and since he doesn't have a moto yet, he asked me to transport him. Told him it was going to rain like heck in a few minutes and wouldn't he rather wait till tomorrow?

He just laughed and said he knew the weather and the clouds much better than I and that it wouldn't rain for at least another two to three hours. Well, we got about ten minutes down the road and all-heck-broke loose from the sky. With him on the back, I couldn't get to my rain gear, plus it didn't feel right putting it on with him not having any.

But after several minutes of being soaked to the skin and with no sign of letting up, I suggested we return to his bureau and take up the matter tomorrow. He decided maybe that would be a good idea. As we headed back, the water level in my rubber boots finally reached the top (just below the knee) and began spilling over. We arrived at his bureau, but drove on past to his house as he said he wanted to get into some dry clothes. I expected to be invited in or at least to stand on the porch till the storm passed, but he jumped off and cheerily waved me on.

The idea of getting out my rain gear was by that time ludicrous and believe it or not, the roads are safer while it's raining than just after (not nearly as slick), as the water rushes over hard-packed ground. Once it soaks in for thirty minutes, though, it turns into a gooey, muddy mess. So I hot-footed it for home (or in this case, cold-footed it) with my visor up (was raining too hard to see through the visor and the visor wipers don't work), water streaming down my face and chin to run in rivulets to the belly button where the waist band on the britches began to swell as it captured more and more water, delivering it...other places, and arrived home just in time for the rain to stop. Jim for once, had beaten the rain home an hour before and was happily reading a book in the dining room, waiting for me.

Funny thing about jeans and some shirts, when they are ALL wet, they just look newer and not wet at all. He couldn't believe I hadn't been soaked in the storm, till he saw the water running over the top of my boots. Then he laughed till he hurt himself as I stood on the porch and poured a half-gallon out of each boot. Socks, jeans, shirt and undies only needed a little soap to finish the wash-and-wear cycle!

* * *

Jim here:

--Our friend, Elke, just came by with condolences and news of the space shuttle Challenger disaster, three days after it happened. What an awful tragedy. Can hardly believe it, or that we hadn't heard yet. Has made us so very sad. This is when we feel the farthest from home and the most isolated. We were so excited about Christa being on this one. Our hearts and prayers are with the families of all the crewmembers and the engineers at NASA. Send me what you can on the cause of explosion?

Jim

Chapter 46
Chinese Toilets and Charcoal Irons

Dear Folks,

It has been cold enough here to think we are someplace besides Africa. Too much rain. It's supposed to be the short dry season, but someone forgot to turn off the spigot, because we've had more rain this month than in the rainy season.

Everyone says it's not normal and should quit anytime. In the meantime, it's wreaking havoc on our pond construction. Can't build ponds when you're knee deep in flowing mud. So, we've had a few light weeks, with lots of muddy moto trips but not much actual work.

Weather changes in Texas don't hold a candle to Burundi. Example: Monday morning it was cold, 42 degrees, with thick fog, mist and drizzle rising up out of the valleys, limiting visibility to about ten feet.

I picked up an agronome (agriculture extension agent) at 7 a.m. and we nearly froze on the hour motorcycle ride to a new pond site. An hour later, down in the valley, I was shedding three layers of clothes under a hot sun and cloudless sky, down to just a t-shirt and jeans. By noon we were climbing up out of the valley and back to the moto, hot and sweaty in 80-degree heat.

I turned around to view our half-day's work from the heights and nearly fell over from the sight of a horizon-wide line of huge black thunderclouds racing toward us.

We jumped on the moto to take the agronome back to his office, but only made it a few kilometers before Jezebel coughed, sputtered, died-- out of gas. (Someone had pilfered my last half-tank, and no, they are not lockable, and at the price of gas, I am surprised it hasn't happened before.) So we struggled on down the path, wheezing and pushing Jezebel in the hot still air and looking for some to siphon ourselves (air and gas).

We finally found some guys willing to let us have their three liters (so I purchased the one gal at double the price–and strangely enough, it was the same amount missing from my moto, but it could have changed hands three times before I got it back), and just as the storm hit with a vengeance. We had two choices--we could get soaked now and 'get out of Dodge' before the commune turned into a river of mud, or wait out the rain and struggle home through mud wallows a foot deep. We chose the first option and only got soaked. I dropped the agronome off, hit the paved road and hotfooted it for home.

And learned something new.

At an altitude of 5,500 feet, on a moto in the rain during the 'season of hunger', and going fast, your fingers freeze to the throttles and you can't undo them. The storm outran me once more (they take short-cuts through the mountains and don't have to stick to the roads--dirty trick), and oh me, it had hail in it. I sought refuge under a big mango tree, but it still found me.

Had to pry my fingers off the throttles and quick-tuck them under crossed arms to keep the hail from beating them black and blue. And learned something new.

Black plastic moto helmets make perfect echo-torture chambers for thousands of nickel-sized hard balls of ice. Wham...Wham...Wham-Wham...Wham-WHAM-WHAM-WHAM--!

It's so loud you want to just scream and rip the thing off, as it threatens to destroy your hearing, but then there's your head to think about--and well, you get the picture. Still not sure which is worse, the noise or the little balls of ice whacking my not-so-hard head. The storm finally eased up and I followed it slowly all the way home, grateful I was on pavement rather than muddy pistes (pees-ts).

It took an entire thermos of hot tea and an hour scrunched up under the covers to get warm again. By 4:00 p.m., it was sunny and warm as Jim rolled up in much the same condition having had a good rainless day of work in the other direction. By 6:00 p.m., another storm had blown through and by 8:00 p.m. the stars were out and it was cold again.

We've begun trying to use the new solar water bag you sent, during hours the sun actually shines, but have to keep a close eye on it in our back yard, as those 'who-provide-for-themselves' are very quiet and very quick.

* * *

Jim ran into the Chinese again while he was out working this week, the group with the porcelain Ceramics Project. (We'd heard rumors they were going to make dishes, cups, etc., and didn't think there was much future in that, but he found out today that their project is for making toilets, bathtubs, sinks and tiles for export--and it should be a great success when it comes about, as most of the surrounding continent needs them).

We went by their house today and invited them over for dinner (There are eight of them now--so had to dig into our pantry stores for extra food).

The 'Chef du Mission' (Chef--doo--miss-ee-ohn, means head honcho-- and listed as their Chief Geologist), Zhu Jia An, is a great guy and through his interpreter (the Assistant Engineer, Li Fan Bin) we discussed in French (made us feel better about our language skills, as only one of them speaks French, and no Kirundi) the clay available, the design for a kiln, and lots of other things, including a kind invitation to visit them in China when we are through here! (They handed us their business cards and were amazed we didn't have any of those either-- barbarians that we are.)

They asked about my clay pipe project, and suggested I mix in a fine sand for added strength instead of the 'grog' (crushed fired clay) as it takes time, energy and money to produce the grog. Really great guys. But I digress. They have discovered there is enough pure Kaolin (that's primo clay in porcelain-talk) in one valley alone near Ngozi, to last their project five hundred years. They've taken bore samples down to two hundred feet and still found pure, perfect clay!

They hope for the factory to employ ten thousand people when they are going full swing and discovered Burundi has all the raw materials plus a cheap labor force (similar to China) with a ready market in surrounding countries.

It will take two to three years to design and construct the factory and processing plant, plus the electricity has to be made available from the hydro project for firing the kilns, but overall, very exciting! A big boon to the local economy and stability for the nation if they can add to their exports.

Since we didn't have videos or business cards, we gave them the address for the two video stores in Buja for movie rentals, and an invitation to the American Club, which has movies on Tuesday and Sunday nights. They invited us back over to their house after dinner to watch Chinese movies again and we popped and took some of the popcorn you sent. It was a great hit with fresh melted butter and salt.

The five films were very dramatic and tragic, the good guy rarely won, romance was very chaste and all about unrequited love, and they all involved lots of martial arts footage with people leaping and floating through the air and fight movements everywhere. The filmography was beautiful, and we laughed, cried and cheered right along with our hosts. (They had English subtitles, so it was even better). Wish we could travel home through China to see these guys again. Great folks.

* * *

--Back to our weather. The rain really causes a problem with clothes. It takes an average of three days to dry something enough to even be ironed in this rainy season). Sylveste used to run out and grab everything from the line before a rainstorm, but now, often as not, he just leaves it out there, stands at the window and shakes his head. (It's just as well, as the extra rinsings help take out some of the excess soap.) Wet or dry, clothes are brought in each evening to mildew overnight on a red plastic chair, then put out again the first dry minutes the next morning to continue the process.

About the third day, they undergo the torture of the charcoal-heated iron (this is a heavy iron canister in the shape of a regular iron, but with a hatched lid on top of the iron cage and a wooden handle. You heat charcoal up on the Wretched Thing (imbabula), use tongs to drop red-hot coals into the iron hole, latch the lid and presto-zippo, an instant hot iron with one temperature setting--scorched.

Sometimes our clothes get scorched and sometimes they're lucky and only get mushed out of shape (sometimes irreparably--I have/had/have a cotton sweater which now reaches down to my knees and out in all directions--sort of using it for a blanket-bag at the moment).

My underwear have all succumbed to having the elastic scorched out of them and I keep gathering the stretched parts up to sew them tighter. The zippers all have teeth missing (replacement zippers come only in assorted astoundingly bright colors in Buja), and Jim's underwear, which began as briefs, now resemble boxer shorts for a really, really, really big guy. We've had to use the economy-sized safety pins we brought to fasten them tight enough so they won't fall off under his jeans.

It's an adventure every time we put on something newly washed and ironed and something to laugh about, though we've taken to washing and closet drying the more delicate things ourselves so we can keep a few nice things for trips to Buja, formal presentations, or an unexpected trip to hospital.

--I can't remember whether we told anyone about Bot flies. They are prolific and have this bad habit of laying eggs in the moist material and folds in clothes out on the clothesline. If everything isn't well ironed (scorched), the larvae hatch in your clothes (while you're wearing them) and burrow into your skin to make big open tracks and sores. (Makes for great dinner conversation). Treatment can be painful and the scarring permanent if they're allowed to fester too long.

--Speaking of food--just popped a fresh Swiss chard, tomato, onion and goat-cheese pie (quiche) from the sand oven and I'm looking forward to dinner and a quiet, warm, dry evening with my honey.

Hope all is well with you and yours,

Love and a hug,

Jim and Anita

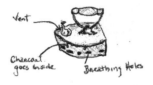

Chapter 47
Concussions and Other Things

Dear Uncle Duck and Aunt Nita,

I had a minor accident last week resulting in a mild concussion, so I'm on three weeks medical restriction at the moment, confined to House, and finally have the time to catch up on correspondence.

--I was minding my own business, not driving fast at all through one of the new small villages (resettlements) popping up on the steep mountainsides everywhere. The path through the new village is very narrow, only wide enough for two people abreast, with houses on one side and a sheer drop-off down the mountain on the other.

Directly ahead of me was an elderly man on a bicycle moving verrrry slowly. I beeped my horn several times to give him plenty of notice that I was coming, but he must have been deaf, because he didn't seem to hear the horn or the moto.

Wary, I slowed way, way down to almost stall speed (should have stopped completely), but just as I drew up even with his rear tire, he turned to look, panicked, and veered right in front of me, a few inches off my front tire. I hit the brakes, but continued to slide in the mud and had one second to lay the bike down to avoid running over him. I was going so slowly, I should have been able to hop off and do a controlled lay-down and it shouldn't have hurt anything but my pride.

Unfortunately, I was on the very edge of the 'outside' lane and as Jezebel and I tipped over with no place for my feet, we followed gravity's rule and slid off the side of the mountain, upside down. The helmet somehow came off taking both of my earrings with it--darn it! (My only pair.) Then a tree jumped out and whapped me over the head.

Within seconds, dozens of other heads popped over the side of the hill to see if I was on fire, then a ten minute discussion ensued as to how they were going to get me and the moto back up the mountain. Meanwhile I was upside down with my leg trapped under the frame, so I couldn't move. Took eight or nine guys to hoist it back upright and topside, and another couple to pull me up, though I'm not really sure how many as I was seeing double.

After dusting myself off and determining that the elder was OK, just scared (turns out he really is very, very old, very deaf and was very gracious--he didn't ask for any compensation for scaring him, and everyone took a consensus and agreed it was his fault in the first place), so I decided I was good enough to finish the day's work.

The moto wasn't hurt at all, which was both surprising and very important (after civilian and personal safety, of course) since work depends on having one. (Nice soft green stuff to slide on, and it was smarter than me and avoided the tree.)

I've had a mild headache and nausea for a few days, and the slide downhill took some hide off my arm, but the double vision was gone within an hour and I feel OK otherwise, so not to worry. But I really miss my earrings. Hope someone finds them and makes some money from them.

--Almost before I got home, the entire village of Ngozi had heard about my fall. Our German friend Elke asked her compatriot, Dr., Michael, to stop by and check me out. He deemed me mildly concussed and suggested a week of home rest. Unfortunately, another expat stopped by the house to see if we needed anything from Buja in the way of groceries and discovered I was laid up for a few days. They told someone, who told someone, and the next thing you know I get this angry 'SUMMONS' by phone at the Post Office to descend to Buja by bus immediately for examination by the P.C. nurse.

I was forced to have a head X-ray in Buja, and would you believe, it showed nothing in there? (The bumpy bus trip down and pressure changes from 6000 ft. to 2000 ft. and back up again were harder on the headache than the fall itself. If I'd really had a problem, the bus trip alone could have set off an aneurism, but hey, what do I know?)

--In fairness to P.C., by the time they heard the news of my accident it had grown way, way out of proportion, and they'd caught some unnecessary flak and misplaced concern from some of the ex-pat community about not taking care of their volunteers. Not fair to P.C. at all.

Nor did P.C. know or give me a chance to explain that I'd already been examined by our friend, Dr. Michael (who has more medical knowledge and experience than all of us combined), or that I'd had two prior concussions in real life and that this bump didn't begin to compare.

--Where I came to butt heads is with my sorry attitude of--"I was all right, not bleeding or broken, so what's the deal?" And that's why I've been put on house (ar)rest for three weeks instead of just the one--because I failed to keep the nurse informed. I appreciate their concern, but think someone needs more volunteers to worry after.
Oh me, Mea culpa, learn another lesson in communications and on with life.

--The worst part? It has been beautiful pond-building weather (the best we've had since we've been here) and I can't leave the house--Poo.

--The next worse part? Jim is now unhappy too, because he had to take my place at the fish conference in neighboring Rwanda for five days, then again in a journey down to the southern part of the country to do a survey of a potential pond site for an independent organization (as a favor from P.C. to another development agency, so another five days lost).

So we both missed out on the last of the good weather and the chance to finish our first ponds before the BIG rainy season. And it struck with a vengeance this week. I've just been cleared to get back to work and there's no place to go. Too wet. DRATS!

--Wish there was as much interest with this cursed diarrhea as with the concussion. It's been non-stop with both of us for over two months now and coincides precisely with the move to the new house, so we're looking into our very unreliable water source as the probable culprit (though we boil and filter all of our water twice before using).

As a last resort, the nurse has asked us to take three samples each to send off to the States for analysis. If we continue to lose weight, we'll have to journey to Nairobi for further tests. Could be something as dumb as Amoebas and they just haven't found it yet. (Apparently very tricky little critters to pin down?) Crossing our fingers (and legs).

Sorry to sound so bitchy, just tired of being cooped up and of not being able to make our own decisions or run our own lives, but then, it's what we signed up for. It isn't P.C.'s fault we are so old and independent, but it does appear to annoy them considerably.

* * *

--Speaking of spills, one of the other 'fishies' took a spill two weeks ago in the rain on an oil-slicked road and bruised her ribs. She's also off her moto for three weeks--bummer (seems to be the magic number).
To add insult to injury, she was spending a week in Buja to escape the boredom of being cooped up in her house with no work to do, and was asked to be in a style show to raise money for the local orphanage.
Kind-hearted soul that she is, she agreed and they gave her some very

nice dresses to wear with four-inch heels at dress rehearsal.

Now, fish people are accustomed to hiking boots, rubber wellingtons, and tennis shoes or sandals, and this particular volunteer is tall anyway, so she almost always wears flats. Out she walks in the four inch heels, pretty as a picture (she really is) and steps in a very big crack on the rickety runway, falls off the heels, bounces and falls off the not-so-sturdy stage, and is now hobbling around with a sprained ankle and re-bruised ribs. Life in the tropics is tough!

* * *

Farther afield, and rarely ever the four-inch heel type, I've spent my injured time gathering materials for the rabbit hutch. I found some chicken wire in Buja and talked Jim into looking for a claw hammer and a new saw when he was there last week (our old saw, the fine-toothed one that barely bends green wood is now a wall ornament).

He discovered an adult saw in the Buja market with big teeth, for actually sawing things into pieces. Can't see doing everything the hard way or primitive when we can afford a few tools to help out, so the hutch should be ready for bunnies soon.

* * *

--We just heard. Jim and Michael (fish-guy in the next Province over) will be getting bigger motos next week, bumped up to 185 cc's. Their 125's don't have enough power to haul them up and down steep mountains or through mud holes when they start picking up fifty pounds of icky-mud on each wheel. The other two fish-girls will get the fellows' current 125's, which are now broken in (or down?). I get to keep my Jezebel as we're quite fond of falling together by now and I've almost got the carburetor down to two clean-outs per day. (Suzuki usually has a good product and reputation. I haven't figured out the equivalent for 'lemon' in Kirundi for this one.)

Did I tell you how she got her new name? We changed it from 'Samson' to Jezebel because she doesn't like altitude, cold weather, wet weather, dust or hills, fouls her nest (carburetor) at every opportunity, and betrays me at the very worst of times.

We've calculated I spend as much time on the side of the road cleaning her spark plug and carburetor as I do working the ponds. But it's either that or push her up every hill. Anyway, all this transportation re-distribution leaves one moto extra for the P.C. nurse in Buja. The whole compliment of P.C. can now have skinned shins, rugged elbows and frapped heads for commiserating together.

* * *

Secondary Projects: I'm about midway through writing and illustrating a fish-culture booklet for our farmers and the local extension agents (with a great deal of assistance and re-writing from our French tutors to put it in proper grammar and syntax) and sponsored by a grant from our new best friend, Catholic Relief Services.

It will be in French with page-by-page accompanying translation in Kirundi, using cartoon drawings and simple technology terms to illustrate requirements and techniques. I hope it will help our farmers, any future volunteers, and explain our project better to any interested agronomes (agriculture extension agents).

--The overflow pipe project is coming along. I have half a dozen short clay pipes drying in the house and almost ready to fire in the kiln I haven't built yet--

--Oops, belay that thought. I just heard today of a kiln I might use down the road a bit at the brick factory. I even have a contact name, so yippee!)

--We've planted several new high-protein fodders (gifts from the German goat project) along the outer slopes of a few pond dikes to see if we can't get bigger fish, faster using the fodder as a supplemental food source (more about this later).

--We visited a cloistered convent out in the country with friends a few weekends past, who sell perfect honey, beeswax candles and strawberry jam. You walk up, knock on the door, a peephole opens up and they take your order. When it's filled, its passed out through a sliding panel and you leave. Cool.

--This last week, we met two delightful nuns (one Irish--full of mischief, and one Belgian--sweet like sugar-candy), and they invited us to Mass on Monday night, as it was to be in French. Yippppeee!

--With my Monday pond site cancelling out, I was home working on my clay pipe project early Monday morning, and decided with no one there (Sylveste was gone to market and the gardener was off sick), and with no visitors likely as it was a work-day and the start of a new week, that I'd treat myself to a quick clay-pack facial and hot towel soak to freshen my skin.

I put water on the tiny kerosene stovelet to heat (we don't use it too often as it's expensive to run), wrapped a towel around my head and had a half-inch of clay over my entire face, when I heard this little tap-tappy-tap at the front door.

I waited, hoping whoever it was would go away, but no, there it was again. More persistent. Tap-tappy-tappy-tap.

Oops, no water in the bathroom. I grabbed a clean washcloth, wiped hard and fast, then jerked the towel from my head and ran to answer the door. It was Sister "sugar-candy" to tell me that the French Mass had been canceled. Disappointed with the news, but delighted to see her, I invited her in to visit, but after only a few minutes she asked, "Are you not feeling well?"

"I'm fine. Why?

"Well, uh, you're looking awfully pale."

I reached up to feel my face and my fingers came away coated with a fine grey powder. Uh-oh.

After a nice visit, some hot tea, and exchanging a few more pleasantries, she took her leave. Back in the bathroom to resume my beauty pack, I nearly croaked at sight of the ghostly specter leering from the mirror. Yellow-red eyes, grey white skin and hair sticking out in all directions, I looked like a stand-in for the queen of Halloween.

Hot water, hairbrush, and pink-scrubbed face later, the wraith in the mirror took on a more human and familiar appearance. Poor Sister Sugar-candy. She's probably still wondering if it's contagious.

Well, gotta go, it's raining again and the leaks in the ceiling are calling for more pots.

Love and 2 hugs,
Your namesake and Jim
(alias the ghostly goblin of grimy gulch, and hewe)

P.S.

One question we still hear every day from dozens to hundreds of locals, young to old is, "Do you have a job for me?"

A young man (16 years old) followed me around for an hour yesterday asking over and over for a job. He said his parents and entire known family were all dead, though I couldn't understand his Kirundi words as to what they had died from, other than tragically, and that he was alone in the world. He had no place to live, no relatives to protect or teach him, and no hope.

It broke my heart to turn him down. All I could offer was the handful of dried fruit I'd brought for lunch and some FrBu ($). We shared a few quiet moments as he ate and I offered to put him in touch with the nuns or priests we know for at least a place to live.
But he was angry, hurt, and didn't want charity, or understand that we truly didn't have work for him. After all, we were white and rich--we already employ three men, and must have all the money in the world. So why wouldn't I give him a job?

Felt so very bad to turn my back on him and others like him. I have to keep telling myself that we are doing as much as we can with the fish-farming and secondary projects, one step at a time. And that someday, maybe it will trickle down enough to help others, just not to that poor young man at this time.

Chapter 48
Ants, Pants and other Wonders

Dear Bill and Theola,

We received the tax forms intact this week. Thanks! But Yechh! Guess I know what we'll be doing this Sunday.

Speaking of the rainy season, it finally arrived and struck with a vengeance. It is too wet to work! The average rainfall is around eighty-five inches per year, but it can go fifty inches or more either way, drought to drowning, and feels like we've had that much already. Buckets and buckets! (Both inside and out, as we still have a leaky roof and have to keep emptying and moving the catch buckets.

Our clothes and shoes are mildewing instead of drying. The cement floor stays cold and damp most of the time. We have a fireplace, but House II is so big, the ceiling so high, and the windows and rooms so drafty, it actually gets colder when we start a fire. The fire creates such a draft you can feel cold wet air being pulled in through the closed windows and doors like a steady breeze that could suck you right up the chimney. But sometimes we bundle up, light a fire anyway with smoky peat from the Irish bog project (just for the cheery red glow), stand in the draft and pretend it's warm. (The peat, which was to have helped schools and business become more independent, turns out to have too much 'ash' content (in part due to the aluminum?) and doesn't burn well. Too sad for the country.

--Since the start of the rainy season, we've read nearly the entire P.C. library, laid out flower beds, planted some high-protein fodders obtained from the goat project (to see if the fish like them and if they will seed-multiply on their own)--and it is still raining. At this rate we will accomplish more in secondary projects than our primary.

* * *

On a lighter note, the other four fish-volunteers appeared off a bus through the downpour this weekend to discuss our next six months of work. They are a rowdy, fun bunch! Best of all, it was good to confirm that what Jim and I find frustrating, they are experiencing in kind, also, and that it is not just because we are 'old guys'.

We are finding many things in common like the comments and questions we endure from the populace:

"Why do you speak French so funny?"

"Why don't you speak French?" after you've been conversing in French for an hour.

"Oh, I see you've gained a lot of weight!"

This is usually and immediately followed by another someone saying,

 "Why are you so skinny? You must eat more."

"Do you have trouble finding pants because you are so short and heavy?"

A story from the weekend:

--Sarah is our youngest volunteer, enthusiastic, and has energy and talent to spare. She moved to a new post last month, on the sunny plains to the northwest of Buja near the Zaire border, and has had a terrible time with army ants at the new place. She didn't sleep much the first few nights, carrying on a war of attrition with a dragoon of ants that insisted on swarming over her bed the moment the light was out.

Next, she developed intestinal problems (she described them a bit more graphically) from the change in water. She was sitting on the throne in misery when her new puppy-turned-gangly-monster came tearing into the bathroom and piled all four long legs, body and huge tail helter-skelter into her lap.

Startled at first, then sympathetic, she held onto him (since she couldn't get up at that particular moment anyway) and said, "Oh, poor baby, what scared you– Hyh?!!!!!...What the..." and quickly put him to the floor. He was covered with stinging scurrying ants and had deposited not just a few on her! She said their pincers are so strong it takes off chunks of hide when you pull them off. Ouch! Poor both of them.

Not exactly her week, she caught a ride into Buja to type her monthly report, but her knapsack full of clothes and two five-gallon gas cans disappeared along the way. Oh, me.

Returning to her post, she discovered someone had broken in and run off with all of her tools and money.

Guess we are all developing a different sense of humor, because as she told us, though we commiserated, it was also just too funny and everyone laughed deep and long rather than cry. And in spite of the misfortunes, she still has a good attitude and is doing a great job with the beginnings of ponds popping up all over her province. Hope we get to see them! We donated some of our shirts to restart her wardrobe, but not much we can do in the pants department as we only have two pair left each. She will have to find some replacements in the Buja market. One thing, life is never boring here.

* * *

--We met our landlord the other night. Rain was busy pounding new holes in our tin roof when we heard a loud knock at the door. I walked to the entry, looked out and up, and up, and up again, to see a giant in very nice dress clothes stooping down to peer in.

I opened the door and he introduced himself in a pleasant deep base voice with, "You don't know me, but I know you. I am the landlord". So we invited him in, thanked him for the water barrels and took him on a tour of his house as he pulled out a big stack of bills, flashing them briefly and told us he'd brought money to fix everything we wanted or needed in the house. Then he began saying his goodbyes and the money disappeared back in his pocket.

Seeing we had a limited audience, Jim jumped in and said, "Well, there-are-a-couple-of-things-we-could-use-a-gutter-to-catch-the-rain-a-fence-to-keep-out-thieves-and-wanderers-the-roof-leaks-and-a-toilet-seat-and-."

Our landlord responded to us over his shoulder (as he stooped low under our seven-foot door frame), "Oh, no problem. The next time you are in Buja, just give me a call and I will personally go with you to select a new toilet seat."

After he left, we studied each other for a moment, got the wooden one out and went back to sawing and sanding.

* * *

--I finally got around to melting down the bees wax we purchased at a local convent and mixed it with some motor oil as you suggested. It cooled to give a fairly decent modeling wax and I hope to sculpt some animals after we've visited wildlife parks on vacation.

--We have lots of local visitors now. Almost too many during this rainy season what with all the extra projects we've planned. People think that if we are home, we are not doing anything, middle of the day or not. Don't mind fish business at all, that's what we are here for, or even the occasional social call during the day, but complete strangers arrive at 9:00 in the morning, ready to drink a case of sodas and beer and chat all day!

* * *

--Thanks, thank you and thank you--for hanging in there to sell the house for us. We didn't know we'd be asking you to make a career of it. Hope we are still friends by the time our tour is up. You've put up with a lot for sake of 'our adventure', and we owe you more than we can ever repay.

--Oops. Gotta go. It looks like a sliver of silver is showing on the cloud tips and we might actually get some fish work done today.

Love and 2 hugs,
Jim and Anita

Chapter 49
Falls and Flour Sacks

Dear Mom and Dad,

Mpore! (Em-pore-ee, or I'm sorry). Excuse and pardon us the three weeks we haven't written. We have just been too busy and too tired to do much but work, eat, and sleep. And to top it off, our dear P.C. staff has dreamed up mandatory reasons for us to come to Buja to 'relax' a few times too often.

Weekends (Saturday afternoon after work to Sunday night)--our normal time to slow down, catch up, rest, write letters, etc., have been taken from us. Never thought I'd be complaining about having too much fun!

We have developed the habit of drawing the curtains and locking the door on Sunday mornings so we can have at least three or four hours of quiet time, but that didn't stop the vegetable vendors from tap-tappy-tapping on the windows at 6:30 this morning. We finally gave up, bought some beautiful pineapples from one then had a steady stream of vendors arriving till 11:30. We are most grateful for the fresh produce, but missed our quiet Sunday morning.

After drowning our sorry attitude in a bowl of popcorn, Jim is out working on the moto's, and I decided to write letters in lieu of cleaning the rabbit cages or several other odious projects. Will do them later.

--To answer your questions, the work is often frustrating, but there are more than occasional rewards. Like when you see the proverbial 'light bulb' go on in someone's eyes as they comprehend a new idea or possibility. And even more exciting is when they carry the idea farther and come up with an innovation on their own. This job allows us to use all of our background, education, experience, and creativity, and it is possibly the most challenging thing either of us has ever undertaken. For example, in building their ponds, the only tools farmers have are hoes and machetes (occasionally the odd shovel). Transporting soil

from the deepening hole in the center of the pond site to the growing
dikes at the perimeter can create quite a problem, even though the pond
may be only fifty or sixty feet across.
Though men and women transport anything and everything on their
heads, only WOMEN carry dirt that way, so of course it is impossible
for men to do that.

They have been asking us to provide wheelbarrows and shovels (not
exactly within our budget, or theirs--therefore not considered
appropriate technology). Their alternative has been to practice what
they do in the communal labor parties--to get a line of men starting at
the hole and ending at the dike, each with a hoe. They pass the dirt, one
hoe-full at a time from one guy to the next. Slow, inefficient, backbreaking tedious, plus one hoe-full of dirt ends up being a teaspoon by
the time it's been passed that far.

--So, after much fertilizing, an idea sprouted. I bought a couple of
empty, heavy-duty, large (fifty pound) woven-plastic flour sacks at the
local market (like our gunny-feed sacks at home but made of fiber and
tough plastic), cut two small holes in the corners of the sown end,
inserted two poles through them and out the open end, and voila! We
had an inexpensive, ready-made, two-man, litter-style wheelbarrow.

The farmers attending the first demonstration went wild. They had
so much fun moving mountains of dirt as opposed to hoe-fulls that they
got silly and began playing 'dump truck'. Gears shifted, horns honked,
and races were won that day, all without benefit of wheels, engines, or
fossil fuel. We have both accomplished more work and moved more
dirt at our ponds in two weeks than in the last four months.

In addition, Catholic Relief Services (hereafter known as CRS and a
wonderful, practical development organization) just happened to have
eight bales of extra sacks we purchased for a nominal fee. We will sell
them to our farmers for less than they can buy them in the market, and
they can fold their wheelbarrows up daily and take them home!

Why sell it to them, you ask? We have found that if they have to
invest even a small amount of money, they take better care of whatever
it is and aren't asking for free handouts--as long as the price is fair and

the same for everyone.) And the monies go back into the fish fund for nets, tools or supplies for the ponds.

I also wrote a request for grant money (and received) from CRS to purchase shovels, one for each pond, so things are really looking up.

--Speaking of motorcycles, we have had no accidents for over a month now. Hurray for us! Our fellow-fish-colleagues have not been so lucky though. Mary hit an oil slick on a paved road at sixty km/hr and took some hide off. Sarah, who's not quite tall enough for her new 125cc moto, came to a halt with no footing in sight for her legs and tumped over. And after traveling over 120 kilometers on rough, pitted paths one day last week, Michael found (as he cruised up into his yard) that he'd lost the nut and cotter key off his rear axle with the axle sticking out two and a half inches on the other side. He is sooooo lucky the wheel didn't fall off...well anywhere. That could have been Really Scary.

But the humdinger was Dann, who spends the least amount of time on a moto. He is in charge of the fish-station, so doesn't get to travel as much and has taken to surveying the station's ponds from his moto of an afternoon, on top of the dikes.

Somehow, last week, his attention was momentarily diverted and he said the next thing he knew, he'd slipped off into one of the compost pits. Now, in general, pond compost enclosures aren't the purest smelling things to swim in, but he's been exceptionally lucky to secure an abundance of fresh manure and stomach contents from a nearby slaughter-house, so his pits are very 'ripe'.

He said there wasn't a soul around when he went in, but by the time he came up for air he was surrounded by a half-dozen howling workers. They were laughing so hard it took another half-dozen to help pull him and the precious moto out. He was so fortunate to come away with only a dislocated shoulder, Ouch, and not to have been impaled on the compost stockade. But even worse than the fall is all the teasing he's taken because of it.

Jimani (Jim and I)--would never give anyone a hard time about something like that--but we have formulated a specially labeled Christmas gift of Eau de Compost cologne in honor of the day.

* * *

--Speaking of manure, we bought a ton of it for our garden. The purchase came about one evening after work when this handsome young fellow knocked on the door just before dark and asked if we wanted manure for our garden.

We told him, "Sure, how much is it?"

He confessed, "It is $10. But we only sell it by the ton, and do you have some scales to weight it on?"

Hmmm. We decided on a ton, and after much discussion and computations, Jim figured a ton of manure would be about twenty wheelbarrows full. The young man agreed and said he would have it delivered--if he could use our wheelbarrow. Since we didn't have one, we borrowed one from our Canadian friends, and the next day two guys showed up to begin hauling. (Notice--one wheelbarrow--two guys--we'd agreed to pay for the labor--you would think we had never bargained for anything before.)

The good news is, we now have a nice, smelly, soon-to-be-more-productive garden plot and are very grateful for the serendipities of life.

* * *

--Speaking of mice and men, we have a pet mouse: a little teensy-tiny thing about two inches long, including the tail which is one inch of the two. He comes in under the inch-high crack between the back door and the floor at least half-a-dozen times a night. We have to watch where we step to avoid mushing him/her/it?

He usually stays near the pantry, but the other night he came skittering into the living/dining room area to visit us, where we were slowly going blind trying to read by kerosene lamps. I tried to herd him back into the kitchen, but he took off with his wheels spinning a hundred mph for every inch of floor he covered and headed for the front door. I opened it to let him out with Jim warning me I was setting a dangerous precedent.

"You'll put him out for a walk, and he'll probably scratch to get back in within five minutes."

Sure enough, he made the tour all the way round the house and was easing under the crack at the back door in record time.

Now what is it that makes big, noisy, ugly rats in the attic so awful, and little, teensy mice in the pantry so darn cute?

With love and two hugs,
jimani

P.S.
I purchased our shovels with CRS (Catholic Relief Services) grant

money, but discovered a new problem. None of them have ledges built in at the top of the spade for placement of the foot, just a really sharp edge, which cuts our farmer's feet. They had resorted to bracing the end of the handle against their bellies and pushing with their bodies. Not good. So we gathered all the shovels up, applied for and received another small grant from CRS and had wide ledges welded onto the top of the spade as a place for bare feet to bear weight down on the shovel. MUCH Better! Our farmers are very happy and continue to be more and more productive with every innovation. God Bless the CRS

.

Chapter 50
Fish Bowls

Dear Mom and Pops, (alias, hey you guys!)

Guess what's better than popcorn, faster than a speeding banana biker, more powerful than a bottle of Primus, and able to leap small minds in a single bound? Give up? Three issues of POPULAR SCIENCE and an OMNI magazine! Terrific day! First Dad's letter, then the package of magazines. We were lucky enough to have them all delivered on a Saturday after work, so we drew the curtains, locked the door, and jumped up and down for half an hour before we could settle down to reading every word, every ad, every page!

So many things to tickle the mind! Any and all future issues you might wish to send this way would be consumed, digested, appreciated, and shared with others forthwith.

Using innocuous brown paper with no labels seems to be a good way to send them, because they arrived 'toute de suite' (toot-te-sweet) or quickly, as in a timely fashion, big emphases on the arrived part.

* * *

The good news: Fish business is moving fast now. We have both finished our first model brood-fish ponds and will put water in them this week. If there are no leaks, we will be bringing fish up from the fish station, hopefully on Thursday, April 24. Our first FISH! Yipppee! With news of fish coming, we suddenly have many more ponds under construction and the big completion push for them will come in the dry season June-July-August (will it ever arrive?).

The bad news? Jim took his first serious fall this week (the first one with injuries). He has been laughing at some of my spills, thinking and saying I'm just not a very good rider. But he's convinced it can happen to anyone now. He was easing his new, heavier, 4-stroke Honda moto down a steep slick road in the rain and the back end just squirted out from under him, no warning, fish-tailing him right down onto his side with the moto on top, no effort at all, the road rising up to meet him before he could blink.

Unfortunately, his left knee is really swollen and bruised and we have been keeping ice packs on it as fast as the tiny freezer in our kerosene frigo can make them. The doctor says it looks like only stretched ligaments, and he should be fine in two or three weeks, but no moto riding until then. And he was so looking forward to playing some volleyball and trying wind surfing on Lake Tanganyika at the volunteer conference this week. Bummer!

Now he's got me wondering if the ratio of body weight to moto weight on these slick roads doesn't have something to do with stability. If you're much lighter than the moto, and riding higher on it, is it less stable and does it have more of a chance to do what it wants? His new moto is heavier and the ratio of his body weight to it is approximately the same now as mine. Hmmm.

* * *

We were called down to a three-day conference in Buja to discuss policies, procedures, problems and projections for the coming year. (How's that for a list of P's?) Though it interrupted work (again), it was informative and we learned some things. And we even had a bit to contribute to the knowledge base this time, with the bonus of HOT WATER and SHOWERS three times a day! We were rained out of the beach activities, so Jim didn't miss much after all with his bum knee. We even saw some first-run movies at the American Club.

--Speaking of them, The American community has adopted all of Peace Corps staff and volunteers and they are constantly feeding us, doing things for us and offering their homes when we come to Buja. I don't know how we can ever repay or thank them. They have all been super kind.

--We have planned our vacation for September or October (we can take almost a month at the end of our first year), and are looking forward to sights, sounds, and collectibles in Kenya and maybe Tanzania. Some of the purses, carvings, rugs, and baskets we've seen from Tanzania, Kenya, and Zaire are outstanding. (We are already collecting baskets, hats and carvings from here to send home.)

--Guess we are getting the six-month-on-post-blues, because vacation and time off really look good. The people and work are great and we wouldn't trade this for home right now, but life in a fish bowl and lack of privacy can get on the nerves.

And when we stop to think about it, it has already been a year since we left home what with fish and language training lasting five months;

and it was two years before that since we'd had any extended time off, much less a vacation. No wonder we are tired.

* * *

--Three weeks later. It rains cats and dogs every day. When we are actually able to work, we draggle back in covered with mud from head to wheel. Poor Sylveste just shakes his head sadly at us--probably at the thought of scrubbing it all out--again.

--Jim's knee is almost back to normal from his fall three weeks ago, and he is happily back on the moto.

--I hurt my lower back (same old place, lumbar three and four) trying to lift Jezebel out of the mud after a minor fall last week, but after two days in bed with a hot water bottle and some of your leg-exercises-for-backs, am almost back to new. We've both curtailed some of our visits to the farther sites because we fall too much when it's this wet and slick. On the positive side, it has given us more time to work on secondary projects.

--And lest you think that our motos aren't very good, or that we're not very good on them, they are actually made for off-road--dirt bikes in fact, with big knobby tires and are quite sturdy and easy to handle, only around two-fifty and three hundred pounds.

It's just that the narrow roads and even narrower paths are hard-packed red clay powder with a thin sheen of dust on them, and the first drops of rain (plus the buckets thereafter) turns those clay roads and paths into slick-slippery-slidey tilted sheets of glass with no traction. And it's really, really easy to fall down. No effort at all.

* * *

Projects:

--The fish booklet in French is finally finished and on it's way soon to Buja for grammar correction and official translation into Kirundi! Yipppee!

--The newly discovered battery acid and saltwater method of tanning hides works and makes them soft and pliable! (and saves us from decimating the blackwater tree)

--The rabbit hutch built itself and is ready to be full of bunnies

--And the USDA sent us a requested Tempeh starter to convert soybeans to bean curd (tofu) and soy sauce (we have a bottle of beans fermenting on the window-sill at this very moment).

--With all the indoor work and not much physical activity, we will be glad when the rain stops. At our age, it takes no time at all to go to flab, though we continue to lose weight.

Also, we have gained the reputation of being great cooks on The-Wretched-Things-with-sand-oven. The American community from Buja and our fellow-volunteers have begun dropping by on weekends in this no-work rainy season to sample our pizza, quiche, chili, bread, rolls, ice-box pickles, barbeque (in the pressure cooker), biscuits, cornbread, soups, salads, pancakes and omelets--and to play cards and games. They always bring smiles and supplies or provide money, so we are not out our own limited funds, and the visits break the monotony of seven days per week of work and rain.

--A good day. After four months of diarrhea, gas, discomfort and weight loss, PC medical has finally determined we do have Amoebas and have started a 10-day treatment with a new drug (for stubborn cases)--though not sure it's worth it as the effects of ridding ourselves of them seem worse than the original.

--A cute, quick story from our Kenya/British tea friends, the Outrams, who stopped by 'for a bit of a visit' the other day. They have a quaint English saying for needing to go to the bathroom. "Do you need to spend a penny?"

They also have a rather tall and large friend who announced recently he was coming to visit them. And he did. As he exited his car (all eighteen stones of him or about three hundred sixty pounds), he pulled not only his luggage from the rear seat, but a brand new plastic toilet seat.

Robin, in his droll manner, asked him, "What do you think you're getting on with that?"

His friend replied, "Well, it's very embarrassing to go visiting here and break your host's toilet seat, so I take a spare or two everywhere I go!"

Man, could we relate. The imported plastic seats in the Buja market are so thin and flimsy a child's weight can turn them inside out. With that reminder, I dug out our wooden one and started sanding again, and it is almost ready to paint. Jim wants to make a lid also, and have me paint the inside so it opens up to the shark's mouth from "*Jaws*". I'm thinking more of a hippo, but we'll see.

* * *

I squandered two hours under the tin porch roof of a farmer's house yesterday waiting for the rain to let up, visiting, listening, and watching a group of men play a game of cups and stones in hollows in the dirt (sort of a combination of Chinese checkers and backgammon called Mancala).

Later, as I climbed on Jezebel, they cautioned me to be careful and not fall, clucking around me like Mother Hens. I eased out at a snail's pace, and the pond chef sent two guys slip-sliding on either side of me to make sure I didn't fall! They trotted along for over half a mile till I hit firmer ground, just out of reach of the fish-tailing moto, saying,

"Sawa...Sawa...bukebuke" (sah-wah, sah-wah, boo-kay, boo-kay, or, OK...OK... slowly...slowly), "Take it easy here, watch out for that hole there," and finally waved me on my way. Made me cry. These people are so special!

In the meantime, think of me the next time you pay ten dollars for a jar of mud to put on your face! I'm getting it for free!

Love and two hugs,
Jim and your #3, (Me2)

P.S.

We had a real treat from visitors this last weekend, a former volunteer is working up in the last remnants of the high-altitude rain forest in the country, on a 'chimpanzee park' to preserve both the forest and the chimpanzees.

And a former college friend of his, Joyce, stopped in to visit his project. Currently on leave from a New York university as a specialist in 3-D computer graphics, she draws brain cells, neurons and other things on the computer for use in teaching and research. Wow. Both a scientist and artist, she took her training at Duke in biological anthropology and anatomy, and is a very cool person.

Two years ago, she traveled Australia and New Zealand to write and illustrate a children's book on the local wildlife and people (**Wallaby Creek).** She has illustrated for Cousteau Society publications, and is currently traveling Africa to write another book, and also designs postage stamps. My idea of a Renaissance Woman! It was great to talk 'art' again, like a breath of fresh air. Gives me something to dream about for life after fish farming!

See ya!
P.S. 2

We hitched a ride up to the tea factory Sunday afternoon to bid our British friends safe journey for their upcoming vacation. The two wildlife volunteers and five Germans from the hydro-dam project showed up and we ate, laughed and played a number of games. A new one for us was tying two long pieces of twine onto two spoons and dividing up into two teams, boy-girl, boy-girl, in each line. At the word "GO!", the spoon went up through the britches, shorts, and shirts of the men and down through the shirt, britches or skirt of the women with the string following after--first spoon through to the end of the line wins! The trick is that the string is always just a little bit shorter than the line and you end up all bunched up like standing dominoes. (If you try it, be sure to use soft cotton or nylon twine as we used scratchy hemp and several of us have 'twine' burns in the most unusual places from enthusiastic team members who pulled too fast!

Twining away in Africa,
jimani

Chapter 51
Coffee Beans

Dear Mom and Dad,
Jim here:

Rain, Rain, and more Rain. All day. Every day. It is severely restricting our work, and just when things were beginning to take off-- sigh.

It is also the beginning of coffee season--the ONE source of solid income our farmers have during the year--so we'll lose their fish efforts for the next two months anyway while they harvest.

As the green berries ripen, hillsides are transformed from a verdant emerald green to pockets and splashes of deep ruby red. People turn out by the hundreds to hand pick each single berry and haul them to the processing factories where they are fermented into Burundi's AAA Arabica coffee for export.

* * *

--Great news! Tomorrow morning I pick up our first batch of fish from the station. In spite of accidents, interruptions, and bad weather, we have three ponds ready to be stocked.

Normally we'd stock fingerlings, but the fish station has an abundance of brooder-fish, so we've decided to make our first three ponds breeding (reproduction) ponds. This should make our farmers immediately independent from the fish station. As more ponds come on line, they can sell the fingerlings they've produced to the new fish farmers at a profit and build production ponds for food for themselves at a later date.

Becoming independent of the station is important, because it's very expensive to maintain and to transport fish from there. We also have no guarantee our program will continue after we leave (or are asked to leave prematurely--rumors are always rampant), so if our farmers are independent of government aid before then, it should be better for the country, the farmers, and the fish.

Our new 'brooders' should only require a couple of weeks to settle into their new homes and we should start seeing the first reproduction around June or July! Truly exciting times.

* * *

--The kids here are great! They are always looking for something to make into a game. In general, if it's round, there will be a kid rolling it down the road with a stick. Plastic lids off paint cans, old tires, bicycle wheel rims, wire hoops, wooden disks, handmade bamboo hoops, even a bicycle chain sprocket (bumps a little, but so what?)

They even build their own wooden scooters with seats, not-so-round wooden wheels, and marginal steering. You'll see them push, pull, or drag the scooter to the top of a hill, jump on, then do this kamikaze run down to the bottom, screaming in delighted terror and laughter and Lord protect anyone in the way.

But my favorites are the toys they make from wire. Wire cars with real steering controlled from a long stick. Wire trucks and scooters. Wire men on bicycles with banana regimes stacked on. Some of them are really ingenious. Wish there was some way we could safely package a few to send home.

* * *

--We have Fish now! The farmers are so excited. Two of the ponds developed minor leaks in the dikes after the fish were installed, but we were able to repair them without draining.

Until now, we have been most concerned about the water temperature. It stays so cold most of the time and there has not been much sun with this year's heavy rainy season lasting eight months instead of three. The fish won't grow well or reproduce if the temperature stays below seventy-five degrees.

But good news! Even though water temperature coming into the ponds is at sixty-five degrees, once it's in our shallow ponds for a week or so (with no leaks or addition of new water), it warms to almost eighty degrees! Good news, indeed.

We have good plankton blooms (the food source for our filter-feeding fish); good composting pits in the corners of the pond (food source for the plankton) and oxygen levels seem to be holding very well. Plankton provides food and oxygen for the fish, and fish and compost provide CO_2 and food for the plankton. It's a great closed-loop system! Farmers also throw termites, insects, and rice bran into the water for extra goodies and protein when they can find it.

These fish are not only hardy, disease resistant, fast growers, omnivorous and oxygen-deprivation resistant; they are also mouth brooders. When a female is ready to produce eggs, the male seduces her. He fans out a shallow circular nest in shallow water on the mild 3:1 (three to one means for every three foot out, you go one up) sloped dikes.

Streaks of red appear along the male's body, enticing the female in to set up house. She enters the nest, lays her eggs, and backs off. The male immediately covers them with sperm, fertilizing them, and he backs away. The female reenters and scoops the eggs into her mouth, aerating them there until they hatch one week later. She does not eat during this time. As the babies or 'fry' hatch, they dart in and out of her mouth, seeking safety and refuge for another week at the least sign of danger until they are strong enough to survive on their own. Neat fish, Huh?

* * *

News, Bits and Bites:

--We've just received a note from P.C. They volunteered all of us 'fishies' to give a fish seminar to the local extension agents--not sure of the politics involved, only that there must be some, as there wasn't a whisper of this at our conference. The hardest part will be doing it in adequate French. Our French is good enough for the few of our farmers who actually speak smatterings of it, as they don't do much better than us, and they are very forgiving of our mistakes.

But the extension agents have had an education, schooling, taught to be competitive and are critical of poor language skills. Anita and I should learn an awful lot from this.

* * *

--The saga of the toilet seat continues. Installation has been delayed due to too many other projects interfering.

* * *

--P.C. sent us over here with fish netting for a seine, but without weights, floats, or sufficient rope. The rope we can find in Buja. But I spent last Saturday afternoon taking apart a car battery to recover the lead contained in it for lead weights for our seining nets. Next I melted the lead over The Wretched Thing and used rolled portions of the tin from the sealing lid of the NIDO powdered milk can to make tubular molds. I placed cut bamboo lengths in the center of the tubes to provide the hole, and set it all in a wet clay mold for support. Poured the melted led into the molds and Voila! Lead weights--ready-to-use.

The homemade weights turned out fairly nice, and we've decided to use my empty plastic Kodiak tobacco cans for the floats. We rescued some Styrofoam packing 'peanuts' from the PC office in Buja to stuff inside the cans, added a little of our handy-dandy Duct tape to seal them, and we're now set to go. May not look like store bought, but should do the trick.

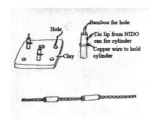

Thanks again for all the popcorn and letters,

Jim

P.S. Anita here:

Just a quick story--I was coming back from my far-far-far-away commune the other day, slushing through mud and puddles, and finally made the last long, slippery climb uphill to the highway, relieved I could see pavement ahead. But as I pulled over onto the dirt shoulder to let traffic go by, I heard a huge hisssss from the rear tire. Oh man, when I took the tire off and found TWO punctures, not just one, I sat down and cried, because I only had one patch.

Phooey--what to do? With almost thirty kilometers still to go, the sun was setting and I couldn't leave the moto there or it wouldn't be there to come back to. I couldn't push it home without ruining the rim. Just before despair arrived, a truck full of weary workers topped the hill going the same direction I should have been, slowed, stopped, looked at my flat tire and asked if they could give me a lift? What a wonderful gift! The back end full of workers hopped out and cheerfully loaded my moto and me and off we went, chatting merrily away about the vagaries of tires and long days in the rain. They delivered me right to my door but refused to accept payment for their kindness. The full package of cigarettes was gratefully passed around however, and I was glad I'd bought them that morning. My eternal thanks to the driver and his 'guys' for rescuing me.

Chapter 52
May Day!

Dear DeLea and boys,

Sylveste and I finally had time to finish the rabbit hutch today and it should be ready to receive seven healthy, furry critters on Monday. But it's still raining and fish-work is piling up on us with all these no work, workdays.

On a brighter note, our first fish are installed in three ponds now, and they love it so much (after a personal interview) that they are ready to make babies already, as in AS WE SPEAK.

* * *

--Finishing up an incredibly hard day last week at one of my ponds, I stood looking over the completed dike, trying to capture a feeling of accomplishment. What I captured instead was the sense of something tugging at my right rubber boot. I looked down to see one of my favorite little tykes, Frederico, dumping pebbles into the top of the footwear.

Turning and crouching to his level, I grinned and asked him what he thought he was doing? When he saw me at his size, his eyes grew big as saucers, and he ran screaming at the top of his lungs back to his Daddy.

But when I sat down to empty my boot, he padded up behind me again and dumped dirt down the back of my shirt. This time, his Daddy couldn't save him. I swooped him up high in the air and threatened to throw him to the hippos, then kissed him quick and gave him back to his Papa before he could even think about crying.

It was all in fun, and he was still laughing, but you have to be careful. We are told a common bedtime story here is how umuzungus eat bad little children, and most of the kids keep a firm margin of escape handy when we're around!

* * *

--Today is May Day, the National holiday to celebrate the working person. Everyone gets the day off and there are parades and drums, dancing and drums, singing and drums, eating and drums, drinking banana and sorghum beer and drums and oh, yes, soccer games galore and drums. Drums are a mainstay of life. We wake up to and go to sleep with the sound of them. Life seems to ebb and flow with the beat of them, and people walking, running, or working seem to do it all to the rhythm of the drums.

Every celebration, every event, every dawn, every dusk is greeted with, bid adieu to, and seems to be infused with the pulsing cadence and flow of them. The deep bump-boodleump-boodleump-bump-bump sound works its way into your mind and soul, and something is missing and empty when it stops for any length of days. Any memories we take home from here will have the sound of drums interwoven into the tapestry.

--There has been way too much rain for anyone to work much (except for the coffee harvest which goes on rain or shine). The weather actually cleared off for a few days last week, but alas, we couldn't get out to our farmers. The gas storage docks/facilities in Buja are in a low-lying area by the lake. Too much rain, runoff, and flooding has put buildings in the area under four to five feet of runoff mud and water. The road is washed out and the storage tanks are now floating with no way to use them till they settle back to earth, thus there is no gas for us or any one else. So it's back to hoofing it and secondary projects.

If you can find out what a cubit is, please send directions for ark building.

Love and a hug and a prayer,
Jim and Anita

P.S.
Speaking of things that float, remember the gun patrol boat in the movie, The African Queen? You know, the one Bogart and Hepburn sank on Lake Tanganyika? Well, it's still here, alive and well, and in service as a ferry on Lake Tanganyika for people and equipment, (and looks remarkably the same as it did in the movie--before the blow-up part).

Chapter 53
Fish!

Dear Moms and Pops, (carbon copy, group letter again--sorry)

My favorite group of farmers (i.e., my first farmers, the ones who had the courage to take a chance on me when no one else would) finished their first pond last week. They filled it with water, had a big leak, spent a week digging out a portion of a dike and repairing, then put water in again, filled up the compost pit, got a plankton bloom started, and Jim and I brought fish to them on Wednesday, the fourth.

They were so excited. Seven farmers with all their families and kids running around on the dikes, saying, "Look, there, there they are! Aren't they beautiful? Look how big they are!"

These particular fish had been in one of Jim's ponds for a month, but they couldn't get the temperature up, because his farmers didn't want him to know they had a leak in the dike and kept adding fresh cold water. The fish hadn't grown any in that month and there was no reproduction. So we seined them out early Wednesday and transported them by moto to my first pond. (Will replace his from the fish station as soon as his guys fix their leak.)

The water in my pond was some fifteen degrees (F) warmer and they took off like they'd been shot from a cannon. (Usually there is a degree of shock and acclimation, but within twenty minutes, they'd checked out the new pad and were up at the top looking for food.) Phenomenal!

My guys were so nervous and excited that they slept on the dikes the first three nights after installation to guard their new treasures from hungry thieves and curiosity-seekers. Five days after installation, the fish were already making nests in the shallows for babies. The pond chef, Antoine and his partners are on top of the world. I am so happy for them.

--You asked about language progress? Well, this group doesn't speak French (well, none of my farmers speak French, but these guys actually try to help me with Kirundi). We spend the rainy quarter of our time on Kirundi lessons under a tin roof on a nearby porch and the sunny three quarters on construction.

They are a really sharp group, always trying to figure things out, understand why things should be done a certain way, and coming up with novel solutions to a problem, like weaving filters over bamboo over-flow pipes to keep bad things out and good things in. (And, yes, we discovered a nearby source of bamboo and are using it for the overflow pipes, so there goes all my work with the clay cannon balls-- not a big loss--and I provided free entertainment for Ngozi residents at the time, so all is good.)

--Anyway, back to our story. Today, I'd promised to take photos of them, and they arrived with their hoes, flour-sack wheelbarrow, their one shovel and wonderful musical instruments to celebrate. After a few serious camera shots, (they are always serious for photos--standing up stiff and straight with no smiles--They won't allow me to take candid shots at the pond, of anyone--They shake their heads and wag a finger at me if I try, and have told me each time that "photos are for serious!")

But today after photos, they exchanged the hoes and shovel for instruments. Music filled the air as people spilled out of the banana, taro and manioc groves, and the fields, to dance on the dikes and look at the fish. (For the last six months of construction, these guys have been the laughing-stock of their neighbors, especially for working with a woman, or hybrid-woman, but also for their hard, foolish work *because-everyone-knows-all-you-need-is-a-hole-in-the-ground-to-raise-fish-and-you're-not-even-getting-paid"*.

But today the ridicule stopped and the neighbors aren't laughing any more. Nope, they want to build ponds of their own. And the fish seemed to know it was all for them, because they were up at the surface looking around with their big black and yellow eyes to see what was going on, when ordinarily they'd be at the bottom burrowing into the mud at the first loud noise. Don't laugh, but I think they responded to all the 'love and happiness' going round.

--The band? A tin can with goat hide stretched over it as a drum, a small seven-inch slab of wood with metal tines and beads mounted on it (sounds like a cross between an out-of-tune piano and a guitar with loose strings), a beer bottle with stick, and the most interesting--a bow (as in bow and arrow) with a gourd attached to it for resonance and a little stick to pluck and draw with, like a one-string viola.

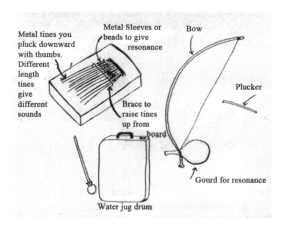

Metal tines you pluck downward with thumbs. Different length tines give different sounds

Metal Sleeves or beads to give resonance

Bow

Plucker

Brace to raise tines up from board

Water jug drum

Gourd for resonance

Re-reading this, it doesn't sound like much of a concert, but maybe it's one of those things you have to experience to appreciate. We played, clapped, sang and danced on the dikes for over an hour. It was wonderful! My favorite little tyke, Frederico, with his short shirt and bare bottom, bounced up and down and shook to the music like a pro. If I don't accomplish anything else, it's all been worth it for the success and joy in this one little corner of the world, just this day.

I know Jim feels the same about his one reproduction pond. A farmer came up to him the other day and said, "Thank you, umuzungu. Thank you, Monsieur Jim. For bringing the fish and teaching us about ponds. It's the first program we have ever had just for us, all our own, and we are glad you are here."

I cried when he told me.

* * *

Last Sunday we took some time off to see the National Sports Competition for the military (held here in Ngozi). It was an interesting exhibition, though we had trouble seeing very much of it. Most of the people there were my height or taller, and it was difficult to find a good viewing area--I'm five foot six and a half inches. Even Jim had trouble seeing and he's six foot one inch. We took what we hope are some good photos of athletes doing hurdles, pole vaulting, high jump, sprints, marathons, javelin and discus throwing.

The President was supposedly here, but was seated in a special tent so far away we couldn't see. Since we saw so little of the competition, we enjoyed watching the crowd watching the sports. They pressed in from all sides and in their excitement kept edging onto the stadium field.

Armed soldiers had to keep frapping them (gently) with sticks and pushing them back with billy clubs to keep them off the track so the events could be run. Excitement and enthusiasm reigned!

The kids climbed every tree available to the very top, with fifteen to thirty kids to a six inch-diameter tree. Don't know how the trees or the kids survived.

Well, enough for now. Think Fish! And wishing you love and lotsa
                              hugs,
                              Jimani

Chapter 54
Toilet Seat Tempos

Dear Carol,

These poor people. I don't think they are ever dry or warm during the rainy season. I just watched a group run by in a downpour. Raincoats are non-existent. With only tiny Chinese umbrellas available for the wealthy, there is no way not to get soaked to the skin even in a minor deluge.

We've been here nine months, on post seven months, and are hitting a low in mental energy. There is no privacy, quiet time, or any time that we're not being watched, questioned or visited.

The worst part is, they don't understand why any of that would disturb us. It isn't part of their culture to be alone or not talk constantly. They are born into large extended families in small houses, together night and day, with noise, talk and laughter going on incessantly with siblings, parents, aunts, uncles, cousins, friends, neighbors--like background noise.

In fact, I think one of the worst things that could happen to them is to be alone with no one to talk to. Most days we do OK with it, but once in awhile, when someone gets too pushy, insistent, demanding, or in our faces with the chatter, clatter, chatter, and we ask them to please be quiet or come back another day, there's this tremendous look of hurt in their eyes and we know they simply don't understand.

--It has even affected our intimate time. Vyance has radar ears like a fruit bat and wakes from a sound, snoring sleep instantly to patrol the grounds if he hears any unusual noises at night. Even with the windows shut, sound carries in this big echo chamber of a House II, through the attic and down into the garage. One particular steamy night we'd left the windows open: lying in bed, cuddling close after, well, you know--and nearly jumped out of our skins at the sound of a delicate cough outside the window three feet away.

Guess he was afraid we'd wake the neighbors and was letting us know we should hold it down. We waited till the whisper of his footsteps died away then exploded into embarrassed hysterical laughter.

--But some days, it's difficult to be culturally sensitive and you just want to tell them all to go home and be quiet (we don't, but we'd like to). Most all of our group have hit a low and are thinking of how long the next year and a half appears. It seems to be a widespread pattern among volunteers after the honeymoon, excitement and newness wear off and the reality of living in a totally alien culture sets in.

* * *

--Our toilet seat is finally finished and we have only to figure a way of installing it without the correct hardware. Coming soon to a theater near you! No more falling into the hole!

* * *

--Sunday--one week later. We worked in the rain every day this week, but the sun blossomed and bloomed today on our day off, inviting us to soak some warmth into our bones and write letters in the back yard. While we were there, a spectacular mushroom exploded from a round white ball and burst open to liberate a bright red three-tiered crown. Remember those firecracker nubs called "Snakes" that, when lit, would uncurl and fluff up into black snaky-looking things? Well, the texture and size of the mushroom is like that, only a bright, fire-engine-red on a white stem. Wish we had a reference library! (No worries, we won't be eating it, just would like to know what it is.)

Till next time.

Think good thoughts and work hard.

Love and two hugs,

Hey you and what's-her-face

Chapter 55
Trouble in Paradise

Dear Mom and Dad,

(We've asked Shirley to mail this in the States as we never know if or when they are monitoring our mail, especially now. We're taking a chance to let you know all is not well in Paradise, but please, no reference to it in letters sent here. Will let you know in-between the lines how things go.)

I could say it all started with the U.S. bombing of Libya, but that wouldn't be true. That was just the spark that set off firewood stacked up and ready to burn.

Just after the bombing, we had a short visit from Shirley, (Uncle Con and Aunt Dorothy's assistant pastor. She was here to visit our boss, her former college roommate--small world!).

Unfortunately, we didn't get to spend much time with her, as her trip coincided with our first fish seminar (held here in Ngozi with the six fish volunteers, twenty local extension agents (agronomes) and our local sponsors from the Department of Water and Forests).

What a disaster! Mid-seminar, the agronomes formed a small rebellion, walked out and wouldn't finish the very conference they had asked for. Why? In part, because Peace Corps wasn't paying them $1000 FrBu/day spending money over and above their expenses to attend the seminar? (Seems this is common for the larger, more well-funded development organizations, but a first for Peace Corps and this seemed a little steep.)

The agronomes complained to our Governor and to their director and it passed up the line until it ended in a push-pull between our bosses and theirs in Buja. Seems they were making a National point at our expense. They don't like the U.S. bombing Libya (one of their trading partners) and while an appropriate technology program for the masses is OK, it apparently should also put additional money in other programs, vehicles on the road, and support the bureaucracy in a direct way, like most of the other development agencies.

The outfall had fallout and they've now cancelled the four new fish volunteers that were due here in July. There is also angry talk that our own Visas will not be renewed at that time either, so we may be coming home a year early or transferring to another country. Am sure there's even more involved, but that's all the grapevine has delivered.

Unfortunately, we also learned this week through the grapevine that the Ministry may have been coerced into accepting Peace Corps from the beginning by a well-meaning U.S. official. The country thought it was the beginning trickle of larger projects and that U.S.A.I.D. or others would then be bringing in vehicles, jobs and bigger dollars--that industry and infrastructure would flow in to oil the economy and all the machinery, as it has done in so many neighboring countries.

To their dismay, they find it's just us and we are only bringing in appropriate technology to help people help themselves (at a grass roots level, which means mostly farmers, at first. At the same time they see the U.S. pouring money into nearby countries, (especially--or should I say exclusively--the ones with vast natural resources the U.S. has vested interests in). They are currently feeling very under-valued and under-appreciated and we are not playing the game right.

--We've also just learned that CRS (Catholic Relief Services), a huge supplier of food aid and money for developing countries--just uncovered a large theft and hijacking ring among distributors here (a multi-national theft ring--not necessarily Burundians) that has siphoned off over sixty percent of their incoming commodities for the black-market (as in not reaching the people it was intended to reach).

In protest, CRS has shut down their offices and may be pulling out of Burundi altogether. (CRS has been a big supporter of our program and provided all the seed/grant money for our flour-sack wheelbarrows, capping of springs for clean water, shovels, rabbits and fodder projects, so we are doubly saddened to hear they might be leaving.)

But the saddest part is that our fish program (which unfortunately, the Auburn University and U.S. fish experts have all proclaimed wouldn't work because it was too cold, at too high an altitude and wouldn't return enough for the time and effort invested) is, in spite of their dire predictions, working.

In fact, it's working so well, we've calculated that just the ponds we have started now can produce over fifteen tons of fish per year, just in Ngozi province, in a place where there was little to no protein before, without taking anything away from current food, rice, tea or coffee production.

So today, we are damning all politics, politicians and PhD's! It is the country overall and our farmers, their wives and children and neighbors, and eventually the country who will suffer from all this nonsense, while all sides are drawing lines in the sand. What a mess. So much for the good news. Poo.

--The bad? I fell again on the moto the day after the failed seminar. I was on my way to the far, far commune, the one with the really bad roads, somewhere in the direction of Rwanda, going downhill on a blind curve, with sheer cliff on the right and sheer drop-off on the left. A dump truck came roaring up around the corner on my side of the road in high gear, and since there was no place to go and the driver's ride was ever-so-much bigger than mine, I opted to lay the bike down, trying to slide under him. (One of the disadvantages of wearing a helmet and riding a two-cycle engine is that you can't hear anything else coming.)

Fortunately, his brakes worked and his tires came to rest very snugly up against mine without damaging the moto. The underside of a giant truck is very interesting from that perspective. Had no idea all that stuff was under there.

The poor driver was as scared as I was and jumped out to make sure I wasn't dead. The fall and slide mushed my knee and it has looked like a small watermelon the last couple of days, but nothing broken or permanently ruptured, just sore, so no worries, and my body protected the moto from scratches and dents. The new gravel from the road did a bit of cheese-grater-thing through my clothes and took some hide off one elbow and the bum knee, but hey, the scars will make for good war-stories to tell the nephews and my knee and elbow look worse than the moto!

* * *

Sorry we don't have better stories, but it has been a difficult two months. The emotional roller coaster seems to be picking up speed with all the new uncertainties. We were better off not knowing all the roadblocks and politics our P.C. staff has had to deal with from the very beginning, both from Washington and from here (and to give them credit very much overdue, they protected us as long as they could, leaving us to simply work).

It was more fun when we were ignorant and just doing battle with the elements and motos, enjoying the work with our farmers and the local administration.

Wishing you good health, joy, peace and abundance in your lives. Will write again soon.

Love and lotsa hugs,

us

Chapter 56
Grasshoppers

Dear Folks,

Lots of little, itty-bitty, news bites.

What a miserable, rotten day. I have on a long sleeve shirt, a sweater, a jacket, and I'm still cold. (We should have brought our red Texas flannels to keep warm!) And it's raining to beat the band, not to mention our tin roof.

Our open garage is an open invitation to poor souls caught out in the rain, and they literally use it as a port-in-the-storm, which we never mind. But being locals, it's not long before they are yelling and laughing and carrying on, making a noise that rises above the clamor of rain on tin.

And bless his Heart, Sylveste trots out periodically to remind them we are home working today in the HOME OFFICE and could they be a little quieter? Which works well for five or ten minutes until the crescendo builds again.

--We had two inches of hail day before yesterday, so our garden isn't producing much right now. In fact, I'm not sure it will recover. Big broad squash and Swiss chard leaves make great targets for little icy cannon balls. A layer of hail still covered the ground three hours after the storm. Can't stand to think what it's done to everyone's crops, as they are already short of food nation-wide and dependent on this season's harvest.

--Garden compost pits:

You dig a pit, build a wooden or bamboo frame around it (to prevent anything or anyone falling in) and cover over the top with branches to prevent the compost drying out during the approaching dry season. I completed a covering for OUR pit just before the hailstorm and ran for the house. As we watched the second inch of hail mount up to flatten the garden, Jim put his arm around me and said,

"Gosh, honey, I sure am glad you got the cover over the compost pit. Think of the damage it would have done!"

What a clown.

--Coffee: Families are busy, wet, and cold in this coffee and rice season. Many kids have colds or flu, and pneumonia and dysentery are evident everywhere. But in spite of the wet and chill, they're happy, because this is the one time of the year for the money to come in. The hillsides have turned from a verdant green to brilliant scarlet with shiny clusters of ripe coffee berries, and everyone is picking like crazy to deliver it to the coffee factories, overseen by our Belgian friend, Jan.

--There are three white beans inside each red coffee berry. Once de-hulled by machine, the beans are dried on long, flat, raised wire screens on the open hillsides above the factories and turned with rakes periodically to expose all sides to the sun. Once dried, they are rolled gently across the screens to remove a silver-colored husk, then dumped into vats for the fermentation process. (Good fermentation determines the final grade or quality of the coffee.) They are then re-dried, packaged and shipped out.

Burundi grows one of the top-ranking Arabica coffees in the world, AAA, and it is used to 'upgrade' lesser coffee beans from elsewhere. The other volunteers tell us it is the best coffee they have ever had, and not being coffee drinkers, we'll have to take their word for it and bring a bunch home for you. It has a nice aroma and a very good reputation on the international market, though none of the Burundians we know drink it.

Nope, they all like STRONG hot tea with lots of boiled milk and buckets of sugar. Have become accustomed to the milk, and actually miss it when it's not available, but can't handle the sugar.

You know me, your 'pickle, olives and salt girl' is still alive and well and shivering in Burundi.

--Coffee harvest will last through to July and everyone is celebrating these days. There are no local banks for the farmers, and robberies are apparently frequent, so people tend to spend money as fast as they earn it. Much of it goes for the basics of new pots, pans, tin roofs, hoes, clothes, etc. But a portion of it also buys beer, or the ingredients for it. (We have to be careful how many invitations to farmers' homes we accept during the workday. Banana beer and motos don't mix well.)

--Another thing we've learned. Never ride a moto with your visor up and your mouth open. Bugs don't taste good.

--**Rice harvest season** is also upon us. Valleys are sheathed in a lush green carpet, the slender heads just beginning to turn a beautiful golden ocher. Tiny new thatched grass huts (pointed beehives) dot the valleys, with men and boys emerging from them intermittently from daylight to dark, guardians of the harvest. These sentries come to work armed with tin pans, lengths of cloth and sticks, and spend most of the day banging pans, yelling, waving cloths, or throwing stones at grain-stealing birds.

Great therapy for the aggressions--This culture seems to prize the appearance of meekness, manners, graciousness and acquiescence to an extreme. The more in control, gentle, or softer one's voice is, the more sophisticated and aristocratic one is considered, and the higher one's status in community. Unfortunately, they are so well controlled that exhibiting anger or emotions is greatly discouraged from childhood, and all of these pent-up, well-controlled people have few ways to vent normal human anxieties.

Much is released into laughter, physical exercise or labor, but much is also simply not acknowledged. As a nation, they risk sudden, unbridled emotional releases and violence from all that bottled up tension, and being expressive Americans, we don't understand how they keep a lid on it at all.

--But I digress. Rice is a recent agricultural addition and not without problems. Of all the things they don't need. It seems there's an indigenous microbe that attacks just as the grain forms, resulting in big golden heads, but with only a few grains inside. It is not feasible or economical to use chemicals (I hope it never is, as the last thing they need is more pesticides in the untreated water systems–they get enough through the DDT wash-off from the coffee trees--courtesy of the U.S. and Japanese chemical giants--and yes, even greater quantities are still being marketed to developing countries long after being outlawed in the U.S. and Europe).

--Various international development groups are working to develop a resistant rice strain, but it may take years to work out. In the meantime, rice production is only a third to a half of what it should be.

* * *

--A funny, ignoble bird has wandered into our back yard. Large and clumsy looking, it prefers to walk rather than fly and is called a white-browed coucal (koo-kowl). It's also called the water-bottle-bird because it sounds like water coming out of a bottle, only more musical, descending and ascending the scale. It is a haunting, distinctly African sound, blending in with the morning drums and fading out with them at night, and we shall miss it when we are gone.

* * *

--Rain-Rain-go-away, Come again...next year? Speaking of go-away, there's a bird here called the 'go-away bird' (the white-bellied variety), due to its loud and penetrating sheep-like bleating call: "Gaaway--Gaaway, Gaaway--Gaaway".

* * *

--We decided not to go to work today. The rain-on-tin has made us deaf, and we must be blind too, because we can't see the road, and well, we were already dumb. Besides, none of our farmers would be working fish today in this rain. If they are working at all, they are working coffee.

--Jim's been having fun with a math problem the last four or five days. An administrator from a small valley near his ponds wants to turn the valley into a small lake for a hydroelectric project for the province, but their first dam broke from the backpressure of so much water. Jim's been calculating water flow vs. weir (overflow) size for them.

Only problem is, every time we go down to the valley to look, there's more and more and more water in the river, and he's been forced to readjust his calculations again, and again. He has pages and pages of graphs and numbers that make my head spin. But it's so neat to hear him chuckle or watch his face light up when he makes a breakthrough, and it exercises his engineering talents.

--I sent my completed fish manual to Buja this week for our language professors to correct the French, then they'll make the dual translation into Kirundi, and we hope to have it published soon for distribution to local farmers. I've included simple drawings and illustrations and the manual will take a farmer from choosing a good pond site through construction--to pond management and harvesting.

It isn't perfect, but it's better than nothing and will certainly give them more information than our own abysmal language skills have done thus far. Oops, ran out of black ink again. Honestly–you'd think someone would invent a lifetime pen. Only about one in every five of those we purchase here even work, and then not for very long. We're too far from the ink-factory and no telling how ancient they are or how far they've traveled overland to get here. But we've used up the last of the Paper-Mate refills we brought with us, so it's back to the Burundian Blues.

--Oops, found a refill with some ink left in it.

--Great news! Jim's brood fish are making nests to have babies already, after only two weeks in the pond! The co-op should have fingerlings ready to sell to other farmers in about two months. I hope to see reproduction in my ponds within the week. We're excited and pleased with results thus far, and the work is beginning to look worthwhile.

* * *

--We finally tested positive for amoebic dysentery, and have started on a new medication, but honestly don't know if it's worth it. The "cure" has increased the symptoms by double or more. It's probably a good thing it's raining today, as we can't venture too far from the necessary room! Still don't have our toilet seat installed permanently, but we carefully align it on the rim each time before we sit, and pretend.

* * *

--This poor country. Suddenly there's a grasshopper plague covering our Northern region, winging in from Tanzania. The pesky crows are being useful for the first time since we've been here. Our Belgian friend, Jan, was by today and said he'd seen a swarm of grasshoppers yesterday that covered an entire valley of rice.

Soon after he left, waves and squadrons of grasshoppers turned the skies grey and the crows have gone berserk dive-bombing and gobbling them up right and left, till they're too full to fly. But even the crows can't keep up with the inundation, and there is fear the current vegetable, coffee and tea crops will be destroyed. We hear entire valleys are being stripped bare in the areas farther north of us.

But ever vigilant, our farmers are catching sacksful of the fat critters to feed to the fish, so maybe something good can come from it. Too bad we can't freeze-dry or dehydrate them for future use--not sure they would stay dehydrated with no way to store them in nearly one hundred percent humidity. Maybe mix them with something? Someone told us they taste good stir-fried--but probably not like chicken?

By the way, keep forgetting to thank you over and again for the pressure cooker you sent. It's our most valued possession here and the only way we can make use of some of the beef and all of the 'rubber chicken' available. (Made some barbecue with one in the pressure cooker last week and shared with another volunteer. She was delighted! And our Canadian friends were so impressed with it, they had Trudy's mom bring one out when she visited!) Lots of company here on the weekends in this rainy season, so all of your care packages have been shared and appreciated.

* * *

There's another gas shortage and we're on rations, which we used up, so we've not been able to get to work since Tuesday. Late Wednesday afternoon we caught a bus to the next village over, Kayanza, and started to hike the fifteen kilometers (~ 9.5 miles) up to the tea factory. We kept glancing over our shoulders as a huge black line of clouds crept up on the horizon, then raced toward us and closed in on all sides. It was suddenly darker, colder and gloomier and you could see it was raining like heck just the next valley over and coming to get us.

The road was being widened and under construction, so the mud holes were almost as deep as the big dump trucks and graders working on them. We caught a ride with a dump truck for a few kilometers, then walked another few as the storm overtook us. Ponchos donned and pulled over us and our backpacks, we sloshed through knee-high mud looking like lumpy walking pyramids.

A huge transport truck pulled up behind us, picking up half-drowned surveyors and offered us a ride the last ten kilometers. We climbed in the back to sit on hard benches that weren't tied down to anything and a sagging leaky canvas cover overhead that was almost like being out in the rain. Diesel fumes rolled in from the exhaust, while every bump we hit bounced us, the seats and the twenty other guys about a foot in the air, and brought a torrent of collected water down from the holey overhead canvas. The chauffeur raced up and down valleys and hills and around curves, then forgot about us and missed our turn-off.

We trudged the half-mile back up the hill in pouring rain to arrive at the base of the 'usine-du-the' (tea factory). We walked and walked and wound around and round past mountains and valleys of iridescent green tea bushes (they are planted solid like hedges, with no space in between, like a beautiful rolling green carpet from a distance).

Heavy mist, bouts of rain and clouds at eye-level in the cold crisp air isolated us from the rest of the world as we wound up and up and up another two kilometers and three to four hundred meters in height. We arrived finally at our host's yard just as darkness settled in, looking like a pair of drowned rats. (The banana bread I'd brought was a little the worse for wear as it had been sat upon once or thrice by others in the bouncing truck.)

Robin and Gayle welcomed us at arm's length and insisted we have a hot bath before supper. They handed us both a drink, and banished us to the bathroom.

I was just settled in with suds all over my hair and face when their 'trick' door popped open giving everyone a good clear shot from the living room. Jim jumped up and ran to close it, but it happened again thrice more, once with me and twice while he was bathing. Then our hosts took a quick bath and though the door to the living room was now shut, we heard the bathroom door 'pop' a couple of times on them. Quite a conversation piece!

A hot meal, good conversation and a decent night's sleep improved our spirits considerably. Next day, we did a tour of the tea factory and the new hydroelectric reservoir, then climbed on Jill's moto (new forestry-wildlife P.C. volunteer) (she'd left it at their house for a quick trip to Buja and needed it back in Kayanza the next day, where we left it for her). We caught a lucky ride back to Ngozi with an ex-pat, discovered new gas rations had been left for us, climbed on our motos and were soon headed out to work. A refreshing break from life in a fish bowl.

* * *

--Jim recovered the lead out of an old car battery (free!) by melting the plates and has fabricated enough molded weights not only for our fish nets, but supply two of the other volunteers with weights for their seines! It was a fun project for him as he made the molds from scrap pieces of tin and placed them in some of my clay with a small piece of bamboo in the center of each tin cylinder bound by copper wire to hold its shape. He poured the molten lead (melted in an old saucepan over the Wretched Thing) into the molds and let them cool. They turned out perfect lead weights that fit snugly on our net rope! Yeah for Jim!

--But bad news, he also fell again yesterday on the moto and mushed his left ankle--Not serious, but will be off of it for a couple of days till the swelling goes down.

* * *

--In case you're wondering what the stuff is on the back of this page, I was using a carbon paper to send the same letter to Jim's folks, only I put the carbon in upside down on this last sheet--oops.

--Uh-oh, what's that? Do my eyes deceive? I can see the road! The rain has stopped. Birds are singing—and, oh—goodness—what's that bright light? Can it be? The Sun! (Which will last about an hour, as there's another big black line of clouds racing in from the East). Oh, well, great duck weather, though there are no ducks here. Think I'll go stand out in the back yard and soak up some quick rays before they disappear. Wishing you all the silver linings from our clouds. More later.

Hope all is well with you both and keep those cards and letters coming.

With love and 2 hugs,
ijiima and aahh-nneeeee-tah

Chapter 57
Toes, Woes, Frogs and Frapping

Dear Mom and Pop,

One week later. No news on our status here. Hopefully everything will blow over and we will just keep on working and not be thrown out. Don't know how the U.S. bombing of Libya affected P.C. programs in other countries, but it has created distrust and hard times here, as much among the European community as the African.

* * *

--On a lighter note, work is really picking up. With the dry season finally arrived, the coffee season almost over, and fish installed in three ponds, everyone and ten of his cousins have heard about us and want to build ponds. We suddenly have twenty-one new ones under construction and more to come. (Plus, using the flour sacks as wheelbarrow-litters for dirt moving has cut construction time from five months down to one–which pleases everyone. Yipppeee!).

The other fishies are having the same pick up in interest, so should have more than a solid program going by the time our replacements arrive next year--crossing fingers and toes that there will be replacements.

--It's raining again! It's the dry season by the calendar and if I go out this minute and ask someone on the street why it's raining this time of the year, they'll look me in the eye, soaked to the skin and say, "It's not raining. This is the dry season. It never rains in the dry season, you know."

Can't tell yet for certain, but I think it rains so very much more in the wet season, that when the dry season arrives and it only pours, they think it's not raining. Or maybe the Kirundi is more qualifying and it doesn't translate well into French? But I have this sneaking suspicion they just don't know what dry, warm or sunshine means.

At least it's good for the garden. (It did semi-recover from the hail.)
We've garnered four large zucchini, scads of lettuce, radishes, Swiss
chard (makes a great quiche), tough hairy spinach, an interesting, mild,
watery, climbing-squash called a chayote that is more prolific than the
rabbits, and rhubarb. Not much else doing well yet, but our compost pit
is looking great from all the yard whackings and rabbit poop, and we'll
soon have enough to enrich the entire garden.

It's getting greyer and darker and this no-rain rain is flooding the
driveway (Sylveste just confirmed our suspicions--he says it's not
raining--this is the dry season, don't you know!)

We haven't had water to the house again in two weeks, so I think I'll
go out in the back yard and take an imaginary bath in this no-rain rain
with fake soap and see what the neighbors say. Might get us a quick
ticket home?

* * *

One toes:

We were out together at a pond the other day seining for yucky
frogs (slimy little critters that eat fingerlings) and had shed our hiking
boots and socks to put on wading tennies. This instantly drew a crowd
of about fifty people, and we couldn't figure out why they were all
pointing and talking in amazement about our feet. Kept hearing them
marvel over the fact that we had five toes on each foot!

Our Canadian friends enlightened us that evening. Umuzungus also
used to be called 'one-toes' because they only left ONE big print in the
soil, had only one big toe to each foot, and had to cover up this
deformity with horrible contraptions called shoes! Our farmers now
know at least two umuzungus in the world who have all toes present and
accounted for. Or it could be that they'd simply never seen white
tootsies before.

--A little more about the frogs. The ones that are bugging us are of
a particularly odious variety, with the dubious grand name of Xenopus
(Zee-no-puss). They are small (only two and a half to three inches
long), with arrow-head shaped bodies, ugly (dull, dirty-brown-and-
black-leopard spotted), have beady eyes planted close together on top of
their heads, (and you know what they say about frogs with close-set
eyes!) and are slimy (this is the worst part).

They are so slimy; you can't stomp on them (they just ooze out from under your feet), grab hold of them (they shoot out like cannon balls from a closed fist), or otherwise entrap them (they stretch out all thinny-like and spurt).

Their slime gets in the fishes' gills, suffocating them, AND THEY ALSO EAT FINGERLINGS. Wicked, wicked, wicked creatures--just doing what they do.

In the last two months, they've managed to nearly decimate the entire fingerling population in all of our ponds, including those at the fish station. Our program depends on being able to produce our own fingerlings, so this is a serious problem.

Our fish station volunteer bought and installed expensive metal frog traps, and is hauling out as many as a hundred and forty frogs every two hours. We've installed a few baited underwater traps for them to drown in, but our most successful method has been to seine them out just before we stock the fish.

Farmers can't afford to buy the metal traps, but Jim found a man in Kayanza (illegal trip over there on the moto) to weave some from grass and bamboo using a metal one as a model, and we'll see how they work. The funny part was that our PC boss, Mona, ended up at the same place a week later, and the man sent Jim's finished traps with her to give to him.

"Hey, Jim," she asked, handing him the traps. "Know anything about this? The guy in Kayanza asked me to bring it to you." Uh-oh.

In the meantime, we've been seining.

--This is a circus in itself. As usual, any activity out of the ordinary draws a large crowd:

--So, you explain you will be seining out frogs, not fish, and that you would appreciate the crowd's assistance in 'frapping' any that escape the net (they love this idea and trample each other in the rush to find good 'frapper' sticks).

So, your farmers slowly draw the seine through the water. It gets heavier and heavier, and the crowd begins to murmur in anticipation. Your guys struggle and strain to pull the massive load up on to the dike, when of a sudden, someone in the multitude yells, "AMAFI!" (FISH!)

The crowd transforms instantly into a mob. They pounce on the net, knocking you and your guys down onto the muddy slippery slope of the dike. You and your crew claw and scrabble to keep from sliding into the pond headfirst as the rabble-rousers tear open the net in anticipation of a fish feast. Thousands of slimy, slippery, squirrely, squirmy, nasty, beady-eyed, wicked little frogs begin jumping, twisting, sliding, scrambling back down the dike over your muddy bodies to the safety of the water.

Screams and shouts galore fill the air as the mob realizes its mistake and they hurry to get out of the way of the twisting mass of shifty, tricky, sneaky, cunning little horrors.

The melee is over almost as soon as it's begun. Mortified, the mob shrinks to a crowd once more and looks sheepishly in your direction. There's nothing to do but try again, so you and your guys pick up your muddy, slimy selves and start over.

This time, people stand eager and ready, their frappers poised for the assault. Once more, the heavy bundle of netting and tangled, contorted, distorted mass of plunderers flounder up on to the dike.

Frogs begin oozing through the mesh and the fun begins. The roar of the congregation signals frapping time and a hundred sticks explode into action--SPLAT! WHAP! SNAP!--with frogs and mud detonating in all directions.

Fortunately, most frogs are still contained in the net, and your guys quick-hurry-up drag them over to the deep, newly dug hole and dump them in for burying. (It is also expedient to escape the range of the frapping sticks quickly, as brown muddy toes are easily mistaken for brown muddy frogs.)

Much yelling, shouting, seining and laughter later, you calculate you've seined well over 35 kilos (seventy-five pounds) of frogs from one pond.

Your farmers are happy and secure with the knowledge that they have a (relatively) clean pond to receive their new fish next week. The crowd is happy because they've redeemed themselves and had a great time.

And you're happy because the caked mud drying over your entire body should produce the most beautiful, well-toned skin in the country!

* * *

--Thanks so much for the new long-sleeved shirts, which arrived yesterday! That should do us for the second year here. Many of our old ones have fallen victim to our muddy work, the charcoal iron and Sylveste's tender ministrations, plus we shared a few with one of the fish-volunteers when most of her laundry disappeared on a trip to Buja.

--Well, gotta go feed the rabbits. Cute little dickens, but all they know how to do is eat, poop, and make babies. Can't get any one of them to retrieve a stick or fetch the paper!

Love, hugs, and prayers,
Hewe and aahh-nneeeee-tah (alias the FFSN gang)
(Frog-Frappers-Society-of-Ngozi)

Chapter 58
Akagera

Dear Folks,

Hi! Greetings from Burundi! Bwakeye! Habari! Idigowannaginni Little Earthlings. Amakura maki?

Bits and pieces:

Only news here is frogs by the thousands eating our baby fish, and dry powdery dust by the tons. We thought the arrival of the dry season signified not getting so dirty or grubby, but all we seem to have done is replace red mud with red powder. It works its way into your hair, mouth, nose, clothes, maybe even the blood and brain. Only time will tell.

* * *

Mike's (fishie from next province over) Mom was here visiting for a few days. What a trooper! He hauled her over one hundred fifty kilometers on the back of his moto to see ponds--on her second day in country. You have to be a dedicated Mom to do a thing like that and still be smiling! We had them over for dinner and really enjoyed the visit.

* * *

We've had some more 'learning' experiences with our farmers. We'll make an appointment, show up at the appropriate time and no farmer. They are such an accommodating people, they wouldn't ordinarily dream of pinning anyone down to a specific day or time. When we do it (very rude), the want to be equally direct, but without hurting our feelings.

"Yes, umuzungu, I'll be there. Certainly."

If you question them as to why they didn't show up (another rudeness on our part), or why they didn't tell you they had other plans, it often turns out it's because they didn't want to disappoint you--didn't want you to feel that there was something else more important they had to do. Interesting cultural differences, yes?

* * *

We had arranged with P.C. for a weekend trip with our Canadian friends to travel to Rwanda (they had a conference scheduled there), but the conference was cancelled at the last minute, and we'd been looking so forward to a short break from our ten-hour days (had planned to spend them at a quiet Monastery while our friends were at conference.

When Elke (German goat project) heard the disappointing news less than an hour later (remember the-faster-than-a-speeding-bulletin famous grapevine?), she offered us her 4-wheel drive Toyota Land Cruiser to tour Akagera animal park in Rwanda so we wouldn't waste our expensive four-day cross-border visas.

Since it was almost the weekend, (late Thursday) we gratefully accepted her offer, tossed food, clothing, sleeping bags and cooking supplies into the vehicle and ran (illegally, as Peace Corps hadn't given us permission to leave the country by ourselves and we're not supposed to be driving anyway). We promised Elke not to have a wreck and try not to be caught.

The Rwandan border crossing was uneventful, but the lights went out from a power outage just as we drove into the capitol of Kigali. We used braille to find a place that had a charcoal brazier still going and a bite to eat, then drove back out of the city to spend the night in the truck at an abandoned filling station (we couldn't find a hotel with all the lights out--every dark street and building looked the same).

With hopes renewed the next morning, we drove back into central Kigali, had a great breakfast at a cafe', gassed up, and headed out in a widening circle around town, looking for and finally finding the teeny, tiny hand-written sign pointing to the park road.

Leaving the well-maintained paved road, the last thirty kilometers became a dusty, rutted path into the park, but we picked up fresh avocados, tomatoes and roasted peanuts from road-side vendors to round out our pantry.

In our hurry to leave, I discovered I'd forgotten to pack the Wretched Thing and charcoal, but we were fortunate enough to find and purchase a large shallow metal disk to cook on (like a heavy cymbal), hoping for some small bits of wood in the park.

It cost us 7800 FrRw ($78 dollars) to enter the park (really expensive on a volunteer salary for two nights and three days of camping).

The good news? We drove through the park gates and into another world, another time. The immediate peace and quiet were incredible. Suddenly, in the space of one kilometer, there weren't a million people around, no human sights, sounds or leavings. Just incredible, perfect silence and solitariness. Monkey, Baboon, Impala, Eland, Topi, Duiker, Bush and Reed buck, Defassa water buck, Marabou storks, long-legged Giraffes, shy Elephants, Fisher eagles, Lion and Zebra wandered in and out of camera range, all of us lazy and tranquil in the heat of the afternoon.

A small path between two lakes lured us off the beaten track to the top of a hill. It beckoned and pulled us to the top of the world; a world of red-blue haze cooling slowly into darkness as the sun vanished beneath the horizon. The absence of humanity did as much for cleansing our spirits as the quiet--for where we camped, there wasn't sign of another soul as far as the eye could carry or the ear hear.

African bush sounds floated up to us on the evening air while we gathered wood and made a small fire for handmade flour tortillas to enjoy with guacamole salad and hot tea. The evening lullaby of grunting hippos, the deep "hhrunka-hhrunka" of lions, laughing hyenas, and the ever-present bullfrogs soon had us yawning, stretching--and looking for a bed.

Ground sleeping didn't seem to be the ticket though, for the first thing we'd found in camp was a large remnant (five foot long, three inches around) of a viper snake skin. The small truck seemed to offer the best protection from the unknown and we crawled in and slept 'curved' for the night.

Early next morning, the tsetse fly population knocked on the door and introduced themselves. The size of a large horsefly, they can fly at speeds of up to forty km/hr, (twenty-five mph), and they attack any and every thing that moves, with a bite like a mad hornet. (Jim still has big red welts from them.)

We discovered if we stood perfectly still and didn't move or breathe, they wouldn't bother us, but, of course, eventually one has to breathe, so there they were. Mosquito netting taped over the windows (thanks to advise from Elke, and our handy-dandy Duct tape which has been useful since the day we landed) allowed for air and visibility and it kept the flies at bay, but they followed us all day, buzzing and charging the windows like bulls on Toreador day.

A bit after mid-morning, we traveled slowly through a thick copse of trees, briars and tall grass and decided it was a nice shady place to pull over, turn off the vehicle, wait and watch. Within fifteen minutes, a pride of lions sauntered slowly by the Landrover, barely giving us the once-over before they stretched out some thirty feet from us. The adults began to groom themselves and sleep while the young cubs stalked each other in the grass, allowing us an amazing view into their daily world.

But all too soon, a great noise and cloud of dust in the distance warned us of approaching 'tourists'. The lions gave us a shared disgusted look, stood and disappeared into the grass as if they had never been. The cloud of dust roared up and a large white bus screeched to halt while passengers leaned out the windows to wave and shout, "Avez-vous vu les lions?" (Have you seen the lions?) We shook our heads slowly (as we knew the lions were well away by now and would not be found by this noisy group) and the bus roared away, thankfully taking its dust-cloud and chatter-clatter with it.

After that, we avoided the few tourists in the park whenever possible, soaking up the silence and serenity of nature like thirsty sponges. A perch high up on a hill covered with trees called our name in early afternoon. Towering a thousand feet above a vast plain and waterhole, it was as if we had a special invitation to set up camp.

We passed the afternoon sharing the binoculars, sitting on the bluff, feeling the warm sun and breeze caress our skin, watching animals come and go to the waterhole way down below. A lone vehicle appeared in the left distance, drove up to the waterhole and a camera crew climbed out, set up shop, filmed for an hour, loaded up, then disappeared off into the right distance, all with no sound reaching us in our little heaven.

Time seemed to slow to a halt and stretch out into eternity. The unobtrusive hush of life in the bush, the ebb and flow of all life, the natural order of living things. It made us wish for a simpler time, one we wouldn't have to leave or go on vacation to find. Not much conversation; words seemed unnecessary--just a quiet floating back to earth and a new perspective on our role in the greater scheme of things. A good last two days.

Refreshed and renewed, we headed back to Ngozi with joy and energy for our work-a-day world.

Gotta go. With love and lotsa hugs,
ijima and aahh-nneeeee-tah

Chapter 59
Games and Bread Dough

Dear Carol, alias C.A., alias one of 'the little kids', alias Twerp, alias
Uncle Bing's favorite little niece, alias grasshopper, alias Jumping Bean,
well, you get the idea,

Guess what came in the mail this week? All the goodies you sent.
Only took eleven months to get here. Thanks for everything! We shared
our good fortune and treasure with the other volunteers. Surprisingly,
everything still tasted fresh!
Catching up:

--To repay Elke for use of her vehicle, all she wanted was our
family recipe of gooey chocolate frosting (fudge) so we showed her and
the Belgian nurse and his wife from Madagascar the recipe for our brand
of 'fudge'. They've been making platefuls of it since and hope they
don't O.D.

--A PC volunteer math teacher from Gabon passed through this
week on her vacation. She was one of the eight who were turned away
last year at the last minute, and she wanted to see what she'd missed.
She was really fun and funny and we are glad to know she and the others
landed somewhere after all, but so sad she wasn't posted here. The
education system missed out on a really great teacher. She also brought
news of fish-volunteers we'd trained with and it was good to hear how
they are faring.

--We spend much of our meager spare time making vacation plans,
as much for a mental break as anything. Not sure where we'll head yet,
but it really doesn't matter. It's all new, so it will be terrific whatever
comes along.

--We just finished a fresh pot of hot tea with some of your goodies
and speaking of the local AAA tea, it is a proudly owned government
business. They have a right to be proud of it as it is truly the best we've

ever tasted, bar none; smooth, clean, no aftertaste and no big caffeine buzz. We'll be sending all we can home.

--We don't get to spend a lot of time with ex-pat's, but the ones we do are refreshing to be around, people who can laugh at themselves and have a good time doing simple, silly things. They keep us going, and we're so lucky to have them close by and for friends.

* * *

Dust:
--It has finally started to dry up. Rain is more intermittent and there is far less of it when it does happen. So we have been busy, busy and busier during this beginning of the dry season, with lots of new pond constructions. We're working a good ten to eleven hard hours each day and collapse most evenings after supper. There are even days we don't care if we ever see another motorcycle, much less get on one, though they are indispensable for our jobs.
Must admit though, we are disgustingly healthy. Moto riding wears off what climbing up and down hills doesn't, and my behind hasn't been this small in years. The Turtle Tushies progress.

--Just one week after the rains stopped, everything began turning brown (except the trees, bamboo, and bushes) from lack of water. Now, two weeks later everything is covered with a fine red silt kicked up from the dry clay roadbeds (including trees, bamboo, and bushes).
If we're unlucky enough to get stuck behind a vehicle or even another moto, we're covered from head to foot with silt and look like invaders from Mars. Even just walking along the road launches off puffs, eddies and clouds of fine red residue. Hair doesn't come clean till the second or third rinse, and our clothes are taking on the same dowdy, ironed-in red color as the roads, a ground-in color (no pun intended) that even Omo soap doesn't fix.

There's a parched dusty haze hanging on the horizon and entire mountains have disappeared from view until the rainy season returns.

* * *

In the continuing saga of Sylveste: at their offer of help, we sent him over to the Canadians' house to learn to make yeast bread from their cook. We thought it might be easier if he learned in his own language from a fellow cook, and also because our efforts have not been very successful.

All went well on the scheduled day. Trudy said the guys laughed and giggled and got flour everywhere and turned out the best bread their cook had ever made.

Sylveste came home, recipe in hand, excited, telling us happily about his good day, and ready to try his new skill.

We reminded him he'd have to start early the next morning, as he was using the electric oven, and electricity goes off at noon. (Yes, we now have electricity for two to three hours per morning. Too bad we're out working and can't enjoy it. But Yipppee anyway.)

Excited over the prospect of fresh bread, I hurried home that evening to find four very heavy loaf-shaped somethings, each only two inches high and hard as rocks, and a beaming Sylveste.
Jim managed to saw his way through half of one, but couldn't eat it and we had to pitch the rest.

It broke my heart to tell the crestfallen Sylveste he'd have to wait till we were home to try again, so we could understand what went wrong. This Friday last, Jim's workday was canceled, so he decided to oversee Sylveste's next attempt. But Jim made the mistake of asking him to cut the recipe in half and only make half as much (thinking that if it didn't turn out, we wouldn't be wasting so many ingredients). By 9 a.m., Sylveste still hadn't started the bread, so Jim reminded him to start soon, and at 10 a.m. found him just mixing the dough, at 10:15 putting the dough in pans to rise in the sun for all of fifteen minutes, and at 10:30 popping them in the oven to bake!

As for halving the recipe, he measured out all of the ingredients and put them into two pans instead of four! So now we have two very, very, very heavy three-inch high loaf-shaped rocks.

I grant you, everyone who has met Sylveste loves him. He is sweet and kind, hard-working and happy all the time, a joy to be around. But they all agree he's a little slower than normal. Most people we've worked with, like our farmers and the agronomes, are quick studies once they have seen a demonstration, and they grasp new concepts readily. But this has also taught us something about development work. It is not enough to show, give, or teach techniques; we have to share and instill the reasons and basic concepts behind the techniques, and that takes time, repetition, practice and patience.

As for Sylveste? When we ask him if he understands what we've tried to teach or show, he says, "Oui, Madame." Or if he has any questions? "No, Monsieur". Guess we'll try again next week.

And that's another thing we've learned from asking ex-pats who have lived in other countries. Many African cultures are circuitous. That is, they rarely approach a subject directly through confrontation, direct statements, or questions. That would be rude. In fact, they are uncomfortable with Europeans and Americans, because in general, we are very direct. And it puts our hosts on the defensive. So, in defense, the answers are usually a short, "Oui, madame", or "No, monsieur", in an effort to be direct also.

One has to be very careful in posing questions so as not to 'lead' people into answering incorrectly. Many whites here criticize Africans for not being able to tell the truth, or answer directly or truthfully, when much of the time it is the whites who have not taken the time to accept, adapt to, or understand a different culture, a different way of being, thinking or posing questions. We don't take the time to socialize, be polite, sit and have tea, or ask after families or local issues before we jump into the work jargon.

* * *

Our farmers continue to give us unsolicited gifts of produce they've raised in gratitude for our help and advice. It would be an insult to refuse the pineapples, avocados, potatoes and cabbage they offer, but it brings tears to the heart to accept. They hardly have enough to feed their own families, and here they are giving us food. We do try to take only one of anything, explaining that one is enough for the two of us and that we wouldn't want such wonderful gifts to go to waste.

* * *

We haven't told you about the men's hats here. They love hats. In all shapes and sizes. The white ruffled nanny cap with puffed-up-top and lace trim is the most unusual and not sure where their love of it comes from.

There's also the black or blonde shaggy fake-fur hat, worn only in the hottest of weather. Then there was a vintage World War I aviator cap with earflaps that we saw last week (which Jim tried to purchase repeatedly without success). But the nicest ones are the hand-knitted yarn stovepipes and bowler hats, usually in shocking striped and zigzag colors, tightly woven and very nicely made.

White 'Nanny' Cap

Fake fur hat

Aviator Cap

Colorful
Hand-Knitted Hat

* * *

--It's cold, blustery and wintery today. We even had some imaginary rain this morning (because, you know, it never rains in the dry season.) The wind is kicking up dust, dirt, and powdery silt everywhere, and it's hard to breathe.

One of our friends refers to the current roadwork going on nation-wide as 'powdering' the roads. And it really seems to be just that. On Communal Saturdays, there are hundreds of work crews out with hoes, pulling dirt out of ditches, off the sides of mountains and onto the roads to spread it around, working it till it's just a fine silky powder. Any vehicular traffic coming along kicks it up in the air, deposits it on the trees, bushes and people, then they go through the same process the next week or month. It does seem to slow erosion. Amazing.

--We're both just trying to stay healthy and accident-free and simply get lots of work done with vacation just around the corner. Thanks again for all the goodies!

Take care, with love and a hug,
ijima and aahh-nneeeee-tah

Chapter 60
Think Texas

Dear Bill and Theola,

Anita keeps saying she wished there were horses here to ride instead of motos. Any draft animal could revolutionize the country. Mules or burros would be great. (Though we understand that serious multiple disease problems prevent draft animals from succeeding.)

In the meantime, fish business is outstanding. We have thirty-plus ponds ongoing (around two and a half acres total), capable of 1500 kg/yr (3300 lbs./yr) of fish--a drop in the bucket when you look at the overall nutrition problem and number of mouths to feed, but you have to start somewhere.

Once we finally finished our first three ponds and installed fish in them, would-be farmers have stopped us on the road daily to talk fish. Hope this trend keeps up.

Anita asked for and received permission from our governor and Peace Corps for us to put helmets and shoes on the new farmers and haul them thirty to forty kilometers cross-country to talk to our already-established fish farmers. That way, they can talk in Kirundi to each other rather than struggle with our broken tongues.

By the time we leave, hopefully we'll have established a networking system where they can support each other and form co-ops and the like.

But hauling these guys is something else. These roads are difficult enough with someone on the back who knows how to ride. But put a guy who's never been on a moto, never been out of his own small region of the country, and haul him thirty-forty kilometers somewhere else at 30-40 km/hr, and it gets wild.

They twist, turn, wave and yell at everyone in sight to make certain they don't miss anyone or anything along the way, and are just as likely to jump off at cruising speed to say hello to someone as anything.

Anita had that happen to her. She said one minute the guy was there, the next minute he wasn't.

By the time she slowed, stopped and turned around, he was picking himself up out of the dust and running after her. The concepts of speed, danger, and impact are foreign until they experience them directly, and even then, it's still all a big game.

All he said when he caught up to her was "Humph!" That means the same in English as it does in Kirundi.

Take care,
Jim and Anita

Chapter 61
Burlap Bags, Rabbits and Wretched Things

Dear Carol,
Greetings little earthling! Amakura maki?

--Fish farming is going well. Though with almost too much work, we're on a downhill slide in energy. Working on the equator seems to sap more out of a person than the temperate climates.

--Sad news. Something has again prevented new volunteers (eight this time--four of them fishies) from coming in this week, or anytime, as in--cancelled indefinitely, but it looks like our own Visas are being renewed for the time being. Hooray!

There are days it would break my heart if we had to leave before we'd finished our two years. And other days, I'd be willing to row home--just gimme' an oar! The emotional roller coaster always seems to be in high gear, whatever the reason, and we find ourselves looking for some consistency in our lives. We can take the first one hundred changes to the day, but for unknown reasons the hundred and first often tips us over the edge.

* * *

--I dropped my bike today. Nothing serious--one of those dumb moves on newly distributed marbles masquerading as fresh gravel on a 12% grade downhill and blind corner, but I tore a brand new, used pair, of perfect-color dirt-brown corduroys in the process, and managed to break three of the four turning signal light housings on my bike (one front -- two back), and put a dent in my gas tank.

I, me, myself, didn't get a scratch, but dropped my helmet on a rock just after I'd picked up the moto, and broke the chin guard, so there goes some of our vacation money for a new helmet and signal light housings in Nairobi. In the interim it's fix it with Goop Shoe-Goo®.

Ruining my new-used cords was almost the worst news. I'd spent an hour bargaining for them in the market last week and they still cost me twelve dollars. Then, the first time out in public, I put a twelve-inch gash in the thigh. To add insult to injury, returning home to change caused me to miss half of my appointments today. Bummer.

I was happy to see Jim pull up to the house soon after me late this evening. He gave me some T.L.C. and a "Tarn-sarn, baby, Tarn-sarn."

* * *

--The rabbits are growing and thriving and we expect two new kindles at the end of this month. We should be ready to initiate farmers in rabbit husbandry the month after that. I need to design a pee-proof rabbit cage, however. The one I built is an excellent design--that doesn't work.

You make everything out of 'chicken' wire on a wood frame so 'it' (poop and pee) falls through the wire floor onto a sloped sheet of tin, travels to the end of the cages on the sloped sheet of tin, and drops down into catch pans which are emptied daily into the garden or compost. Neat, huh?

The pellet-parts work great, but those cotton-picking cottontails do everything within their power to eject their pee everywhere but down. They've covered the back wall behind the cages and we have to warn visitors not to stand too close to the front, because their aim is improving.

The other problem is that they climb up into their food mangers and poop all over the food, but that's my fault--I didn't make them climb or poop proof--will fix that part this weekend.

--Finding enough fresh greens for them in the dry season is also a problem. It's a three and a half kilometer walk for our gardener to descend into the valley and collect a daily batch of green stuff (there's a prolific high-protein 'weed' called iconda, ee-chon-da) he collects that the rabbits love.

But--the little furry things seem to be content and healthy as long as we give them fresh food, water and target practice once or twice a day, so we're making progress.

* * *

--Speaking of Wretched Things, I had a small problem the other night. Jim asked me to heat up two big pots of water for our Friday-night 'bath', so I started up the two Wretched Things on the back porch.

The wind (good to start fires) was blowing hard against the back of the house, and sent sparks flying everywhere, so the charcoal caught readily. The Wretched Things soon glowed hot and red and I put on the two pots of water to boil while I fixed supper.

Thirty minutes later, I glanced out the window and noticed it was awfully hazy--no, not hazy--smoky?
The bells went off in my head, and I rushed out to find the entire burlap bag of charcoal on fire! (A full bag stands over four and a half feet tall, two and a half feet around, and costs around fifty dollars, which is a lot of bloomin' charcoal, and now was money going up in smoke.)

I quick-dragged it to the center of the porch and tried to drown it with a pan of water. This only disintegrated the burlap bag and created more smoke and a grey greasy mess. Several pans of water later, thinking I had put it out, I went back inside.

Thirty minutes later I went through the whole thing again with Jim's help--as he noticed the smoke the second time, and we lost the entire bag of charcoal--which is truly amazing, considering all the trouble we have getting small amounts started in The Wretched Things!

By this time the two pots were boiling merrily away, so we left the back porch in chaos and took a hot dribble bath each.

--Golly, did Sylveste have a good time when he arrived the next morning. His face lit up brighter and merrier than a sunrise on the beach when he discovered the two Wretched Things, the blackened mound, the shreds of burlap, slowly piecing it all together.

Howling with laughter, he was off to tell all the neighbors--in all directions. It was almost as good as the saga of the toilet seat! And he'll have even more fun telling our tale to the whole market when we dig into savings and send him to buy another bag of charcoal.

Well, enough already. Gotta get to bed. Work and daylight come early. Take care and do good things.

With love and a hug.
Hewe and aahh-nneeeee-tah
The CCC of N
(alias the Charcoal Charring Champions of Ngozi)

Chapter 62
Private Matters
Late August

Dear Uncle Con and Aunt Dorothy,
Bwakeye! (Buh-gah-kay--Good Morning)
The landlord's been promising for some time to have the many holes and leaks in our tin roof repaired before the next rainy season.
--We arrived home from work yesterday to find two guys on the roof, painting it a bright red (painting, mind you, not repairing). From the sounds of banging and thumping as they dragged heavy boards across it to sit on while they painted, we'll have a few more leaks come September and the rainy season. There's another huge crew painting the fourteen-color patchwork quilt of stones on the front of the house the same bright red, so it will all match the beautiful fifteen-foot poinsettia tree in our circle drive.
--We're using some of our precious vacation money to put up a fence on one side of our overly large yard to keep the neighbors from camping out on it with large noisy parties, deter some personal harassment and regain a semblance of privacy. We figure if we spend $20-$30 per month for four to five months, we'll be able to fence the whole acreage and can walk out in the back yard without anyone bothering us or reporting on us (it must be the most boring intelligence report ever, as we have no time or energy to do anything but work, sleep and eat.)
I guess lack of privacy is the biggest thing we still have to deal with. And in addition to the normal curious, rowdy locals, there's an ongoing anti-white campaign that's growing stronger by the week, like blockages in work for no apparent reason, or official-looking types showing up to stand outside our house and glare in the windows.
We never have a moment we can walk outside or work in the garden or on small projects without a dozen people appearing wanting to

know what we are doing and why, every minute of the day and night, and becoming angry if we don't answer. (Lest you get the wrong idea, this is not their normal friendly behavior, and has everything to do with politics.)

The other volunteers have not experienced the monitoring as much yet and have not been sympathetic the few times we've mentioned it on our rare trips to Buja. Until one by one, they've visited us for a weekend and end up going bananas from being constantly watched. Could it be something we've done, or talked to the wrong people?

* * *

Our work, which was going so well, has reached an impasse in many places (other volunteers are now experiencing the same work stoppages). We heard through the faster-than-light 'grapevine' that it is because U.S.A.I.D. cut funding from some major projects into which money was being poured, and that the government is retaliating.

But it feels like it goes much deeper and wider than that. On July 1st, their Independence Day, the President gave an hour-long speech on the evil influence of all whites and said that by next year they would at last be free from this evil yoke, having expelled all of us.
They are stepping up their campaign against the European priests and nuns who have been here plus forty and fifty years, revoking their visas in record numbers.

And while we know we are on the bottom of the food chain and are ignorant of much that goes on politically here or at home, we are seeing with our own eyes things that don't make sense economically, hearing about important projects that should be sponsored and others that perhaps, should not.

We were cornered by a U.S. official at a recent ex-pat gathering and told that we were extremely naive when he asked after our project. He said, "It takes excess money to make things work and if only one to ten percent trickles down and does some good, we've accomplished our goal."

I hope he's a singular exception rather than the rule. If not, no wonder the world is headed toward bankruptcy.

We can't really blame emerging countries who see money floating around, cars, Landrovers, high standards of living, and they want it too-- and now, like other countries who seem to be swimming in it, not later.

Well...enough! No more complaining. Doesn't do any good and our smiles will keep everyone on their toes and wondering: "Are they sane?"
(If they only knew or understood how simple-minded we really are, that

all we want is to build fish ponds, not fall on the motos, and prove that our project is good for the country, that it builds the economy, and that it can improve the lives of those we're working with and beyond. And most important, that there is absolutely no intrigue or evil influence going on down at our level of work. Even if we had the inclination, we are too tired to be sneaky.)

Love and a hug,
Jimani

P.S.

We'll mail this in Kenya, or with someone headed home, as we don't want to endanger the program. We still hear that mail is opened regularly.

Chapter 63
Safari!

Dear Folks,

It's Vacation Time! We are so looking forward to the next month--not away from our farmers or the work--lest you get the wrong idea--just for some anonymity, quiet time and someplace to lay our heads where nobody knows who we are for a few weeks.

Kenya:

Leaving the country proved almost as difficult getting in. 'Everyone' had told us that it was only a one and a half hour flight from Buja to Nairobi and that we should be there by noon.

Unfortunately, everyone forgot to tell our pilot and we were an hour late taking off. Then there was the diversion to Kigali, Rwanda (not in the flight plan), with disembarkation and a two hour layover (always makes one suspect engine problems), delaying just long enough to take off into a full-fledged thunderstorm that had us bucking and rolling in the aisles all the way to Nairobi, five hours late.

Everyone had told us there was no problem or hassle obtaining a tourist visa at the airport, so we were somewhat surprised to see a long line in front of the booth marked VISAS.

What everyone could not have predicted, was that on this particular day, someone would misplace the stamp and book of visa issues. Bemused, we watched very intense uniformed fellows scurrying here and there for an hour and a half, looking fervently for the lost stamp and record book.

At last, someone arrived with another book and we all surged forward with our U.S. cash to be allowed into the country.

Unfortunately, they'd neglected to bring any change to the booth and we in the queue only had tens or twenties for the eight-dollar fee.

We finally got all but one dollar of our change back and considered that a nominal tip. There was another surge to the airport bank to

change dollars into Kenya schillings, and then another as we all sought
fresh air and freedom, only to be accosted by a dozen aggressive taxi
drivers.

'Everyone' had told us to avoid these guys, who wanted $20 to drive us
from the airport to a downtown hotel.

'Everyone' said instead, to take the airport bus for $2. But with all
the delays, the last bus run of the day had occurred while we were
waiting in line for our Visas. The taxi drivers informed us of this, but
not to be taken in as poor dumb tourists, we decided to wait it out.

--Dark approaches rapidly on the equator, very soon after 6:00 p.m.,
every evening. As dark rapidly approached, we decided to forget
'Everyone's' advice and take a taxi into town, on the wrong side of the
road. (You tell yourself you'll remember that traffic moves in the
opposite direction you're accustomed to, but we found ourselves almost
being run over nearly every day for a month because we continually
looked the wrong way for oncoming traffic. (Slow learners.)

--One thing Kenya has in common with Burundi is stuffing mini-
vans and small buses called matatus (mah-tah-toos) chock full of people,
in layers--with arms, limbs and bodies sticking out akimbo.

We actually tried to ride in one, paid our money to the barker and
everything, and found that even after a year of becoming very strong and
lean, our Turtle Tushies still wouldn't do that wiggle/slide thing in and
down to fit in amongst the other sardines.

Much to the other passenger's relief, we finally gave up and walked
away, walking most places, and only took a cab when it was just too far.
We had planned on joining a Safari immediately, but I required a dental
appointment for a crown repair and the first available was in two days.

Plus, we were so overwhelmed with the bustling commerce of
Nairobi that we spent three days walking the streets, ogling the
storefronts, kiosks and full shelves of stuff-we-didn't-need, peeking into
doorways and alleyways to make sure we didn't miss anything, and
reveling in the fact that not a single person there knew us, or asked us
what we were doing there. It also gave us the opportunity to better
check out Safari offerings and prices.

(Reflection: One of the big cultural adjustments when we arrived in
Burundi was to see all these wonderful storefronts, clean and bright with
polished shiny windows, each with a sign proclaiming something
different: auto-parts, mercantile, grocery stores, but all with nearly
nothing inside, just empty shelves.

Most of the stores in Burundi carry the same imported few items
(no matter the storefront) –tiny tins of Chinese tomato paste, candy bars,

soap, rice and beans, bolts of cloth--and that's all they have. Why? Burundi is landlocked and very much interior to the middle of the continent. All goods must be first imported to the coast, then packed and trucked several thousand miles inland through several countries (each with their own tariff) before it finally arrives in Burundi or Rwanda.

Without a thriving economy, not much is ordered unless it either has a very long shelf life, they have constant and immediate use for it, or it is very affordable.)

--So in Nairobi, the occasional store we actually ventured into would affect us like kids in a toy store!

"Hewe! Come look at this! Parker ballpoint pens! With refills!"

Or, "Hewe, did you see this?"

The clerks, I'm sure, thought we were crazy because we couldn't seem to decide on anything we wanted, just kept picking things up to stroke and marvel at them.

To see such a freewheeling, happy, open economy with people marketing wares in the street stalls just made us smile. Jim was in his element. Everything was in English and he really got into the spirit of bargaining, always friendly and laughing and talking to the shop person, asking where something came from, what kind of wood, stone or fiber it was crafted from, how long it took to make--then finally getting down to some friendly bargaining, not beating them down to the last cent, arriving someplace in the middle where both parties could leave the deal feeling good.

It was as much fun watching him as it was gathering our little treasures for shipping home. I love getting the history and story of things, I'm just not very good at bargaining. Left to me, we'd have been broke within the week.

--The post is another story. We were so 'smart', we'd purchased a metal foot locker in Burundi, thinking we'd fill it half full with their wonderful tea and coffee (which we did), then cart it here to Kenya, buy more art and treasures, and ship it all home, slow-boat-to-China method for you to disperse to family in smaller packages.

Great plan, yes? Wrong. Shipping companies now only handle goods by the 'carton'. That didn't sound too bad when they told us...but..."How big is a carton", you ask? A carton is a 'cargo shipping container'--a huge metal crate just under the size of an 18-wheeler tractor-trailer.

We couldn't find that much to ship home, so off we went to the local Post only to find they accepted only packages smaller than 20 kg.

(forty pounds), and like the Brown trucks from home, couldn't exceed certain dimensions.

Unfortunately, our prized footlocker did not meet any of those specifications. So we rearranged our thinking and packaged up a small ten-kilo box as a trial run. Jim trotted off to the Post while I rinsed out clothes in the Hotel sink. He was back in about ten minutes, but still had our package.

The same Post lady we'd spoken with before, said, "Well, we don't actually accept the packages here, that office is..." (Someplace not close.)

So off he went again in the opposite direction and was gone for a verrry loooonnnng time.

When he finally returned, there was a twinkle in his eyes and I could tell we'd learned something new again. He'd arrived at the Post, weighed in his package and presented it to the sweet young postal clerk, who looked at him with dismay. "But sir, you must have plain brown paper and string covering the outside. Everyone knows that."

Jim was crestfallen and said, "Oh, but I don't have any and the Post is ready to close for the day and it took me so long to find you and this has to go out today," throwing himself on her mercy.

"Well, hakuna matata," she said, soothing him, "No problem, Sir, I just happen to have some wrapping paper here that someone left, and look, here's some string to go around the outside." She helped him prepare it to look just like all the other international packages going out and gave him the projected postal rates for future boxes.

Jim has this affect on women.

* * *

--It was after this experience that we began to notice that Kenyans are very kind, treating tourists like errant children, watching over them, giving 'strokes', being patient and tolerant of all our errant buffoonery and cultural insensitivities. We began to feel like we were the walking 'zoos' and that the local wildlife and the people observed, watched, fed and looked after us.

--The hotel we chose in the middle of downtown Nairobi is so accustomed to tourists that it has a complete locked storeroom for travelers to leave their extra belongings in while they take Safari, which is what we did with our excess treasures, tea and coffee as we prepared to go on Safari, four days into our vacation.

* * *

Safari!

We had a few anxious moments when the hotel one-day laundry service turned into four and then they lost it altogether, (thus my rinsing out things in the sink), so we were faced with starting safari in our one and only set of semi-dirty clothes. We gave up ever seeing our 'duds' again, checked out of the hotel and left for the travel agency. What we did not know is that hotel management had not given up, had in fact sent a cab across town to the laundry and bless their souls, they located, retrieved and had our 'bundle' of clean clothes delivered to us just as we were boarding the Safari bus. Wow, were we impressed, and vowed to return to the hotel with a large tip for our rescuers.

* * *

'Safari' is Swahili for journey, and we began ours with twenty five other campers stuffed tight like sardines into clean steel cans masquerading as a mini-van and a small bus, down great paved roads through the lovely English-style farm-country nestled around Nairobi.

Descending into the Rift Valley, we passed well-kept barns, fields of hay, irrigated crops and tidy brick houses, all of which gradually gave way with the miles, the heat and the diminished rain-fall totals to tin shacks, mud brick huts, and scrub brush in semi-arid desert conditions.

Leaving the highway, we traveled several very long dusty, bumpy hours on dirt roads that eventually delivered us to the first of three bird-watching lakes and hot springs. Not seeing many birds, Jim and I walked down to the lake's edge to stretch cramped muscles and to see what kind of flora and fauna it held.

We made the mistake of swishing our hands in the crystal clear warmth of the lake. Strong alkaline water entered every cut and crack in the skin and began to burn. We jerked our hands from the water only to see them turn white in the air with the alkali coating. It even polished our rings. There's not a bird in his right mind or feather who would stay there any longer than necessary and then, only to polish his nails.

-- As we helped unload camping gear that first evening, Jim and I chose an old heavy canvas tent, while two really funny (in a genuine comic sense) English chaps took a new fancy-dancy lightweight nylon pop-up variety. The drivers kept an eagle eye on all of us to make sure we had what we needed for supper--and didn't wander off.
"Nice tourist. Good Tourist. Are you hungry? Here, have another pancake." They were so accommodating we wondered what we'd done right?

Settling in that quiet first night at the hot springs gave us the chance to chat with fellow travelers (sans road noise and dust) and discover where in the world everyone was from.

One of the English chaps is a foreign attaché in the British Embassy in Saudi Arabia, the other a social services worker in London and a world traveler who wants to be a comedian on British stage--he deserves to be as he really is very FUNNY. We loved his droll humor. He couldn't seem to help himself offering witty comments one after the other, and kept us in stitches and laughing the entire trip.

We also met a young couple we really liked who had just finished their two-year tour in Peace Corps, Seychelles (remote islands one thousand miles due east of Kenya, and near--well, not near anywhere really, just in the middle of the ocean).

On a happy note after supper, we pitched in to wash dishes--then everyone turned sore and tired tushies in for an early night. Soon after, it began to rain. Comfy and dry in our ancient canvas cocoon, we'd almost drifted off to sleep when we heard some rather urgent whispering issuing from the vicinity of fancy-dancy. The whisperings were followed by muffled thuds, whaps, slaps, and curses. Then all was quiet and we slept like the dead.

I awoke early with the dawn and peeked out at the day. Mildly surprised to see fancy-dancy already collapsed and ready for packing, I thought to myself, "My, Self! But those chaps rise early!"

I nudged Jim awake and with no water provided for washing, we strolled down to the hot springs to risk a toothbrush-full of alkali for brushing and rinsing (figured no respectable anti-human germ or bacteria would live in that stuff). Hope our enamel holds up!

Foregoing our usual morning spit bath to protect our outer layer of skin, we wandered back to camp and breakfast. The other campers stumbled from their tents rubbing sleepy eyes at the smell of coffee brewing, including our two British friends from an entirely different tent. Turns out their pop-up fancy-dancy leaked like a sieve and they'd abandoned ship in the first thirty minutes of the storm. In the rush of leaving for drier ground one of them had tripped and pulled the support rods and tent down.

Fortunately, they'd found and pitched the last spare canvas abode in the rain, saving themselves from a drafty, cramped wet night on the bus, and got almost four hours sleep.

The second lake was much the same as the first, beautiful, but bereft of much wildlife. But at the third, Lake Nakuru, we disembarked on a hillside perch a thousand feet above the lake and had a birds-eye view of a huge shimmering pink swath lining the shore and extending out for hundreds of yards on the water below.

With the binoculars we focused in what turned out to be thousands upon thousands of flamingos in undulating pink ribbons that continually swelled and retreated along shallow shores rich with food supply.

Pelicans and funny-looking marabou storks rounded off the view, and directly beneath us in burrowed pockets along the high rocky ledge were some really cute burrowing little ground-creatures called 'rock hyraxes' (like large gerbils--good subjects for sketching), and everyone was happy (it looks like a squirrel or gerbil, but turns out it's the closest living relative and land animal to the elephant! Manatees are a close second. Who knew?)

We were allowed out of the vehicles only at brief stops and at each night's camp sight, and even then cautioned not to wander too far, making us wonder what was out there that we weren't seeing?
--The people we encountered were great, but the most indelible memory of those first three days is of dust. An incredible amount of dust. The one difference we found between the clouds of dust in Kenya and those in Burundi is that Kenya's is grey-white instead of red.
During the first two kilometers of dirt road, everyone aged forty years as fine white layers of silt filtered into the open-air buses, till we all looked as if we'd been rolling around in a flour bin.
It settled on the face, hair, clothes, seats, luggage, sifted into the food, tents, sleeping bags, everywhere and in everything. Emerging from the van or bus at day's end, the first thing we all did was slap clothes, hair and skin, sending poofs and jets of the stuff spiraling off. Great fun!
* * *
--One of the most interesting destinations was on the shores of Lake Baringo at the Jonathan Leakey snake farm (conservationist descended from my heroes Louis and Mary, archaeologists /anthropologists of Olduvai Gorge and ancient 'Lucy' find and fame). The Leakey snake

farm milks snake venom for use in laboratories and universities around the world.

Our group piled out to see a large dome-like wire and metal rebar frame structure enclosing tall grasses and a tree, and a small open-frame shed near the enclosure housing only a narrow wooden worktable. Hot, unimpressed, and tired of waiting for the 'show to start', two guys from New York City in shorts and t-shirts (on their first camping experience--ever) explored the shed, then hopped up for a seat on the work table, swinging their bare legs back and forth, comfy, enjoying the shade and the view.

Our tour guide and the snake farm host appeared just then from up the track and stopped in their tracks, staring at our two fellow travelers. The guide cleared his throat and said, "Sirs, I would not choose to sit up there if I were you." Every head swiveled in the direction of New York.

"Why not?" one demanded, not liking being singled out.

"Well, you see, Sir, that is where we milk the snake venom. I hope you have no open sores or scratches, as one drop is enough to kill a half-dozen people, especially the black mamba venom."

You have never seen two guys move faster--and through the entire demonstration of our host snaring a black mamba in the enclosure, bringing it out to our group and showing us why the two-meter-long, slender, nondescript olive-green-to-brown snake was called a black mamba (its mouth is black inside), and explaining how neurotoxins work and how fast and effective is their poison--these two were continually wiping their hands on their shorts and checking themselves for the list of symptoms our guide and host so graciously gave us.

--Then it was back to the dust. We ate more of it traveling the hundred and sixty kilometers from the northern lakes down south into the Masai Mara game preserve, bouncing around in the van like Ping-Pong balls in a wind tunnel over the rough roads.

We were just getting used to the beat-on-your-head rhythm when we rounded a blind corner. With no warning, an enormous dirt wallow appeared suddenly in our path, opened its maw and swallowed us down whole in one big gulp. The van lurched to a sudden and harsh stop, the engine died and we foundered, sinking slowly down into a foot of powder.

Groans and yelps were followed by sudden quiet as a silky white cloud of puff arose, enveloped us and obliterated visual contact with the outside world.

The sudden stop and skinned shins left all us sardines in shock, giving the driver unfettered time to resurrect the engine. After a few grinding tries, it coughed to life, wheels rocked and spun, then churned us out of the hole, and without much fuss, we were off again like a shot, bouncing left, right and up at every twist and turn.

--Pulling into the campsite just outside the game preserve, Jim slapped off poofs and layers of white from his clothes and face then off-loaded our reliable old canvas shelter. He teased me about looking out for snakes while he pegged stakes outside and I crawled inside to set up the tent pole.

While pushing at the canvas corners inside to spread out the wrinkles and groping around in the dark for the pole, my hand went into something warm, semi-firm, and yukky. I let out a muffled yell, and jerked back a full body-length, bowling Jim over in my haste to return to the light of day.

Picking himself up, he almost laughed then pooh-poohed my fears of a snake, telling me nothing could possibly have survived all day on the roof of that bus. Cautiously reentering to search for the invader, I discovered a lost bag of carrots we'd misplaced that morning. Quite dead now, they'd been steamed to perfection in the plastic in canvas atop our noble carriage in the hot sun. If not for all the dust, and the fact that I'd pretty well mushed them with the first encounter, we'd have eaten them anyway. As it was, we settled for macaroni and cheese and hot tea.
And we learned something. Hot, fermented carrots leave an after-odor uniquely their own in a damp canvas tent.

--Our compatriots from New York were not adapting as well as they might have to their first camping trip. They kept choosing the worst sites to pitch their tent. This time they opted to set up down-wind of the cooking fires and in the lowest spot on the terrain (though it did have the best view, overlooking a ravine and the beautiful vast savannah).
But they were immune to suggestions from our guides that it wasn't the most favorable of sites.

--We were blessed with Masai warriors as guards for our camp that night, in tribal dress--friendly, but aloof--and our guides informed us that they'd been hired because there had been lions reported in the area and warned us once again not to wander off into the bush on our own, as it might spoil the trip for the others.

--We thought this was great fun and done for our entertainment until we heard them 'coughing' outside our tent (the lions, not the Masai) just after sunset, then start that deep Hrrrunka, hurrrunka we recognized as lions, many of them, and close by. Visions of the 'man-eaters from Tsavo' danced through our heads until we dropped off to sleep.

Sometime during the night, it began to rain again, softly at first and then harder. Still dry and toasty inside our canvas cocoon, we had a restful night's sleep, but arose to find two very grumpy New Yorkers, who were first driven from their tent when it filled with smoke from the cook fires, then again from the watch fires, and yet a third time in the rain when the run-off washed out the ground from beneath them and filled their little canvas box to overflowing.

With no extra tents available, they'd spent most of an uncomfortable night wet and cold, scrunched up on the too-short hard bench seats in the bus. They lent reality to the phrase, 'unhappy campers', or one from home, "They'd been rode hard and put up wet." We did feel for them.

--Breakfasted, loaded up and ready to go, we drove into the park just after sunrise across a vast, rolling, yellow-grassy plain, broken only by shallow, tree-filled ravines. We raced through the first two hours, herded and rushed through the living museum until the pressure of finding and photographing the 'big five' was off (elephant, rhino, lion, buffalo, and either cheetah or leopard).

Having accomplished their goal as guides, our drivers relaxed and adopted a more leisurely pace. The wildlife was varied, prolific and exciting: wandering Topi, lions chased zebra and wildebeests, a cheetah stalked and killed an antelope only to have it whisked away by a very rude hyena. Bat-eared foxes peered warily from their holes while elephants and rhinos protected and hid their babies in the bush. We had a great next two days.

Our last day turned up drizzling rain with the beginnings of mud wallows and slick roads (also the beginning of the rainy season when the animals migrate from the Mara back down to the Serengeti), and we had to talk our guides into risking the vehicles in the mud, since we'd already seen the Big Five. They acquiesced only when we promised to push if we got stuck.

Spinning and sliding into the grey blanket, our hearts were merry at the prospect of adventure and adversity. And even with the greyness of the drizzle, there was a soft kind of brightness and light trapped under the low-hanging clouds, matching our spirits.

Out of the grey, the sight of a baby elephant wandering alone and in distress wrung our hearts. Where was its mama? We had just seen her yesterday. The same thought leapt into all our heads. Poachers! We were trying to talk our driver into calling for wardens or taking Baby E. onboard the bus for safety, when he spotted lions stalking a herd of cape buffalo on the other side of the ravine. Ignoring our pleas to rescue Baby E., our driver turned the van toward the buffalo and the bus followed.

There we saw a patient lioness teaching her three young cubs the skill of stealth. But being kids, they were more interested in fooling around and soon had the incensed attention of the outer guard of the buffalo herd.

Our guide jockeyed into a good viewing position and explained that a lion will never win in a direct confrontation with the savage and unpredictable buffalo. As if to verify, the outer ring of sentry bulls suddenly charged the pride. Noses high in the air, taut-muscled bovines stamped anger and challenge into every movement, worrying, warting and chasing the offending cats back to our side of the ravine--except for patient mama L.

She hunkered down into invisibility in the brush.

Nervous, the bulls continued to whirl and snort and search the area. Their sense of smell told them a cat was still near, and at last they rooted her out and sent her packing.

We slowly tracked and followed Mama L. and found the whole pride resting under an immense old tree that leaned and branched out over a narrow gorge at a 45-degree angle. Two cubs faced each other half way up the trunk, playing king-of-the-mountain.

Abruptly, a large leopard, spooked by Mama lion, streaked up out of the hollow. Seeking refuge, he scrambled up the tree, knocking the surprised cubs sprawling to the ground, yowling and clamoring their unhappiness.

Taking immediate offense, the adult lions surrounded the tree, pacing back and forth around the trunk, growling, rumbling, and snarling up at the interloping leopard. Leopard subsequently climbed to the highest, smallest branch that would support him and growled back. Our two vehicles jockeyed slowly around, trying to get a better view of the leopard. We pulled up to the edge of the ravine and craned our necks through the pop-up observation roof.

Cameras clicked and snapped rapidly, until someone asked what we were shooting at. (You wouldn't believe how a large, bright-orange-black-and-white animal can lose itself so completely on a green and grey tree branch!)

Another commotion had us swiveling our heads around to the left as poor Baby E. charged down the ravine, chased and molested by Mama lion. The pair passed literally under our noses and we almost tilted the van over with everyone scrambling up and out again for an aerial view of the drama.

We couldn't keep silent and cheered Baby E. on to safety as he struggled out of the hollow and stopped under the leopard's tree to take a stand. Leopard immediately snarled and growled a challenge down as if to say, "Get lost bub, I've got troubles of my own!"

In a panic, Baby E. slid back down into the gully, and Mama L. took up pursuit again.

Our driver backed around and followed Baby E. toward the buffalo herd, our anxious crew murmuring encouragement all the way. But the lioness attacked Baby E. from behind, raking E.'s tough hide with her claws. Baby E. swung suddenly around, head down, ears flapping, and challenged her with a short two-step charge, squirting (or flinging?) a trunk full of dust into Mama L's face.

Mama L. backed down--as much in caution of us and the nearing buffalo as anything else--and slinked off into the grass. Baby E. wheeled around and made a beeline toward the buffalo herd.

Our guides assured us he would be safe for the night if he stayed with the herd. Don't know if this was true or if they were afraid we'd try to follow through with our threat of bringing him on board the van or bus with us. Short of a revolution and overthrow of our guides, there wasn't much we could do and sadly, we were forced to leave Baby E. behind.

Slowly circling back to the leopard's tree, the driver had just maneuvered into a good position for photos when four new safari vehicles bore down on us from the hills above to see what we'd found. Within minutes the scene resembled a circling wagon train, ready for the last attack.

The lions, thoroughly disgusted with all the notoriety and attention, turned and vanished into the bush. Meanwhile, the leopard moved the last visible vestige of his tail into concealment, and within seconds, it was difficult to believe the drama had ever come about.

The other vans edged closer and close, calling out to us, "What is it? What is it? What do you see?"

Honestly. Tourists.

* * *

--It rained every night and at least once during each day, yet each time we took to the road, it was as if there had never been in all of creation, even a drop of rain in our path. Dust stalked us in the beginning, swallowed us, choked on us, and spit us out six days later on the highway back to Nairobi.

East Africa during the dry season is like living inside a vacuum cleaner bag with the sun installed.

Dusty, tired and happy, we arrived back in Nairobi feeling like desert rats. We invited the Peace Corps, Seychelles couple up to our hotel room to take advantage of a hot shower before they flew out for their roundabout trip home through Australia and New Zealand.

We enjoyed listening to the highlights of their two years and their chance encounter with Walter Matthau, (in the Seychelles to film '*The Pirates*'), and who is apparently just a really nice guy. T. has always been a big, BIG fan of Matthau's, and when they met and hit it off, Walter took them both under his wing while he was there, with an invitation to come visit in Hollywood when they arrived back home. Cool.

We bid them a bon voyage and spent the next day washing tons of dust out of our clothes in the hotel bathtub, unwilling to risk the one-day laundry service again.

That's when we discovered we'd left the address of friends currently living in Mombasa, back in Burundi (former next-farm-over neighbors from my home town--Ha! and you thought no one ever came from there, didn't you?)

Not panicking yet, I looked them up in the Nairobi/Mombasa hotel phone book and sure enough, there they were and we tucked the address and phone number away for later use.

* * *

Eating at a side-walk café that evening, we ran into one of our fellow-fish-volunteers from Burundi, fish-station-Dann, also on vacation. He'd stayed in a B&B where the English proprietor had recommended he take in the island of Lamu for an unforgettable taste of ancient Africa. He said both the B&B and Lamu were super and that we would enjoy.

So, we bought tickets and spent a sleepless, swaying, lurching night on the famous Lunatic Express everyone raves about (the Mombasa-Nairobi narrow-gauge train). We were raving seasick all night, but arrived in Mombasa in one piece, thankful to be on firm unwavering ground again, and thankful too, at not having been snatched from the train by any descendants of the man-eating-lions of Tsavo--which caused a huge problem in the building of the railroad in colonial days (you can read about them in *The Lunatic Express*, by Charles Miller--great book).

Once arrived, we called my former neighbor, and he arrived soon after to pick us up at the train station. When we explained about leaving their address and phone number in Burundi, he and his wife couldn't figure out how we had reached them. They have NEVER been listed in the Kenya phone book. They showed us the only two editions of the national directory (just like the one we'd used in Nairobi) and sure enough, they weren't listed. The angels are definitely looking out for us. They and their three beautiful girls seemed genuinely pleased to have real live American visitors, albeit unannounced. They were very gracious hosts and we had fun exchanging war stories and adjustments to life on the equator as expats.

He enjoys his job as Superintendent of a church school and they love the people and friends they've made, but they were not so fond of the climate of Mombasa itself. At sea level on the equator, it's always hot and humid, and they've been exposed to some of the worst of African diseases, the most debilitating of which so far has been chronic malaria.

They were all very thin and we worried about the long term effects of disease, especially on the girls, but still, we spent a happy two days there before flying to the island paradise of Lamu on the Indian Ocean.

Chapter 64
Lamu (lah-moo)

Dear Family,

We flew out of Mombasa in a small four-seater fixed wing that had suspicious oil streaks running down the side where the propeller and engine joined. I asked Jim if that was normal and he said, "Oh, sure, hon, they all look like that. Not to worry. Hakuna matata."

So I didn't, until in mid-air, a quarter of the time into our flight, big blotches of oil began streaming onto the windshield, blocking our view and coincidently, the pilot's also.

"Uh-oh," our pilot said, and promptly turned the nose down. Not the words of comfort we wanted to hear.

Jim said my eyes were big as saucers. You should have seen his through his bifocals! A brief, bumpy, but safe landing dumped us on a barren airstrip in someplace called Malindi, not to fix the plane but to pour in four more buckets of oil and clean the windshield.

As this method failed to work, and oil continued to leak out almost as fast as he could pour it in, our pilot called in another airplane from Mombasa (much to our relief) and a short hour and a half later we were airborne again.

It was a nervous flight, but we put the near miss out of our minds as the brilliant white sands and iridescent blue waters of the Indian Ocean rose to meet us, with our pilot landing quite safely at the northeastern edge of Kenya on the mainland coast.

Without so much as time to catch our breath or give thanks, the plane door was sprung open as a dozen eager porters jumped out of the thick brush to play tug-o-war with Jim for our luggage.

Jim wasn't about to let go without negotiating for a price and tried repeatedly to ask how much? Ignoring him and unruffled, two of them wrenched our two small backpacks from his hands and trotted merrily off to the ferry waiting to transport us to paradise.

Trotting quickly after our luggage, we were pulled in all directions by porters anxious to show us the many different accommodations and activities available. Jim picked out a man who just happened to look wise and sane, who said sure, he'd take us right to three or four guest rooms and we could take our pick, but not to talk to the other porters as they would most certainly only lead us astray and we wouldn't want that now, would we?

Then he began a nonstop sales pitch on friendly safe and wonderful Lamu, because of course, it was pretty much entirely inhabited by Muslims, and there was no drinking allowed and did we drink, because liquor was hard to get, and were we interested in diving, snorkeling, sailing, or seeing dhows built, or ancient ruins and wouldn't we like a tour starting as soon as we arrived?

We wondered if we'd made a mistake leaving the peace and quiet of our friends' home in Mombasa, but as it turned out, he led us to a very clean, quiet, lovely place in town.

There are no cars or trucks on the island, and most of the population appears to be located in the town of Lamu proper on the waterfront, Lamu Bay.

The town consists of tall, rectangular, white-and-grey hand-hewn coral stone buildings with thick walls and cool courtyards, all interconnected by narrow, dark passageways that wind around in a maze of mystery. The square-topped silhouettes of roof verandas against the bright blue sky are broken only by the domes and towers of the many mosques.

Each house or building is three to five stories high, so that once you're down in the labyrinth it's difficult to find your way out until you learn the streets.

We rented a wonderful room in a private residence with five large apartments in a three-story complex and a central enclosed courtyard. White, cool, clean and neat, each apartment had a private shower and toilet facilities, and all for mere pennies compared to mainland prices. We unpacked, took a nap in the lazy heat of the day, listened to the call to prayer from the mosques (hauntingly beautiful), and eventually wandered out to discover we were only a block off the main thoroughfare.

The food in town was extraordinary and inexpensive: fresh-squeezed limeades, incredible banana-chocolate milkshakes, shish kebabs, fresh crab, lobster, shrimp and grilled fish with coconut rice.

We made pests of ourselves at our favorite restaurant, the Pole-Pole (polee-polee, Swahili for slowly, slowly), stopping frequently for limeades, information, or just to sit and watch the world go by. Blinding white sand and aquamarine, crystal-clear Indian ocean water dazzled and beckoned us to come toast our feet and other parts in their warmth. Unfortunately, we'd forgotten to transfer our sunscreen from the big bags in Nairobi to our backpacks, and in less than two hours, two poor white bodies that hadn't seen much sun in two years, got very, very crispied.

Standing under a cold shower took some of the sting out, but the shaded roof veranda of the house was home for the next two days. We languished in the breeze, read books, wrote postcards, dozed, and tried not to let anything touch our parched red papery-skin.

Poor Jim. In misery the first night of crispy, with no modern remedies available, we decided to try the old-fashioned aid of vinegar to take the sting out, then lotion to put the moisture back in. Silly us. We went down to the market and not speaking Arabic or sufficient Swahili, used sign language to point at our sunburned skin to purchase a bottle of vinegar.

Being a conscientious and considerate wife, I offered to put the newly purchased vinegar on Jim first. It poured out of the amber bottle a funny red color, but in the dim light of the shower room I thought maybe it was just wine vinegar.

Alas, alack, it was very dark red henna coloring dissolved in vinegar. (We later learned that local women use the stuff to dye their skin with temporary tattooed pretties for wedding ceremonies.)

I had his entire back and legs painted before it occurred to me that it wasn't going to come off. Jim was pretty philosophical about the whole thing and not the least bit piqued, until he discovered I had no intention of letting him put that stuff on me.

Husbands can be so unreasonable sometimes! I mean I got it all over my hands, didn't I?

By the third day we were able to walk in the sun again without pain and talked ourselves into a romantic donkey ride across the island to the dhow-building village of Matondoni. A German couple and we arrived at the departure point to clamber aboard four very-low-to-the-ground burros. To avoid dragging parts of the body, we had to bend at the knees and keep our feet pointed up and out at 45 degree angles.

The saddle consisted of a piece of burlap thrown across the donkey's back. Did I say back? In most mammals' anatomy what is recognized as a backbone, in Lamu donkeys has risen to new heights, and can only be described as a razor's edge of spine with two bony sloping sides.

This was immediately perceived by all as being extremely uncomfortable to sit upon, but we grunted and grinned our way through the first half-mile of it.

Jim's cantankerous old stud burro went out only about two hundred yards, then abruptly veered off course and headed for the hinterlands. Yanking and pulling on the reins was almost as effective as dragging his feet, and the King of the Razor Backs showed no sign of stopping. Noting my concern over the loss of my husband, the rear guide reined in and trotted after them. Catching the ol' codger by the nose, the guide drew him up short, (the burro, not Jim) and led them back into line.

Not one to be bested, the King took a few running steps, put on the brakes, and lowered his head whilst his hind end lifted off the ground.

To call this a bucking burro would be stretching things a bit, but Jim still found himself neatly sliding off over the long ears and fuzzy head, the reins trapped between his legs. I looked back just in time to see my gallant husband bent over double, the errant beast's head pushing firmly against his tush.

By the one-hour mark, four of us were beginning to regret the misadventure, wondering why we hadn't taken the leisurely dhow ride around the island to the village. By an hour and a half the other three were walking. Only our guides and I still rode, and I out of pure stubbornness and some foolish idea of getting my money's worth. Every step jarred that razorback into my tailbone and on up into my neck. My brain bravely sent 'this is dumb' signals to the rest of me, but would I listen?

The village finally listed into view and we were given a quick fifteen-minute tour of the dhow building area. One bottle of hot sticky-sweet soda later and it was back to our eager fleet-footed steeds for the return journey.

Pride forced us to remount until we were out of sight of the village. But once safe from laughing eyes, Jim and the other couple jumped off, intelligently trudging the two hours back through hot, soft sand. Not known for my intelligence, I discovered that sidesaddle was slightly less uncomfortable, and managed to stay on into the second hour. But eventually, even I had to admit defeat and abandon burro--but by then my tush was so sore I could hardly walk the last half hour home.

Still in agony that evening, we found it impossible to sit on anything less than two pillows. We had an official 'bum' inspection in the room to see if, or if not, we needed immediate hospitalization. Both of our tushies were rubbed raw in a two-inch square area with radiating bruises already beginning to show, and in the most uncomfortable spots. It took another two days of waddling and wincing to recover.

I can safely say any future opportunities involving these fuzzy little creatures will be herewith avoided; except from a distance, with a camera, and rolling our eyes at any naive touristy comments like, "Oh, isn't he cute!"

We waddled down for breakfast and met new friends--a neat couple from Minneapolis--and agreed to go on a snorkeling trip they were organizing. We accompanied them to make arrangements with the dhow captain, picked up two other couples in the process, with the Captain assuring us he'd find enough masks and snorkels for the journey.

* * *

As the eight of us climbed aboard early the next morning, Minnesota D. asked the Captain if he'd found the masks and snorkels? There was a long pause and the captain said,

"Yes? I found some."

"Some? Well, how many did you find?"

"Almost eight," our captain smiled.

"Almost eight? How many is that? Do you mean seven and a half?"

At this, the Captain roared with laughter. "Seven and a half, that is very funny." Then almost embarrassed, he said quietly, "I found six masks and four snorkels. But it is enough!"

"Four snorkels? How can that be enough for six masks and eight people?"

"Well, maybe we can share?"

And with that we were off. We sailed quickly out of the harbor, still trying to find a comfortable position for our bums, marveling at how one large square sail and a non-aerodynamic, rough wood-plank boat sealed only with shark oil--it gives off a very strong odor by the way-- could move so fast and smoothly through the water.

Anchoring over a coral reef, we took turns using the masks and snorkels, and Jim fell in love with it. Being a natural sinker, he's never been all that fond of swimming (Lake Michigan's not my idea of a perfect learning pool--but even in fish-training with an in-door heated pool, he and two other 'fishies' were natural sinkers. The only way they passed the swimming float-or-tread-water-for-one-hour test, was to grab big breaths and sink slowly to the bottom, pushing back up occasionally for air).

But in the extra salty Indian Ocean, he had buoyancy for the first time in his life and the mask and snorkel gave him the freedom to view the exquisite bright-colored fish and coral reefs below. He floated and paddled happily for a full two hours till we finally had to call him back to the boat for a shore lunch.

(And me? The sunburn from four days earlier went deeper than I thought as sun blisters suddenly came to the surface and burst at my first dive into the ocean. I couldn't exit quickly enough, but the crazy stinging itch once the blisters were open went on and on. Only repeated short dips back into the salt water helped cauterize and ease the pain over time.)

Once we were all gathered back in, our Captain sent his crew overboard, each with a spear and within minutes they had enough fish for all eight of us. He brought the boat to heel near a small tree-shaded island and we waded ashore while the crew built a fire and grilled the fish over an open flame with lemon, salt and hot peppers. But the best part was the rice cooked in fresh coconut milk from the overhead palms, and a fresh tomato curry sauce. We had 'almost eight' forks, so Jim used his Swiss Army knife to fashion chopsticks from some nearby twigs and we stuffed ourselves silly.

Then it was shelling on the beach, waiting for the tide to come back in and more snorkeling. We started back around five-thirty p.m. under a slight breeze and were still floating toward Lamu when the sun set and the lights went out.

The heavens are indescribable to someone who's never experienced them without the interference of ambient light from cities or modern civilization. And on the ocean, with no land or structure as reference point, the blue-black sky expands out and out and farther still--to a dome so vast it's beyond comprehension and fills all your senses with awe.

The millions and billions of stars you never knew were there shed enough light of their own to fill your heart and soul with a brightness and lightness of being.

It was so overwhelming the entire company grew quiet, content to just take it in. As I listened ever more intently, the sound of water gently lapping at the sides of the dhow gradually faded, to be replaced by a distant far-off music. Quieting to the space within, it seemed as if there was an ancient sweet chorus emanating from the heavens, gently surrounding and lifting until it felt as if I were floating in mid-air, a part of them, from them, and realized this truly, was the 'music of the spheres', a sacred moment of communion for a journey lasting into infinity.

Don't really remember docking or sending goodbyes and good wishes to our newfound friends, but Jim says we did.

* * *

Two days later, we took another dhow ride to explore the 14th (or 15th?) century ruins of a formerly prosperous Arab trading town said to have had a population of over 10,000 for two hundred years. Like many Arab settlements along the coast, it was abandoned suddenly and mysteriously, with speculation ranging from loss of water table to war to epidemics of disease.

Our Captain told us this as the dhow wound its way through a narrow channel into a mangrove swamp. To our surprise, he brought us in when the tide was out and we were forced to 'wade' the last quarter mile through brown water that Minnesota D. termed, 'the primordial slime'. His wife and I found something in common in that we both dislike walking barefoot in dark water with slimy oozing mud and other things sucking at our feet.

But this was forgotten when we saw our first ancient baobab trees. Twenty to thirty feet in circumference and forty to fifty feet high, they were like something from dreams and the imagination. Baobab trunks are enormous, but the fat beginnings of trunk, branches and limbs quickly disintegrate into spindly points of nothing twigs, with but a few stubby leaves.

Baobob Tree

One of its nicknames is 'the upside down tree', and they really do look as if they were planted upside down with the roots showing instead of the branches. Or like they were some magical, mystical thick-waisted dancer turning slowly and gracefully to the music of the earth, their limbs and leaves like hair knots or twists swaying to the heartbeat of our Mother, with bells and dangles spinning.

Locals tell us they can live to 3,000 years or more, and tribes have many legends and stories about the Baobab; about it being wise and ancient, that it can provide for all needs, that it is filled with power and connected to the dark and shadowy underworld, or that it is neither born nor dies (some truth to that is that the baby Baobab looks nothing like the mature adult, so they seem to just spring into being from one season to the next.

And though they are hard to kill (can strip the bark from them for multiple uses and they just grow it right back; burn it and it grows right back)--when they do actually die, they die from the inside out and one day just collapse into a mass of fibers. The legends and the baobabs left indelible footprints on our hearts, another image of Africa.

* * *

Alas, alack, our time up, paradise disappeared as the ferry churned away from the island and headed for the mainland. All too soon, we deposited ourselves into a large bus waiting at the end of the airport runway; where literally there was hardly room to exhale during the seven-hour return to Mombasa.

People filled up the seats double capacity, then stood in the aisles double capacity, then tried to climb on top of those standing and sitting, and finally just clung to the outside.

I don't know how those old bald tires held up. And to top it off, it rained on us nearly the entire way. Not to worry, you say, you're high and dry inside the bus? And it is after all, the dry season.

Nope, wrong. The roof was so leaky with holes that almost as much water arrived inside as stayed outside. One stream found its way down the jacket-sleeve of a soldier standing in the aisle clinging to the overhead rack. It dripped in a precise line off his elbow and onto my nose. Never did figure out why he was holding on to the rack. He was wedged in so tight around, that a crowbar wouldn't have pried him up, out, or over.

The driver began to step on the gas at each village or settlement to avoid the dozens of people running out to catch our already overfilled bus. Actually, I think we must have looked more like a rolling cartoon of humanity than a bus, with arms, legs and baggage sticking out akimbo, the various pieces of metal and rubber stuck on only for good looks.

We crossed several rivers with some very homemade-looking bridges; narrow, rickety, and our side always seemed to drop off and leave parts of us hanging out over twenty to thirty foot of empty air. Jim noted my big eyes once when it was dropping off, and said, "Not to worry honey, if we go over, we'll sink so quick, you won't notice a thing."

One river had no bridge at all and much to our relief, rather than try to swim it, we were ordered to disembark. The elderly ferry awaiting us was deemed not safe enough to allow bus and passengers on at the same time, so the bus crossed first. It moved quickly out into midstream while Jim and I stood on the bank puzzling why most of the passengers had plopped down as if to stay for a while. Many ordered brochettes (which even for the fastest chef in the east, takes ten to twenty minutes to cook from fly-covered raw to extra-crispy brown). Many more wandered down the road and off into the bush for some 'private moments' with nature.

We held our ground as the ferry chugged back in a few short minutes, ringing the call bell for passengers. A rush of humanity bowled us over and carried us along in a panic to board the ferry. Those who had ordered brochettes stamped their feet, trying to hurry the cook, then abandoned the food hastily in lieu of the only transportation in sight for the last fifty kilometers.

To our surprise, the bus driver gave the ferry driver the go ahead and we pulled out into the river, only half a compliment strong. People came running back from all directions of the bush, yelling for us to wait, that they had paid their money already.

The bus driver just laughed when we reached the other shore and told us to load up, saying, "Hakuna matata". No problem. Not to worry. There will be another bus along sometime for those left on the other bank, and there will be more room now for those of you who made it!" Interesting.

* * *

--One of the most amazing sites on the return to Mombasa was the miles and miles of cashew and sisal farms. They extended out to the horizon on both sides of the road and seemed prolific enough to provide the entire world with nuts and fiber.

--Back in Mombasa with our friends, we took a few extra days to explore Old Town with its curio and souvenir shops and ancient 15th century Arab architecture. We had hoped to tour the massive stonework of Fort Jesus up-close, as our hosts told us there are ghosts which one can see and hear down in the shadowy inner walls and passages. But the tour coincided with the birthday of one of their daughter's and we opted to help her celebrate at Mamba Village in Nyali.

Nyali is East Africa's largest crocodile farm (8,000-10,000 crocodiles) and also an amusement park, with rides, food, and a movie on the life cycle, behavior, importance of conservation and environmental impact of the crocodile in the East African ecosystem. A birthday party with cake and candles ended a fun tour at an on-site restaurant that offers only the finest in crocodile steaks. Mmmm, tastes just like chicken!

Imagine tanks and ponds and streams of really huge, burly, toothy crocodiles. Loads and bunches of them in all different sizes; swimming, snarling and chomping on dead stuff in the middle of a beautifully landscaped tourist park. An odd paradox.

At the end of the crocodile runs there were--Camel rides! Now, just for your information, a camel's back, while not wholly comfortable, is an immense improvement over a Lamu burro's, and a lot higher off the ground, so your legs don't suffer from the bends.

It was there that I fell in love with camels. What wonderful, ridiculous, amazing creatures. Beautiful, big, liquid-brown eyes. Thick black eyelashes three inches long (without the aid of mascara). Funny lobbed ears and a quivering upper lip that overhangs the lower in imitation of a parrot. A long lumpy neck, knock knees, roly-poly fat belly, and best of all, magical legs that fold up or down on themselves in a most wonderful spectacular scissor-jack contortionist's trick when they sit down or stand up! One of them kept giving me long slurpy kisses with a rough tongue, and I could have spent a week watching and sketching and scratching behind his ears. I climbed aboard with one of the girls as we were led around a very tame corral, but it was great fun and we felt like real tourists at last.

A final few good days and all too soon we were winging back to Nairobi, then Bujumbura and our workaday world. We brought back some Swahili to our work here.

Words like:

pole-pole (po-lee po-lee) means: slowly slowly

hakuna matata (hah-koo-nah mah-tah-tah) means: no problem, the universal response to any and all situations

shuwari (shoo-wahr-ee) means: peacefully

tasubiri (tah-soo-beer-ee) means: I will be patient

Rested, and ready to get back to work, we hope all is well with you,

with love and lotsa hugs,

Jim and Anita

Chapter 65
SCRABBLE, Parties and Nevermores
October

Dear Folks,

Can't remember whether we told you, we have a Technicolor house again with ten very distinct colors (eleven, if you count the chartreuse curtains grinning out the windows). Some workers appeared out of a parallel universe the other day and began painting each of the stones a different color, connecting them all by painting the mortar a bright green, though not the same color as the curtains. It's almost enough to glow in the dark and read by, but unfortunately, it's mostly on the outside and we usually read inside.

* * *

We had just got back into the rhythm of work after our vacation, when company showed up by the droves. Mona's folks (Methodist minister and his wife from Oklahoma) were here and soundly, roundly and thoroughly beat us at SCRABBLE (they are serious players, averaging two games a night at home and thrive on three and four-letter words and timed responses--one minute each). We almost held our own in the card games.

They visited our ponds and her Dad was GREAT. He'd brought a pocketful of balloons and began pulling them out a few at a time, blowing them up and tying them off for the kids. He was an instant success and was mobbed by a hundred reaching arms at each pond site! Our farmers were so impressed with our friendly elders and wanted to know if these folks weren't our parents, when were ours coming to see them?

* * *

--Mona and parents had just pulled out when an Italian volunteer arrived to talk about a new fish culture program they are initiating, and five minutes after him, Mary (another fishie) and her parents and brother (from D.C. and California) pulled in (having rented a car) and we had another full house and a good time playing Euchre and Liverpool Rummy. They left the next morning and we had just settled into some peace and quiet when up walks Dann (fish-station volunteer) and friend Betsey (one of our fellow-trainees in fish training–now on vacation from P.C. in Gabon).

We had just settled in to welcomes and sharing war stories, when in pops Sarah, the fishie from the western-most province, fresh off the bus and ready to party. We stayed up half the night playing Trivial Pursuit and sharing stories with a case of liter-sized beer, having fun...again.

Got them all off on the bus Sunday a.m. and had almost an hour of quiet time, when who drives up but our British friends from the tea factory with one of our favorite former-volunteers, Peter, who heads the chimpanzee project. We had another full day of hearty partying, but we were really glad Monday rolled around so we could go back to work and get some rest.

* * *

We had only put in three straight days of work when we were officially ordered down to Buja, Thursday through Sunday to celebrate my birthday with the whole American community. (Just happened to coincide with the 25th Anniversary party of Peace Corps and the Halloween party at the American Club, but we pretended it was all for me. And since it has rained almost all day, every day, we're not really missing a great deal of work.

* * *

The other volunteers treated us with fried Ndagala (baby fish, like smelt, fried whole) at the Greek restaurant. Afterward, the waiter made a big presentation of half a box of used birthday candles, with his best wishes. Turns out he'd misunderstood the instructions and thought that once he'd installed and lit the first half on the cream puff desserts, I was to get the leftovers as a present.

You could see he thought we were all insane, but he was trying to accommodate the fou's (or more correctly the folle, but whether Franglais or Francais it still means 'crazies') as the cream puffs burned brightly away and everyone sang Happy Birthday. The Greek proprietor found somewhere an old English love song of Happy Birthday and played it on his accordion to cap off a great celebration. (He likes Americans--The only one who does these days, it seems).

* * *

Giving thanks to our Greek host, our troupe moved on through the rain to the ex-pats Halloween party with roast pig and costumes. One of the embassy guys came as a 'flasher' and there were several skeletons, belly dancers, Bedouins and cowboys, a Hagar the Horrible, and Angels. The usual mix.

Mona, our boss, joined in as a 'punk rocker', but made the mistake of putting food coloring on her beautiful blonde hair--took the entire weekend and ten shampoos to get rid of it--Ouch.

We arrived disguised as wild and rowdy P.C. volunteers and hardly anyone recognized us.

* * *

Everyone overdosed on movies at the American club Saturday, played tennis (sort of) at the U.S. Embassy on Sunday (great clay court), and best of all, the slow-boat came in with the packages we've all been waiting for the past year. Spent hours oohing, aahing, lusting over and sharing each other's care-packages, like an early Christmas. The best was our red licorice--what do you suppose they put in it that keeps it fresh, soft, tasty and rubbery for a whole year?

* * *

--We're finally back to working, slipping, sliding and falling down full-time this week and in celebration, seined our first two production ponds of over 3000 fingerlings to re-distribute to our twelve finished and waiting ponds--which means the initial seining and frog traps worked-- so take that, Xenopus! It was so exciting! Our farmers have been on a high ever since, their first money from fish, and we hear the entire country is abuzz with the success. Yipppeee!

* * *

But all those visitors, then the four days partying in Buja, then a full week of soggy-bog work, is why we've fallen down in our writing duties. But no more–or is it nevermore? Or do you have to see ravens to say that? At any rate, we're both back in the saddle with callouses on our bums, and we hereby and faithfully promise to issue at least one sheet of propaganda per week.

Love and lotsa hugs,
Your wild and wooly kids
(Formerly dull-boring-dodders)

Chapter 66
Questions and Questionnaires--November

Dear Bill and Theola,

Vacation relaxed us so much, we thought we'd have difficulty revving up the motors of enthusiasm to go out for work again, but after visiting our ponds and farmers, we're on a real high. We've discovered that leaving our fish alone was the key, as they reproduced phenomenally in our absence. (Just kidding. Actually, seining out the frogs, trapping them in hand-woven grass traps, and having 5 degree warmer water temps during the dry season had a lot to do with it, as it has both inhibited frog reproduction and encouraged fish reproduction.) We now have fingerlings everywhere!

In our absence, farmers followed parting instructions almost to the letter, and we have sixteen near-perfect ponds filled, all with good compost blooms and ready to receive fingerlings! And they will be our own farmer-raised fingerlings from our own local farmers! We are so proud of all of them, we are like first time parents, bragging on them to any who will listen.

* * *

--In the continuing saga of Sylveste: We had promised to pay him full wages while we were gone so he would know we valued his services, and left instructions to clean the pantry, (empty, clean, re-stock the shelves) and make sure he kept the kerosene frigo (refrigerator) running (as it is so cantankerous to re-start that it sometimes takes two or three days to fully re-charge).

We arrived back home with $55 worth of meat and cheese from Buja to last us four to six weeks, only to find that he'd emptied the frigo, shut it off and left the pantry dirty.

Needless to say, all of the things we'd left in the frigo—our $11 bottle of mustard, the $9 bottle of mayonnaise, sausage and hamburger in the freezer, etc., were all ruined and smelling quite strong, as he'd pulled them out of the frigo and put them on the pantry shelf. Plus the frigo was hot and not ready to receive all the perishables we'd brought up. As much as we've grown to love him, we may be looking for a new cook soon.

* * *

--In the continuing up and down ride through life on the equator, some of our analogs (Burundian counterparts) were so impressed with our work that they spread the word, and it reached all the way to Buja. Monsieur le President is visiting Jim's ponds today and mine on Thursday.

Yipppee, we think? The anti-white rhetoric is still escalating nation-wide, we are just not sure that we're included, or if we are considered harmless hybrid-whites, like I'm a new form of hybrid woman, and if that is acceptable. It is very confusing.

--A week later. I'm writing this by lantern light because we have no electricity-- again. The village generator burned out a few days after we left on vacation. Waiting on the parts from Europe means we probably won't have power again for three to five months unless the new hydroelectric dam comes on line before then. (Not holding our breath. Last word was they didn't have enough cured utility poles to string the wire with.)

* * *

--Days later. We are writing letters this afternoon because we have already been soaked and nearly drowned four times this week and decided doing it again today was above and beyond the call of duty. Also, writing letters in the daylight for a change (gloomy and dark though it is) is preferable to going blind by candlelight or kerosene lantern at night.

--Speaking of kerosene, I hardly remember what to call it these days. In French, it's called 'petrol', but that is also English (British) for gasoline. 'Gas' in French means propane, and kerosene in British is 'paraffin', which is wax in American.
So some nights, we put the petrol-paraffin-kerosene in the lamps and go blind. Others, we just sit in the dark and listen to the rain on our leaky tin roof. Sometimes we just practice breathing.

All in all, it is a grand life here! We are back in the saddle again putting new callouses on our bums (not side saddle and our mounts don't eat grass, have fuzzy heads or razor backs, so once again, we are grateful).

* * *

Hurray! Just to repeat myself, we seined our two production ponds this week and netted around three thousand fingerlings to stock twelve ponds! If all goes well, we'll need ten thousand more fingerlings by the end of December to stock the additional forty ponds nearing completion. That translates into almost five thousand pounds of fish by June or July, and will make all the blood-sweat-and-tears (alias slipping-sliding-and-falling-tush-over-teakettle-while-cussing-a-blue-streak) worthwhile.

* * *

--A week later. It has rained every day and half the nights since we've been back. Can squeeze in only four or five hours of actual pond-work per day before we head for home and dry clothes (our poor farmers are always drenched).

Then, it's work in the garden, play with the bunnies, read, write letters, design future dream homes or new frog traps, and wish we were home for Christmas.

--All those unexplained statements and questions from your last letter are driving us crazy with curiosity. Please expound in the next one?

In the meantime, what with no electricity and a good supply of candles, we have lots of opportunities to 'light a candle and say a prayer' every evening. You are always included.

Hope all is well with you and yours. Jim says we have to go to sleep now. Goodbye, with Love and a hug,

Us (sometimes wishing we were 'they' back there)

(other times, glad we are us, here)

(Old-speak for, we're doing okay, mostly)

* * *

P.S.

We were invited to visit the home of the U.S. Embassy Cultural Attaché two weekends ago. He had a clay model he wanted advice and help with, on how to make a mold on it, and we were invited to stay for dinner. We had fresh oysters on the half-shell that had been flown in fresh from Belgium that day, Caesar salad and the biggest fresh shrimp I have ever seen, chargrilled with a horse-radish and butter sauce. This culinary feast was followed by Black Forest cake and fresh vanilla ice cream. The Attachés partner is a former P.C. volunteer and said she's making up for all the things she missed during her service. The food was truly amazing.

Unfortunately, colds and flu have been going around (seem to pick up something every time we descend to Buja) and half way through the meal I became ill and chucked the whole thing. Couldn't eat any more after that (followed the P.C. first aid book, *Where There Is No Doctor*'s advice: "When you are throwing up, don't eat.") and went home in misery. What a waste--for me, anyway. Jim ate till he was overstuffed completely--first time he's enjoyed raw oysters--so was glad for him. Had to send a note of apology to our hosts as they'd gone to great trouble and expense to bring the food in. Will have to make sure I do a good mold on his clay model next week.

Love and a hug, jimani

Chapter 67
Jambo! (Swahili for Hello!)
Friday Nov. 7th, 2nd year

Dear Sis,

"Jambo! (Or Hi, How's tricks?--in Swahili). It is still raining and
still we have no electricity. In celebration of life and family however,
we just opened your generous contribution to our health and wellbeing
of a wonderful-delicious-terrific-once-in-a-lifetime-tin-of-smoked-
oysters!

Yes, your package finally arrived 14 months after it was sent and
we have thus far splashed Jean Naté® into our underwear compartment,
flossed our teeth with super-duper-special dental floss, enjoyed an entire
gallon of Gator Aid, worshiped adoringly (though not opened or eaten)
the almonds, Lifesavers®, Tang® or Kool-Aid®.

We also consumed at first sight and shared the red licorice (still soft
and tasty), magazines and letter (year-old information is still fresh and
new to us!), and bowed three times in your direction for Jim's tobacco.
What a terrific care package!

Most everything has been tasty and none the worse for wear for its
yearlong journey across Africa. Thank you again, for thinking of us.

* * *

--And now for the good work news. You won't believe what
happened in our absence on vacation. Word has finally spread that our
project is for the people, that it works, that there really are fish, that they
are growing and reproducing, and that some lucky souls are going to be
eating farmer-raised fish in six to eight months.

Interest exploded while we were gone and rained fish farmers
everywhere. Jim and I have daily requests by the dozens to please come
and look at new sites and give advice on construction practices. And our
first three reproduction ponds should produce an additional six thousand

fingerlings by Christmas! We'll still need four thousand more from the fish station, but Hooray! It's working!

We now have fifty new ponds under construction, and farmers are actually following our instructions and doing things right. We celebrate each small success with them and let them know they're doing good. It's great to finally be able to communicate, even though it's still very rudimentary and with baby-bantu!

Can hardly wait for the fish book to come out in French and Kirundi. All of the details and finer points we've been trying to get across will be in there, in proper language and with illustrations (thanks to our translators).

They'll have a ready reference when we're not available, or no longer here. It is so exciting these days! We can actually see light bulbs coming on in people's eyes, as they comprehend that this is their program, their fish, and their future.

Sometimes we jump up and down and fall on the ground laughing for the sheer joy of it.

Better close now and get this in the mail. Wish we could send about half of this rain to poor, dry Ethiopia, then we'd all be happy.

* * *

--Days later--We were inundated with company last week. It felt like half of Peace Corps and the British, American, and German communities dropped by with visiting relatives, friends, and parents. We stayed up nights playing Euchre, SCRABBLE, Liverpool Rummy, and Trivial Pursuit, accompanied by lots of food made on The Wretched Things, cases of beer and fish stories.

All those visitors are why we've fallen down in our writing duties. Mea Culpa and we promise to write down a bit every day so we can send words at more regular intervals.

Sending you lotsa hugs, love, and prayers,

Jimani

Chapter 68
Hot Cider

Dear Folks,

It. Is. Cold. Rainy. And. Dreary. Again. Makes the instant hot cider Aunt JoAnn sent us that much more appreciated, and Uncle Barney's cartoon of a Polish snowmobile now hangs in our living room in a place of honor.

Polish Snowmobile

* * *

We just received another batch of brood fish (335) from the fish station to become breeders for reproduction. Each of our nine communes (counties) will now have their own source of fingerlings, with at least one breeding pond in each commune. The first harvest for eating is scheduled six to eight months from now, depending on water temperature and growth.

All total, we've fourteen ponds stocked with fish slated for eating and another ten with breeders for reproduction of fingerlings, with many more under construction. Will wonders never cease?

The farmers have taken to monitoring each other's efforts in a race to produce the biggest, best fish ever. And no matter where I've scheduled a work day, farmers from other ponds arrive to make sure I haven't added any new information; that I'm imparting the exact same advice to the new guys as I did to them--and to lend their own support and experience, as they've found a camaraderie and pride in being fish-farmers.

* * *

--On a sadder note, we've had to put Sylveste on probation. He has two weeks to improve his performance or be let go. Things simply aren't getting done. His memory gets shorter as our workdays get longer. We're wondering if he isn't suffering from some kind of brain dysfunction, dementia or depression (or threats from others because of his good job).

We make sure he gets enough to eat and we also send food home, so it's not low blood sugar or starvation. He is not drinking. Not sure what it is, unless it's another form of work stoppage. He is so very sweet, I would hate to let him go, but we may have no choice. We keep having to re-do his assigned chores ourselves, and frankly, we are just too tired.

Not much news other than hard work, muddy clothes, and farmers running amok, going crazy-happy with enthusiasm, but wanted you to hear from us.

Love and a big hug,

Hey you and What's-her-face

P.S.

"Hey, look! Over there! Umuzungus!" a man close to us shouted. Two hundred heads, including ours, swiveled to look for the 'new guys' in the market square. Sure enough, there were two white strangers looking at baskets and bananas.

The neat part was that we automatically knew they weren't talking about us. Even though we are still two pale-faces in a sea of black wherever we go, we are Jim and Anita now, part of community and not umuzungus.

Skin color no longer differentiates us from the villagers, and we sometimes forget that ours is not black, because we are just like everyone around us. Just people. Fitting in, working, feeling at home and being a part of community. We can't pin down a day or week when it happened. Just one day we were friends and neighbors, not foreigners. At least for Jimani, umuzungu now only denotes a stranger in town, not us as 'white man'.

Man, what a good feeling!

Love and a hug,

jimani

Chapter 69
Banana Beer Bacchanals
December, Second year

Dear Mom and Dad,

I recently asked for and received permission from all the appropriate government entities to have the Peace Corps fish-project truck come up once a month from Buja to expand our farmer exchange program. You remember, the one where we haul farmers around on the back of our motos from one commune to see the ponds and farmers from another.

The farmer-to-farmer exchange has been a terrific teaching aid for them and us, because they share and exchange ideas, problems and they have come up with some great innovations on their own, and in their own language, so they don't have to depend on our poor offerings.

Our work is so much easier when we don't have to repeat the same thing a thousand times to each new farmer. But a truckload at a time will be even better and safer for all concerned.

--Well, on our first big exchange with the truck, we took fourteen of 'my guys' to see 'Jim's guys'. After a good tour of their ponds and some excellent exchange, we signaled it was time to leave.

Jim's guys surprised us by inviting everyone up to a house on top of the hill for a 'little something'. Once there, we all crowded into and around the tiny mud brick house to sit on wooden stools and benches they had borrowed from all over the neighborhood.

Then they brought in a huge clay pot full of banana beer (five gallons) for us to drink. Even for twenty to thirty people, five gallons is a lot, so we drank and passed the dipper, talked and drank and laughed and drank some more.

With camaraderie at a high, the speeches started. Half a dozen guys from each group took their turns thanking each other, us, and our P.C. driver, Girard. (They even provided Girard with sodas since he was driving and couldn't drink.)

Done and almost done-in by the banana beer, we at last climbed back in the truck to go home, waving and hugging. My farmers even had a few tears of good-bye for their newfound colleagues.

If it sounds like I'm making a big deal out of it, it's because I am. Most of them have never been outside their own community. Maybe once a year they see relatives or friends who live more than ten kilometers away.

And most would not consider themselves important enough to be invited to a program, picked up in a truck and driven to the site, have an excellent exchange of relevant information and honored with a party. And they get to keep the fish!

No program for 'townies', no sir. This was for farmers, and the realization was beginning to sink in. They were important enough to have this offered to them. Somebody cared!

What a trip home! All the way, my guys sang at the top of their lungs about how they were the farmers of the cows-and-the-goats-and-the-chickens-but-most-especially-of-the-fish! Then they made up songs on how they had the best ponds, the best fish, the biggest fish, the fastest fish, the smartest and the prettiest fish, the most baby fish in the commune-no-the-province-no-the-world!

We had the rear pickup window open and Girard translated for us while he drove. He and Jimani (Jim and I) laughed and clapped the hour and a half trip back to their community. It was simply great!

* * *

To get back to our story--P.C. staff paid a visit on our second scheduled exchange, as they had heard the stories from Girard and were curious. We had a great day walking to see this pond and that, talking with farmers, and then, with three ponds still left to visit, we were invited for banana beer.

Encore, too much to drink, speeches, friends, talk. We finally finished most of the first pot of beer and rose to leave. But a second group of farmers had been patiently waiting in the eaves, and they herded us further up the hill, where they had laid out mats and benches outside and an even bigger pot of beer (gallons and gallons)! We were halfway through the speeches and everyone was doing quite well, considering, when it started to rain cats and dogs. We quick ran and crammed into the three nearest mud brick homes with tin roofs and sat down to finish off the beer and speeches.

They came up with some good ideas and great suggestions for the program. Our P.C. boss told them she was impressed and delighted to meet such a fine group of progressive farmers. She told them that they had the best fish program she had ever seen, and that they were way in advance of anyone else. (Jim and I groaned inwardly as we saw chests swell even further in pride and our farmer's eyes shine like diamonds with the praise, knowing it would translate into even more work and enthusiasm.)

And sure enough, they've been working like run-away-freight-trains since, and Jim and I are working ourselves to a frazzle. We have over sixty new ponds in construction now, and twenty-six more finished and stocked.

This is too much for just two people to keep up with even though our farmers are terrific. They work so hard to follow directions, and listen so well that our actual supervising time now is minimal, but we've called a halt to new construction and absolutely must get more volunteers to help.

We spend most of our time just checking up on their work to make sure it meets the stiff criteria we've established (solid, non-leaking dikes which have been tamped hard and have three-to-one slopes with a gradual sloping bottom from three to three and a half feet in depth, healthy compost pits, fresh-water filters against invaders, good plankton blooms, good water temperature, etc.)

An unfortunate by-product of all this activity is that we can't spend the time with individual farmers, as we did at first. This is sad because each farmer has his own special gift and energy to give to the program, and there are weeks we wish for the good old days of just last year when we could afford to spend an entire day or week at one pond site.

We miss the camaraderie of getting to know farmers and their families, especially the kids. At the risk of repeating myself, we wish there were more of us.

* * *

Even more good news! Our Governor called us in the other day to inform us that the farmer exchange program has proven so successful that he is incorporating the practice into most of the provincial functions: transporting teachers, record keepers, bureaucrats (office workers) and health technicians.

It apparently is bridging the problem of a slowly-improving, but as-yet-inadequate communications network and giving people insight and support into each of their individual programs, as well as a view of the overall system, with innovations and improvements already creating Provincial unity and positive results.

At least, we think that's what he said. (Our boss confirmed this yesterday, as news of it reached Buja.) Terrific, yes?

Well, best go now.

Take care, with love and two-dozen hugs. Too tired to get into trouble,

Hewe and Aahh-nniii-tah

Chapter 70
The Great Turkey Caper

Dear Folks,

...Once upon a time, long ago and far away in August in Ngozi, Burundi, East Africa, Jim and I stumbled upon a grand white turkey in a Belgian ex-pat's yard (the same one we taught to make gooey-chocolate-fudge--the Belgian, not the turkey). Liberating it from his feathers, (the turkey, not the Belgian and for a price, of course) we shipped it out to the German doctor and his clinic's freezer to await transport at the proper time. The proper time came and the denuded bird was ferried down to Peace Corps for cold storage till the Turkey Day Weekend (T.D.W.) party.

T.D.W. arrived, but the guardian of our turkey (our new P.C. Director, R.) had an unexpected opportunity to see the mountain gorillas in Rwanda and left town.

Fortunately, she also left her back door key with her second-in-command, our boss, Mona, to rescue our bird from the Director's pantry freezer for the party.

Jimani descended early Friday on a kamikazi bus with everything but the kitchen sink tied to our backs to help prepare for the T.D.W. dinner. We arrived safely in Buja (always something to be grateful for) and had the residual grocery shopping done by noon.

I started to work on the cakes, pies, stuffing, etc. (in a REAL OVEN, with electricity and all!), while Mona cornered Jim to work on photocopy material for our upcoming fish seminar, scheduled on the Monday after Turkey Day Weekend. They were late getting home (7:30 p.m.), due to Murphy's Law and complications with both the copier and the seminar material.

Mona is tall, slim, athletic and light on her feet, but some of the other players are not, and she had incurred a broken rib making the winning touchdown catch Thursday afternoon in the American community football game, so she was moving slowly and slower as Friday wore on.

I hopped, and she crawled into the truck and we headed for R.'s house to retrieve the dindon (dan-don, sounds almost like dingdong which is turkey in French, and appropriate, huh?).

I ran up the back steps, put the key in the outer security door and opened it, then was faced with an inner wooden door and a dead-bolt lock, and, guess what, the key didn't fit!

Several repeated attempts later, I said to myself, "Now self, this is really something when a mature, intelligent, capable woman can't open a silly door." But try as I might, it didn't work.

Back down the stairs I went to explain to Mona why the turkey wasn't defrosting under my left arm.

"Second door? What second door?"

Up the stairs to inspect again and sure enough, I wasn't so silly after all--the key just didn't fit. Then we tried the other doors, all seven of them, and the key didn't work in them, either.

Back at Mona's, Jim came to the rescue and decided we were all tired and hungry and needed sustenance. At the American Club, we found the person-responsible-for-keys-to-American-houses, but alas, alack, there were no spares.

We remorsefully toasted to our lost frozen bird with a first beer: the big-size, quart kind, thinking at least the stuffing would taste good. Then Mona wondered if some of the club employees might know R.'s cook, who had locked us out in the first place, and might he have a spare? Great idea!

There followed a twenty-minute discussion-translation in French-Kirundi about what we needed (the key), from whom (Deo, the cook), for R.'s house to retrieve our Turkey-Day-Weekend dindon. Two guys were off in a flash in the PC truck to the rescue, and we settled back to enjoy the evening with friends.

Soon, everyone had heard the story and was buying us poor turkey-deprived volunteers beers, hamburgers and fries in commiseration. An hour later, the truck, the two guys, and the key showed up and we invited them to celebrate with us in thanks, with you guessed it, another beer.

Feeling pretty giddy, we gathered up our large and handy voc-ed-teacher-volunteer, Todd, to take along (in case he had to huff and puff and blow the house down) and the four of us arrived at R.'s ready to at last retrieve our turkey. Visions of giblet gravy, roasted wings and stuffing floated through our heads as we mounted the back steps.

Let's see, put the first key in, open the outer door, then put the second key up to the second door, and--it doesn't FIT! Curses and drat! What was going on? In a panic, we tried the other seven doors and the new key didn't fit any of them, either, again.

We looked at Mona. Mona looked at us. We knew there was only one alternative. Break in.

--Once we'd decided, the fun began. First we had to explain to the night guards why we were breaking in. My wonderful command of Kirundi on top of a few beers had them shaking their heads and backing off quickly to wash their hands of the whole thing.

Whatever it was, they definitely wanted no part of it and they melted away into the shadows. "Crazy umuzungus! I see nothing. I hear nothing."

The second door (the unfriendly one that wouldn't accept our key) had a small high transom window. Jim wrapped his hand in a towel, found a brick, and promptly smashed the glass with all the quietness, stealth and ceremony of a bull in a china closet. (All the more convenient windows had bars on them.)

After so many beers, the hilarity of the situation began to tickle us as we imagined tomorrow's headlines:

P.C. Volunteers and Staff in Jail for Breaking and Entering to Purloin Dindon!

Well, as I said, Mona had a broken rib and Todd and Jim were too big, so that left me to climb through to rescue our poor bird. The transom was way up above my head so Jim and Todd began boosting me up and through. Half way through the transom they got to laughing about how I was going in head first and how funny it was going to be when I fell through on my noggin'. They quit boosting and I was stuck half in and half out of a tight squeeze with no foothold or room to maneuver. I squirmed and gasped till they decided to help double me up crooked and stuff one of my feet through the window. The rest of me followed and I tumbled inside to bare floors and broken glass.

I fumbled around in the dark, crunching glass for a few minutes trying to find the pantry and freezer, when this sweet melodious voice from you-know-who came floating over the transom, "Aahhnneeeee-tah, why don't you turn on the liigghhts?"

This set Todd and Jim off howling again. We haven't had electricity in so long I'd forgotten there was such a thing.

Found the light switch, found a key to the freezer, found the turkey, found a broom to sweep up the glass, and found a pen and paper for

Mona to write an apology and explanation to R. for the purloined turkey and the broken house.

The one thing I didn't find was a key to the second door.

I did find a short stool to stand on, passed the frozen bird up and over and out to the guys, posted the note of apology signed by 'The Four Dindons', then boosted myself up to the open transom.

Almost missed turning off the lights, but reached out with a foot at the last second and plunged the house into darkness once more. Jim and Todd were waiting expectantly, but at my half-way point, they once again got into a discussion, this time over who was going to catch me and how.

I laughed so hard I lost my breath and couldn't move, in or out, so they grabbed me by the arms and pulled me down like a sack of potatoes. Not being lighter than air, I fell pretty heavily and we all ended up in a heap by the turkey.

As we locked the outer door, the guards were nowhere to be seen, so we grabbed our prize twenty-four pound dindon and piled into the Landrover.

On the return to Mona's, we mused about the key that didn't fit; the key that had been wrested from some poor hapless guy, some poor fellow who was going to have to explain to his employer why he'd given a stranger the key to his boss' house.

Suddenly, Mona made the connection:

"Oh, Nooooooo! I know who's key that is. It's my house key! They found my cook, who's Deo's brother, and brought back the key to my house!" That set us all off again, and sure enough when we got there, the key fit perfectly into her back door lock!

* * *

Never knew breaking and entering could be so much fun! Made the turkey taste all that much better. We may have missed our true calling as second story purloiners.

And The Great Turkey Caper has gone down in the annals of our P.C. Burundi history as an all-time high.

--After not sleeping a wink on Mary's soft cement floor once more, Sunday found us all sated, satisfied, and packing off to the small village of Kayanza to give our fish seminar on Monday and Tuesday to the country's extension agents (agronomes).

Unlike the first attempt, it was a great conference with lots of participation, and at the very last minute, the P.C. chauffeur, Girard, roared up with the new fish booklets hot off the press for distribution.

* * *

We were back to work on Wednesday and had a whirlwind week of 12-hour days through Saturday. WHEW! The only problem with leaving for even a few days is that playing catch-up is hard on the body. But it's Sunday again today, it's raining, and we have had no visitors, so we're recovering.

Do hope all is well and we will call you for Christmas. Miss you both bunches.

Love and lotsa hugs,
Hewe and aahh-nneeeee-tah
(alias the Daring Dindon Duo)

Chapter 71
Shoes for Danny

Dear Mom and Dad,

    I have to tell this story to someone, because it won't leave me alone:

    Danny is a small, clubfooted, semi-retarded young man without known family, work, or place of his own. (We are still not sure where he sleeps.)

    He tries to do odd jobs to get money for food, and shows up here daily with an armful of iconda for our bunnies (ee-chawn-dah is a wild herb that just happens to be a high-protein legume the rabbits love).

    We pay him a small amount for his work and he's taken to doing it for others in the area. He wears an old pair of red plastic sunglasses with the reaches fashioned out of bits and pieces of wire. I tried them on once, and they are so scratched, I couldn't see through them.

    He uses a set of clothing we, or others have given him till they drop off in tatters and are replaced--not sure they ever get washed. A pair of tennis shoes four sizes too big for him that are more holes than shoes, cover his clubbed feet. He has indicated that he wanted a new pair, but shoes are expensive, especially for someone like him with no regular income.

    When he came by yesterday (Saturday) afternoon, I told him to meet me at the market place today (Sunday), and we looked at several vendor's shoe offerings until we found a reasonably priced pair that fit.

    A large crowd gathered to see what kind of deal would be struck and approved when I drove a reasonable white-guy deal (not as good as a local, but respectable).

    Danny's old shoes were tied on to his feet with wire and string, and I had to cut them away. Everyone had friendly advice as to which of the many knots or wires should be cut first and there was much discussion and hand waving.

Finally, his old shoes came off. He sat in the dirt and the new tennis shoes were donned, laced, tied, and adjusted. I shouted for the crowd to move back and Danny shuffled out twenty feet or so to try them out.

We all applauded while he made the sign of the cross awkwardly several times in thanks.

I don't know why this kid's story should affect me so much when there are sad stories (and harder ones) just like it all around us, and most kids here don't even have shoes. But it does.

Guess sometimes, in the midst of becoming hardened to overwhelming needs, needs which we can't even begin to meet as just two people, something reaches out and reminds me what we're here for and makes me wish there were more of us.

Thanks for listening.

Love,

Jim

P.S.

Just a note to add to Jim's letter on the subject of shoes. At a pond site recently, one of his farmers (Simeon) asked, "Monsieur Jim, is everyone in America rich?"

Jim said he thought a minute then tried to give him a supportive, philosophical answer.

"Well, Simeon, being rich is really a state of mind. It's all in how you look at things. You are rich in that you have beautiful children and a loving family..."

Simeon waited patiently until Jim had finished. "Yes, Monsieur Jim. I understand all that. But does everyone in America have shoes?"

Jim responded, "Well, yes, most everyone has shoes, but–"

Simeon broke in, "Then everyone in America is rich."

Gives one cause to stop and ponder, yes? And give thanks.

Love and a hug, Me

Chapter 72
Soggy Rubbers

Dear Mom and Dad, alias parents,

It has been a too-busy month, what with a three-day fish seminar, three days of transporting fish, no, make that four days now, and a refresher course in French scheduled for next week over Christmas. It hasn't helped that we've also come down with the flu--again.

* * *

Transporting Fish:

We constructed saddlebags by sewing two CRS (Catholic Relief Services) plastic burlap flour sacks together with top holes to receive two five-gallon jerry-cans, one on either side and fitted them over the moto seats. With fresh, clean water in the cans, seines loaded, dip nets, holding buckets, backpacks, and a tire pump tied on (to aerate the water for the fish), we looked like gypsy vagabonds pulling out of our driveway.

Jim and I seined a holding pond three days in a row to divide and transfer 320 newly delivered, delicate brood fish to five other completed ponds. And every single day it rained buckets and waterfalls on us. We'd wade into the pond to seine, transfer the appropriate number of fish to the holding buckets for thirty minutes to an hour, giving them time to eliminate and calm down then transfer them again into the clean jerry cans of water for transport.

It was cold, wet work. Top that with traveling on a moto in the rain with wet clothes and wet feet, stopping every ten minutes to aerate the fish with the hand pump, and we were two miserable wet puppies.

We ranged from fifty to one hundred thirty kilometers (30-80 miles) on slick, slippery, muddy roads each twelve-hour day. The first day exhausted us, the second was no fun, and by the third, we were ready to quit and come home direct, do not pass go, do not collect two hundred dollars, just hop the first plane to Nairobi and Hello, U.S.A!

(The pond-owners at the holding-pond site had no experience seining, and while we are gradually teaching our farmers how to handle live fish, these were precious breeder fish, in very short supply, and we couldn't afford to lose even one, so we opted to do the seining ourselves, and as a teaching demonstration to them.)

It is times like these, with every muscle aching, your arms and legs jerked out of their sockets trying to keep the moto and one hundred pounds of squirmy, squirrely fish and water upright in a foot of mud and goo, soaking wet and freezing, that you find yourself slipping into language you've worked your whole life not to use--language not becoming to someone with an extended vocabulary and education.

Endearing sophisticated phrases like, "SH..., OH, S--T! Ohhh, man, nobody in their right mind would be doing this on purpose--OHhhh, NOOOO...S..!"

The second day of wet muddy clothes and especially wet socks inside of wet rubber boots got my brain to working. It was impossible to change clothes after we seined, what with two hundred people standing around watching and cheering our every move, even in the rain, but why not take along a dry pair of hiking boots and dry socks, and at least have dry feet?

So, on the third morning we stuffed a pair of boots and socks each into our backpacks and off we went; seined, transferred fish, packed up the motos and were ready to start the transport.

We pulled off our soggy rubber boots, soggy wet socks, and unveiled our secret weapon in the battle against flailing morale--hiking boots and dry socks! Jim was into his in a flash with a big grin on his face. Then he looked over at me. I sat with one foot booted and one foot naked--laughing so hard no sound would come out, just one long wheeze.

Because I have hard-to-fit skinny feet, and thinking I'd be wearing them (the feet and the boots) every day here instead of the rubber wellingtons--I brought two pair of perfect-fit Vasque Skywalk® hiking boots to Africa, same brand, same style, identical in every way, and at 6 o'clock that morning, in the dark, I had packed the two left boots into my pack.

Torture is an inadequate description for intentionally putting back on cold soggy socks and rubbers. My only consolation was that at least Jim had dry feet.

--But the powers that be for 'dry and happy' just were not smiling that day. The skies opened up and laughed all over us just after we installed the last fish in the last and furthermost pond, seventy-five kilometers from home. Jim's leather hiking boots got soaked, his dry socks got soaked, and his dry feet got soaked. And that's when we both caught colds.

But hooray for guardian angels, we didn't fall--not even once. And we didn't lose a single solitary fish, before, during or after transport. Must be getting better at this stuff?

But that's when we also caught the flu--no effort at all--like falling off a log (or a moto as the case may be).

We keep hoping things will slow down to a routine we can count on and handle, but every new pond with fish generates two or three excited neighbors and more new constructions. Great for the country, but it is wearing us down and out, as we've over a hundred ponds ongoing.

Come about March and the real rainy season, we're thinking of hibernating for two months, hang up a "Danger! Quarantine!" sign and hone up on our SCRABBLE and Solitaire skills with hot tea and homemade biscuits.

On the other hand, we only have eight months left and one of those is vacation (if we can find time or energy for one); another will be taken up with the new volunteers (our replacements, if they arrive and are allowed in-country) in July; then it's August and September harvests and homeward bound--so probably no hibernation--or vacation.

* * *

I have a commune that hasn't been real active, but the administrator recently invited me to meet a group of farmers in a promising valley. He ended up doing all the talking while the rest of us listened. He announced we would be working six days per week on a pond, finish in three weeks and have fish by the fourth, and then I would provide them all with Tee-shirts with a fish on the front and the words, 'Think fish!' in Kirundi. Oh, man.

One, I don't have six days a week to give them--Two, the gathered men only wanted to work two days per week. Three, I found out why-- they weren't a private co-op at all, but forced communal labor for a communal pond, with one hundred to one hundred fifty workers to oversee--and Four, I have no Tee-shirts to give. On, man.

The two days I've been there (by 7:30 a.m.), they've only shown up around 9:30 and started tapering off by 10:30. Communal ponds are our most difficult work because we have to generate all the enthusiasm, ideas, energy, and directives, and because we have to be there for every minute of work-time. The ponds and the fish won't be theirs when they finish so can't say I blame them at all.

* * *

--We have thirty-four baby bunnies growing fat and big to sell to our farmers at a very nominal price for their own rabbit hutches (not as a profit for us, but to insure the farmers invest something and will take care of their livestock--and the money goes into a kitty for purchasing more seining nets.

They are so cute and cuddly (the rabbits, not the farmers), and we've really grown attached to them (rabbits and farmers). Have wasted a good many evening hours out playing with them (rabbits) since we don't have a dog or a cat.

--Speaking of dogs, the Canadians are very nice to let us entertain and play with their dog, Jake-the-Rake. No purebred this, oh no. Just your nondescript large black Heinz-57 with lots of teeth when he smiles, and we've spent happy times chasing after the balls he throws to us.

--Jim's been trying to patch all the new holes in our rubber boots, but we are out of "GOOP" Shoe-Goo® (sounds like a 50's song, yes? Goop-shoe-goo, Goop-shoe-goo).

Right now, there are more patches than original rubber, and to be honest, they're suddenly just plain worn out, the soles worn so thin it's like going barefoot. We'll look for some new boots to buy in Buja over Christmas as someone told us there is an imported Chinese variety available. Until then, guess it's just wet feet every day.

--The best news is that we have electricity again! The twenty-four hour kind from the hydroelectric dam. And with electricity comes--are you ready? Water! Blessed Water! And in the pipes where it's supposed to be. They can now pump as long as it takes to fill up our two 55 gallon barrels. It is terrific, and only raises our electric bill a small, affordable amount.

After a year and a half of no inside water and spit baths, and months of going blind by candle and lantern light, we are back to reading till midnight, playing SCRABBLE and cards, and heating buckets and buckets of water on The Wretched Things for nearly real baths.

Can't believe how much difference it makes in our energy levels to be clean, and not have to grope around in the dark and semi-dark of an evening. The cassette-player works again! (We've had no way to re-charge the batteries for these many months.) Had forgotten how music soothes the savage beast, especially ones with cold wet feet.

Well, that's about it for this round. Hope all the holidays are warm, happy, and well spent (with family that is)!

Love and lotsa hugs,
Jimani
(alias Four Wet Socks)

Chapter 73
Of Mice and Motos

Dear Carol,

Can't thank you enough for the Banana Republic pants and photographer's vest. They fit perfectly, and I was down to my last two pair of britches and one holey jacket. These should do me through the end of our program! Thanks, thanks and thank you. Laura and family sent smoked oysters and other goodies, and Mom sent a box we still haven't reached the bottom of and are still sharing with other volunteers. Thanks to all!

On a heavier note, Phooey! The two-month short dry season lasted almost two weeks. It's beginning to look like last year, with no dry weather in store for us. But while it lasted, we had two full weeks of good roads. No boue, no goo, no slopping around in the muck. Then, just as we were getting used to it, in the middle of the night, when no one was looking, or up and around except the rats in the attic, it rained like the dickens. All night. We woke to a cold, foggy drizzle and more rain. It might clear off by noon, but has shot most of what was to have been a good day of work.

Speaking of work, it continues to pick up (in spite of the rain) and we have been especially pleased that our farmers are using the fish booklets to learn not only more about fish culture, but also for studying French and better Kirundi. It may become a small alternative educational tool for those who aren't allowed the opportunity for schooling.

* * *

--Speaking of Jim, he has come up with some good one-liner's lately: He woke up in a morose mood the other day and moped around for the first hour or two while a curtain of rain isolated us from work and the world.

So I asked him, "Hey you–what's up? Where's your smile gone to?"

And just as quick as you please, he pops back, "Oh, I sent it to the cleaners. It'll be back tomorrow." (In a country where there are no 'cleaners', and NOTHING comes back by tomorrow, was especially funny, or maybe you just had to be there, or maybe we're just becoming simple-minded?)

--We have been doing relatively well up to now with work, mostly because the administrators and various functionaires (funk-shun-airs or office bureaucrats, or anyone in authority who isn't a peasant /farmer /craftsman) have pretty much left us alone. Not sure why. Maybe our Governor has intervened, or they are afraid of us, unsure what to do with us crazy umuzungus, frustrated at our poor language skills, or simply wanted to see if we were going to fall down and go boom before they put their eggs into our basket. (Except for two communal administrators and our governor, who have been terrific and supportive the whole time.)

But now that we're obviously doing great with actual results, the work stoppages have disappeared, everyone and his brother is on the bandwagon trying to help, hinder or join in.

And therein lies the problem. We've worked a year and a half with no disputes or problems over land and now all of a sudden everything is a problem and has to go before the administrator or equivalent arbitrator (magistrate) for resolution or arbitration. With land at a premium, and everyone wanting and needing to own a bit, it looks like the next batch of volunteers will be bogged down in red tape, the land-courts and the system.

I know 'the system' exists everywhere in every culture, I just regret seeing efficiency and enthusiasm drop in proportion to the amount of rising interference as the system jumps in to lend a hand, with forms to fill in, registrations to be made. Seems to be a story as old as humanity.

I am just grateful we were in on the first of it; the creative and beautiful part, before things revert to mundane or fall apart from overload.

* * *

--Last week I received a request for consultation and site evaluations in a new region through an assistant administrator in one of my communes (county). I told him I wasn't taking on any more pond constructions and he said fine, that these were already built anyway and they just wanted fish!

Oh, Me! I asked where the particular region was, as I hadn't heard of it before.

"Oh, it's over there," he shrugged a shoulder, indicating an area as vast as Texas, which might include parts of Rwanda, Kenya or Tanzania.

"No, I mean how far is it? How many kilometers? What colline (hill) or region is it next to?" I persisted.

Confusion and a lack of understanding clouded his face, so I must have used the wrong time, distance and tense in Kirundi to ask my question.

But he was helpful in pointing the right direction, "Bugina is just over there--. No problem to find at all."

No problem to find at all turned out to be ten kilometers of pure torture as the road disintegrated to a foot path, then to the width of the moto tire with the mountain straight up on one side and a sheer drop-off on the other and no place to turn around.

"Oh, how do I get myself into these things," I chastised into my helmet.

At one point, I straddled a narrow washed out chasm on a path just wider than my tires. The ravine dropped down five to fifty feet beneath me, (depending on where one started falling).

But that was nothing compared to the rushing stream five feet across, two feet deep and with two skinny poles placed across as a bridge. Two guys appeared from nowhere to stand on the other side, arms crossed, ready to watch the show once they realized I was going to take a two hundred plus pound bike and myself across those two skinny poles. (This was in preference to turning back and re-crossing the washed out ravine, and I couldn't have anyway--no room to turn around.)

And all the while I was thinking, "They want to stock ponds here and every time, every week, I have to face this path?

"Noooo... way!"

--But seeing there were only two poles, there was no place to put my feet or push the bike across. The stream banks were too steep to wade across and water was running too fast. Plus my experience of streams here is that you have the visible one to two feet of water, and then sink up to your eyeballs in boue (mud).

The two guys on the other side grinned, as they too, worked it out, then motioned me to push the bike out onto the poles. They grabbed and pulled from the other side while I pushed from behind, without a word said. The poles only sagged a foot or so, clearing the water by at least an inch and in no time at all, with many thanks to my heroes and a couple of cigarettes, I was on my way again.

Arriving at my destination (determined by the fact that people pointed to the ground and no longer waved in the direction of Rwanda or Tanzania when I repeated the name of the hill), I asked where the local chef was. This question was met with blank stares, vaguely waved arms and Kirundi for, "He's over there somewhere."

Vaguely fed up with vaguely's and running out of daylight, I conceded defeat and decided it was late enough to head home. I was even OK with never having discovered the new 'finished' ponds, as long as I didn't have to return. I discovered the well-maintained coffee road about two hundred yards straight up and parallel to where I'd just traveled, but the farmers just shook their heads when I asked for a path up to the road.

After a few minutes of negotiation and with the help of a dozen farmers, they lifted, ported and pushed my bike straight up the steep slope, hand-over-head and up at last onto the coffee road. I was so grateful--I paid them all the money I carried (the equivalent of about $20 U.S.--or 20% of my monthly salary) and a new full pack of cigarettes, which pleased them as much as it did me.

Hot-footing it for home, I arrived mud-covered and a mess to find our Canadian friends chatting away with something in the driveway that vaguely resembled my husband. Couldn't tell for sure, as whatever it was had been rolling around in the mud and was covered with it from head to toe.

--Now, Sylveste has taken to boiling our socks to get the red-brown stains out and he prides himself on matching up pairs. But he hasn't made it all the way through our inventory yet to get them all back to white, and as Jim shucked his muddy boots off at the door and we went inside, Trudy asked him why he wore one brown sock and one white?

Sylveste was mortified and tried to steal the socks from Jim's feet at the door. We had to reassure him over and again that it wasn't his fault that Jim kept filling up his boots with muddy water. We finally mollified him by asking for some hot tea and bragging to our guests at how well he kept up with the marketing and house chores.

* * *

We spent a fun hour exchanging stories, Trudy and Phil laughing at our moto escapades, while the mud dried and began caking clothes to skin. And we shared their joy at the many adventures of having a first child, sleep deprivation being at the top. Promising a SCRABBLE game soon, they exited with little baby Daniel to let us die in peace.

Sylveste left for the day, too, and I put two pots of water on The Wretched Things, stuck whatever-it-was in the tub and scrubbed with hot water and soap until the skin and my husband began to show through again--though it took two rinsings.

Then came my turn for the rub and scrub, and into some dry clothes, hot chocolate, dinner, and to bed with both of us with a good book. It is so wonderful to have electricity again! Sometimes we turn on all five of the lights just to watch them work, and laugh.

--Bunnies and garden are doing great, one keeping up with the other, so we have wall-to-wall squash and bunnies now. (Not squashed bunnies)

Well, 'nuff is enough. Hope all is well with you and yours and there's not too much ice and snow abounding.

--Oh, yes, speaking of waving vagaries, people see you coming on the moto and have a habit of running helter-skelter down the steep hillsides, tearing through the banana, coffee and taro groves and down to the road, yelling and giving you the national up and down arm-wave sign for 'please stop'.

So, you pull up short, getting your polite refusal speech ready, thinking they are going to ask you to come look at a new pond site. But they run up, breathless, eyes ashining, and say, "Oh, so you've arrived. What do you want?"

And with those parting pearls of winsome wisdom, Happy Valentines
Day!
With love and lotsa hugs,
Jimani

P.S.

Trudy and Phil brought us back each a bumper sticker from their trip home to Canada: "Engineers are Better by Design" and "Artists are Quicker on the Draw". Made us smile and wish for more silliness in our lives...and for a bumper to put them on.

Chapter 74
Little Ponds and Ambassadors

Dear Folks,

On the way to one of my best pond areas Thursday, I saw two small boys frantically waving me down with the National arm wave for STOP. I pulled over and they grabbed hold of my hands, pulling and tugging, indicating they wanted me to go with them, yakking both at once and so excitedly and fast in Kirundi I couldn't make heads or tails of it.

Thinking maybe someone was sick or in trouble, I allowed them to pull me across a large marshy area and a short way up the side of a hill near a new construction site my farmers hadn't yet shown me.

Then I noticed a small fenced off section with water in it. Curious, I went to investigate. A whole slew of kids appeared magically from the coffee groves and descended upon me, gesturing wildly at the two who'd brought me and chattering all at once in high gear, so I could only catch half of what they were saying at first. But slowly, the story unfolded.

By himself, the son of one of my farmers had constructed a fish pond, HIS SIZE: two meters square, with baby composts, perfect three-to-one slopes on the tightly compacted dikes, a canal for water lined with rocks to prevent erosion, a filter to keep unwanted fish species out, and a filtered bamboo overflow pipe for heavy rains! He even had a plankton bloom growing in his tiny compost pit! To top it off, he'd built a fence around it to keep out thieves and people with big feet.

But the most impressive part was the money he'd worked many months for to buy four fingerlings. Talk about crocodile tears. I sat down and cried for happiness. It's one thing to teach their folks, but this is already the second generation! What a great kid. Oh, me.

I shook his hand, congratulated him on a perfect pond and promised to bring baby fish out to him next week, along with a Hershey's chocolate bar to celebrate his courage.

Think it was my very best day here.

* * *

--On the more difficult side--I've had one group that has consistently not done as well in their pond construction, often taking shortcuts that don't work. They were in too big a hurry to put water in the pond last week and merely piled the last dike high with dirt and mud. When I arrived to look at it, water was pulsing out from under the dike.

Pointing this out to them, I explained they either had to tear it out completely and start over, or dig a shoulder-wide vertical canal (ditch) completely down through the center of the dike and put in a compacted eight-inch-wide core of clay, top to bottom, to stop the leaks.

When they began to argue with me over the extra work, I made the mistake of stepping off into the gooey mess to illustrate the fact that it wasn't well-compacted, and before I could blink, went in up to my chest in boue and goo, like quicksand on Wolf Creek, except messier.

After they fell on the ground and finished with some hysterical laughter, they realized I wasn't climbing out and it took four of them to pry me free, the problem being to release the suction on my only pair of rubber boots without leaving them in the hole. It is not the first imitation of an earthworm I've done, but I have done it more gracefully. By the time I'd been dragged out onto terra firma, they were convinced I was right and began reconstruction.

* * *

The U.S. Ambassador was up to see us this week. He met with our Governor, toured some of our ponds, had lunch with us and was off to see Michael, the volunteer in the next province over.

As there are no handy restaurants here, I'd asked in advance if there was anything he couldn't eat and had been assured by both the Embassy and Peace Corps that anything I provided would be terrific and not to go to too much trouble.

I had a nice veggie Swiss Chard quiche ready to pop in the sand oven over one of The Wretched Things when our group arrived back at House from the pond tour, and quick-stirred up some biscuits to bake in the other one while Jim and Mona entertained the Ambassador.

But when I set the steaming offerings on the table he got the funniest look on his face, followed by surprise, then embarrassment, then disappointment--all in a flash, before his Ambassador-face fell back into place. It turns out he was allergic to tomatoes and onions and wasn't that fond of goat cheese or Swiss chard, so he graciously feasted only on the biscuits and butter.

Well, phooey. I did ask, and wish I had known. I could have at least had the makings of a cabbage or fruit salad, or splurged on ground meat and cow cheese, or even pate' and crackers (one of the stores in Buja serves up a goose liver pate' which we can't afford, but yummmy).

It was great for us to have some official U.S. recognition, though unfortunately I'm sure he will remember the tiny meal he ate, and the big one he couldn't.

Till next time,
Hewe and aahh-nneeeee-tah

Chapter 75
Letting Go

Dear Mum and Pops,

A belated Happy New Year and Happy Anniversary. Another week gone by and no letters written. We almost have an excuse. We caught colds and the flu at Christmas while in Buja and the colds have hung on and on and on, till we are both worn to a frazzle.

We haven't had the energy to do much but go to work, come home, eat and sleep. We are going to spend what is left of the weekend inside with hot toddies, dry clothes and some expensive wood in the fireplace (preferably lit and toasting our tootsies the whole time).

The dry season has begun, such as it is, and it has turned really cold at night. Mornings we can see our breath almost as frost until around 10 a.m. It only rains every third or fourth day and not gully-washers, just enough to keep the new garden alive. We have been eating squash, carrots, broccoli, cauliflower, spinach and Swiss chard from the garden till we can't hold any more and the coffee expert, Jan, brings us tomatoes, carrots and leeks almost every week. So there is no reason for us to have colds, but we do.

We took some fifteen pounds of zucchini down to folks in Buja over Christmas only to return and find two more bushels waiting for us-- most were about two feet long and four inches thick! We shared with all of our neighbors, sent some to other volunteers and still had bunches left over. Have served it stuffed, baked, fried, casseroled, souped and raw.

But alas, alack, just when we thought we couldn't eat another one ever again, mildew caught up with the garden and in the space of about three days it is all gone till we replant in two months--and the 'season of hunger' is upon us--again.

* * *

Our Canadian friends, Trudy and Phil and little Daniel, went home for six weeks in October and November, to Canada. They were only back for two weeks in December, then gone to India for two weeks to attend a Baha'i conference (their faith), so we have really missed them. (Two plus, years worth of vacation.)

We've been furiously catching up on SCRABBLE, jokes and good times since they returned, but just learned they have accepted a transfer to Goma, Zaire, in March and will spend the next two months turning their development programs over to others and preparing to leave. They have been such a bright spot in our lives and we will surely miss them.

We have had a new gardener since August whom we've been pleased with--bright, industrious, honest--did a great job on the yard, the rabbits, the fence, flower beds, etc. Gave him a raise mid-fall, and a good Christmas/New Year's bonus, almost up with Sylveste. But we came back from Buja on January 2nd to find he'd been drinking the whole ten days, not done any work and left the rabbits to starve (thank goodness Sylveste put a little food in every couple of days).

When we tried to find out what was going on, he became angry and belligerent, even yelled at us. If it had just been a bender, we would have given him another chance, but he wouldn't calm down, so we had to let him go and ask Odance to come back.

The whole affair has made us so very sad and we still don't know what triggered it. Guess we never will. Do so wish we had better language skills, but our coffee-friend, Jan, tells us only the priests and nuns who have been here thirty or forty years and who work daily within the language, culture and politics, truly understand.

Well, off to bed with us. We should have purchased another blanket over Christmas for use in this drafty, damp bedroom. Even with two blankets and 'spooning', we have a hard time staying warm.

Don't know how our farmers or their families manage to survive.

Love and lotsa hugs,
Hewe and aaahh-nneee-tahhh

Chapter 76
The Great Cabbage Caper

Dear Carol,

...We sped down the tortuous highway, dodging giant cabbages that launched themselves in suicidal leaps from the over-loaded truck ahead, right, then left, then right again. Deadly projectiles of sentient sauerkraut, they seemed possessed of internal radar tuned in precisely to our front tires.

From our post town of Ngozi to the thriving metropolis of Bugarama and its three hundred twenty four stalwart citizens plus one PC volunteer, we stealthily descended some ninety km down country, then ascended (as Bugarama, at 6,879 feet, is actually 900 feet higher than Ngozi at 5,974 feet), to lend moral and technical sustenance and support to our fellow-fish-friend and volunteer, Mary. Of course, we also wanted to partake of her invitation to enjoy some newly acquired Irish Cream, or even some hot cocoa spiked with brandy, but that was a secondary consideration.

We cringed down into our helmets and rain gear with each passing vehicle, hoping against hope we wouldn't be recognized or run into or over by some P.C. staff member. (Staff members, who should, by rights, be slaving and suffering away in an office in Buja, and not out larking around on a dreary and overcast weekend.)

Yet we were wicked with glee at the prospect of breaking the rules by taking the motos out of our province for business and pleasure. We had asked permission to view Mary's ponds on our own time to lend encouragement and support, and been refused twice, so of course, we finally felt obligated to go of our own accord.

--Light mist and fog shrouded the verdant hills, bringing to mind shades of England and Sherlock Holmes. We rounded a bend and there it was, just ahead--a speeding vegetable truck, careening around corners and screaming down the straightaways, evidently practicing for the local Le Mans. And it was loaded to the gills with giant cabbages that bulged out between the metal bars of the three enclosed sides, its engine straining under the weight of a ton of vegetation.

Hanging, swaying and occasionally swinging from the overhead bar at the back was a young man trying to keep his feet braced on the cabbage heap. But each bump and twist and twirl in the road caused the load to shift, and try as he might, the kid couldn't keep those green bowling balls from obeying the law of gravity. At irregular intervals, one and three at a time, they launched themselves in desperate suicidal leaps to freedom, splatting at 60 km/hour into our path, creating an obstacle course of flying shards and cabbage hearts.

Rising to the challenge, we twisted and turned, oscillated and swerved, biding our time and waiting for just the right amount of visibility and clearance. Dodging a sudden eruption of flying cabbages, we zoomed around the maniacal menagerie in a gleeful burst of speed, leaving them to be swallowed up in the thickening shroud.

--We rolled into Bugarama at last, two inconspicuous umuzungu figures on bright blue and red machines that sounded like World War III, sneaking unobtrusively past what looked like the full complement of 324 stalwart citizens standing by the road to watch the world go by in the drizzle.

We cautiously made our way up the last hill toward Mary's house, only to come to an abrupt and grinding halt. There, only 300 yards away, parked in her driveway, was a shiny new white Landrover belonging to--someone from Buja! But who? Friend or foe? Someone who would laugh at our escapade and join in the conspiracy, or someone who would turn us in and get us sent home at this late date for breaking moto rules?

We quickly shut off the engines and dismounted, quietly pushing the motos to the back of the house, praying that Mary's big, friendly dog was no better a watch-dog than the last time we'd seen him. Very quietly, we unloaded our gear, hid the motos safely in the bushes and calmly walked around to the front to see who was there.

Mary and two nice-looking-clean-cut-all-American-types met us at the door. Her first words were, "Oh, my God, what are you doing here? Didn't you get my message? R. and T. (our P.C. big-boss and her husband) are on their way up to see you this weekend! You'll be caught and hung from the nearest yardarm! Get out of here!"

With that pleasant and welcoming greeting, we asked her to explain herself. The last communication we'd received from Mary through the grapevine had been on Thursday, saying the coast was clear: our boss, Mona, was in Nairobi, our poor ad-min, Terry, was sick with malaria, nurse was in Rwanda, and R. our head Chef, was holding down the fort in Buja as the only staff member on duty.

All plans of mice and men collapsed however, when Terry got better and R. decided to come see us anyway, on Saturday or Sunday, rather than the following Tuesday or Wednesday as she had planned.

Too late and too dark to start back, we decided to get an early start Sunday morning. Also, we knew they weren't in Ngozi waiting on us or we'd have passed them on the road...maybe.

And after all, I said, we were visiting for fish work purposes (all considerations of extra benefits aside), and we'd already put in our half day of work Saturday before descending, then wondered if that rationalization would actually serve, save or hang us.

At that point, the larger of the two huge guys extended his hand and said "Hi, I'm Scott!"

The other introduced himself as Charles.

"And what do a Scott and a Charles do," I asked.

"We're the new Marines for the Embassy." They'd landed only a few short weeks before, but had already decided that things were a little too dull in the capital city and had come exploring on their first day off. They readily became co-conspirators with us, promising to help run interference if possible, then left all too soon for a night on the town.

We spent the evening fish-talking with Mary and discussing what we would do if R. showed up early Sunday before we left.

Well hidden, the moto's were locked and no problem, but what if she offered to give us a ride back to Ngozi (as she was sure to do) so we wouldn't have to ride the bus? There was no way we could explain then, why our motos weren't in Ngozi when we arrived.

We decided to do the courageous and honorable thing, and crawl under the bed or into the Zamu's hut or hide behind a door--if she surprised us. A great evening later, we sipped our way through hot cocoa and played Yahtzee, laughing and talking 'fish stories' from the last year and a half.

Sleeping in till 6:30, we had a leisurely breakfast, shopped in the vegetable market, and then decided, what the heck, we couldn't have come all that way to give support and encouragement and not actually see Mary's ponds. Taking our careers in hand, we mounted up and went to ooh and aah, and were not disappointed. They were worth the effort and risk--really beautiful ponds.

Gone for three hours, we arrived back to an empty house, but with two new sets of tire tracks having invaded the driveway in our absence.

Jim and I looked at each other, knowing who had been there, but not when.

We couldn't leave immediately or we might catch up with and pass her on the road. On the other hand, we didn't want her to sit outside our house all afternoon either, so we waited another half-hour, loaded up, hugged goodbye and thanks to Mary, and were off.

Rain and drizzle cloaked the return voyage, thank goodness, keeping visibility to a minimum, and was uneventful until we arrived in Kayanza, the province and town next to ours.

We sneaked slowly and discreetly up into Michael's yard, relieved not to see the Peace Corps Landrover. However, instead of a key to his door to retrieve the fish-seining net we'd loaned him the week before, there was a note in the secret hiding place, bearing words of gloom and doom.

Bad news, guys. R. and T. arrived here around noon. Knew you guys weren't home, so Jill and I invited them on a picnic to give you some time. Bad move on my part! The picnic place is on the road to your house, so we may meet you coming back! Sorry, wasn't thinking.

We should return around 3:15, so if you're here around that time, lay low and sneak around us. Good luck! Love, Michael

We looked at our watches--then at each other--3:25 p.m. Oh, No--! We raced for our bikes and lit out like lightning, praying for fog or drizzle to hide in. Covering half of the thirty-two km's home, we spotted them dead ahead. It was too late to duck off on a side road, so we bluffed it out and drove right past. I couldn't resist the temptation to wave and got a positive response!

Michael (fishie) and Jill (the new chimpanzee project volunteer--great personality) said later they nearly died when they saw me do that. R. was either being nice or really didn't recognize us due to the poor driving conditions, because she has never said a word.

We put it in high gear and dispatched for home without further ado. Minds in a- flutter as we arrived, our version of the Keystone Cops ensued, rushing to make up the guest bed, put away all signs of our journey, straighten, shove, push, hide, take inventory of pantry, wave good-bye to Jim as he expedited fresh groceries from the market, accelerating at every turn before the mind went into total shutdown and tilt from the overload, light the turn-the-house-colder-fireplace-with-smoky-peat, put on the tea and some music, change clothes, put up groceries Jim hauled in, and sit down to be casually reading books just as they pulled up into the yard, stroll out and say:

"R.! T.! What a pleasant surprise! Welcome, and come in this house!"

We celebrated the evening with their good news of being expectant parents (first child). Yipppeee for them! Unfortunately, T. had some questionable wine on the picnic (or maybe it was just the flu) and he headed to bed early.

We will never be sure if R. saw us or not, or if she'd rather believe it wasn't us, the goodie-two-shoes of her bunch of ruffians, or that she simply chose not to call us on it. But whichever, the powers-that-be continue to smile and protect us, and it will be awhile before we have the courage to transgress the laws of the land again. (Like at least a week!)

With love and lotsa hugs,
Jim and Me (alias The Patched Cabbage Kids)

Chapter 77
Rats, Bats, and Taxes

Dear Bill and Theola,

Have been sosososoooo--busy. The rainy season only pretended to start last month and we have been working ten to twelve hours a day since. Verily, we are ready for the rainy season.

We need the rest. Never thought we would say, "Work is going too well."

We did receive the latest Popular Science and the Reader's Digest from you! Devoured them both like popcorn. You always know just what will brighten our days here and make the time shorter till we come home. Thanks for being there!

* * *

I stopped by an administrator's bureau (office) the other day to give an update on the fish program in his region. He wasn't there, but his Secretary was, who told me they were keeping a close eye on me, the farmers and our work, and began reciting the current statistics of the program. Only problem was, they were all wrong and I made the mistake of informing him. The shock and horror that came over his face was alarming. He barked at some poor soul to run get the latest reports for the Governor and presented them to me in black and white as proof that the figures were correct.

"Yes, I can see all of the numbers and figures typed in, Sir, and a very nice job of typing, but with respect, unfortunately, they are not correct."

Again, horror and shock.

"But, madame...madame...but...

"Not to worry, I have the latest figures and we can fix them." So we spent the next thirty minutes going over the figures, ponds, collines (sites) and farmer co-ops and correcting them. Instead of a total of ten ponds, we came up with ten ponds stocked, four completed and awaiting fish, and another twenty under construction.

Hope his administrator is happy and he doesn't get into trouble for changing official reports.

* * *

Our weight is holding just about right, not too thin, not too thick. Guess it's because we eat a lot of goat cheese and wheat bread. Can't all be 5'10", svelte and blonde. I mean, some of us don't even have much hair.

Things could be worse. We could have fifteen colors on our house again instead of three, and the rats playing in the attic could just as easily be playing under the bed--or we could have bats in our belfries instead of the rafters.

So, as I say, we are doing pretty well, except that we just received our tax package from you with all the house sale stuff in it to figure out. Looks like we can't even come to deepest Africa and run away from the IRS.

Honestly, they have probably already established branches on all the other planets in the solar system, nay, the galaxy, just waiting for us to show up:

Dear Colonist (s),

You failed to file your 102034 SXT form before you left Earth. The penalty for failing to file within the prescribed period of time is computed on the chart listed in the appendix to form 102034 SXT, that is form 1021 ASXT. Please file your penalty in triplicate before the below listed date, and teleport your penalty plus interest immediately to Earth headquarters, as well as compu-filing the original with the bureau on Mars, with any amendments forwarded to Andromeda. Failure to comply with any and all of these regulations will result in your immediate ejection from the protective air lock and your surviving family members will have to deal with a representative from the Special Agent IRRS (Internal Revenue Robot Service) and suffer the due consequences.

Very Sincerely Yours,
Iwant Your Money
Special Agent
IRS Bureau, MARS

* * *

--Well, so much for lighthearted, soul-cheering, pick-me-ups. It is late and we have a long day again tomorrow. Just wanted to say thanks for all the letters and goodies, and to let you know we are alive and well (sort of), and living in Africa (verily).

With love and a hug,
Jim and Me
* * *

P.S.

Just wanted to add a note to Anita's letter. Fish business is still going great with first harvests expected in May-June, then weekly harvests starting July-August. We may even get to eat a few (if we're willing to pay our farmers for them), but our replacements had better arrive with track shoes on to keep up with the work. We've heard they're due to start their stateside training April 15th, arrive in country in July for the language training, and be here on post September 1st to overlap us by about three weeks.

We were asked to consider extending our tour by another year (we would get 30 days home leave in between). Depending on the day we think about it, we vacillate between uh-uh, No Way, and "How can we leave our farmers to someone else's care?"

On the other hand, we've also been thinking if we continue development work, we might rather work in a job that provides a vehicle with at least two doors and a roof, no more motos. We're pushing our luck on the accidents and don't want any permanent injuries.

Love,
Jim

P.S. 2--Sent you some pili-pili (hot pepper) seeds for you to try in your garden. We've grown to love the taste of the little buggers, hot, smoky and all, a different flavor from the chili pequin hot peppers at home.

They grow here about a meter tall and wide. Will be interested to see how they grow there, or if they sprout at all.

Chapter 78
TV Stars

Dear Mum, Dad, and siblings,

It has been so busy, we are both ready to be buried where we stand or run away from home! The real rainy season still hasn't hit yet. It rains hard one day, followed by four or five days of hot and dry. Most unusual. Hope it isn't the start of a drought. The country can't afford any natural disasters.

We've had only one weekend off since January and used it going to Buja for Mona's going-away party last weekend (our P.C. boss--She has accepted a new position in Togo. Sad day, and we will really miss her, as she's been our front-line defense and protector on the bureaucratic front, as well as a friend.)

Didn't get much rest of course, and I came down with malaria the following Monday. Took the 'cure' and still had four days in bed of bone-rattling chills and fever.

Back out to work on Friday and Saturday, weak as a kitten and still don't have much steam, but our schedule is too full to take any more time out.

* * *

Hey, guess what? We are TV stars! Yep! The National TV station is filming a special on the fish program and Ngozi Province is being spotlighted. Burundi Television was here on Monday to set up for the shooting on Friday. Friday arrived and they spent the day with our farmers, the fish ponds, the governor, and local administrators, and say they'll be back in July to film our first big fish harvests as a follow-up. Our farmers loved it.

The crew filmed ponds in all stages of construction and management and we even had a fingerling harvest, with our guys doing a great job, looking very professional as they seined, sorted and readied the little ones for transfer to a neighboring pond. The program will air this week sometime, and though Jim and I won't get to see it, we're hoping Peace Corps can videotape it for us.

They asked me to give a presentation for the filming, which scared me terribly (fear of public speaking), but after a short brain-freeze, I made up a large flip chart, complete with color drawings of the pond construction and fish-growing process and had it ready to use (in French) before the camera. Even with a local language professor correcting my presentation speech beforehand, am sure half the things I said were unrecognizable, and certainly not 'proper' educated French. Well--at least the pictures were pretty.

* * *

--One week later. We now have over one hundred forty ponds and, unfortunately, a few more every week--not through our own efforts as we are refusing to take on any more--though we hear about new ones every few days.

We have no authority to stop the farmers from constructing ponds or selling fingerlings without our oversight--sigh. So we've begun enlisting the help of local ag-extension agents to help monitor the established ponds and oversee the some management and construction, but it's difficult for them, since they won't be paid for their assistance and they have not been given directives to add the fish-program to their work duties. But for the most part they are interested in learning about aquaculture, have shown enthusiasm, and a few of them can see we are making progress).

--There are also some strange rumblings going on in Buja. The Ministry has requested but not approved our replacements and we are trying to incorporate the local hierarchy (two years ahead of schedule) into the program. We hope to give our farmers the best chance of continuing if we are not replaced. Politics the world over is just weird and interferes with a lot, yes?

Normally, a new fish program runs for a minimum of six years, with three successive groups of volunteers at two years each.

The first, like us, introduces the technology, makes sure it's practical, economical, doesn't interfere with other agriculture, uses appropriate technology for that particular region and insures there is sufficient interest (usually one to five sample ponds).

The second group incorporates the hierarchy at all levels, teaching local extension agents monitoring practices, reinforcing good management and harvest techniques.

The third fine-tunes and expands the program, assuring that it can run independently of both volunteers and--or local government.

We're doing all three at once, not by choice or plan, it's just the way things are turning out. Not complaining, just running out of steam while we're having fun on the way to the earthquake!

* * *

Bits and Pieces:

--We just had our farewell dinner for Trudy and Phil, our Canadian friends. They are moving to Goma, Zaire tomorrow and we already miss them. We hope to take a week's vacation soon and help them get settled in, build shelves, rabbit hutches and chicken coops in their new home, and squeeze in a last few games of Scrabble and Yahtzee.

--Sad news. Mona, our P.C. boss, left last week in a transfer to Togo to another job with Peace Corps.

--Mona's boss, our new PC director, R., is expecting her first child and will be leaving soon to spend the last three months of pregnancy in the States. Surprisingly, neither of them will be replaced any time soon, so that leaves our super-star Admin-officer, Terry, stuck with all of us and doing the job of three people, plus closing out the fiscal year in July. She might go crazy. (She's hosted some great get-togethers for the volunteers at her house and has a standing offer to cut the guy's hair, which is perfect because the barbers here mostly know buzz-cut.)

Except for emergencies, it looks like we will be on our own more or less for the next four to five months. Do you think they know something they are not telling us?

* * *

--We just saw the taping of the TV program on our fish ponds. It was great! Our farmers looked so professional. And thank goodness, they dubbed over my presentation in French with a deep Burundian bass voice translating it all into Kirundi, so no one will know different or have to listen to me!

--Bit of sad news. Jim shaved his beard and mustache this week and he looks like a Dutch-Polish guy again. I tried hiding his razor, but he just took mine. Guess I'm stuck with the clean-cut all-American Dutchman again. Oh well, can't win them all.

--April 5--another week and haven't yet finished this letter. Everybody in Peace Corps showed up this weekend and ate and drank us out of house, food, and beer. It was good to touch base and English-speak, but Monday saw us dragging our tired tushies out to the motos looking for enthusiasm.

--It is especially quiet this evening because Jim is down in Buja having a boil lanced on his neck and procuring antibiotics for it. Not serious, but it has been very painful for him. I'll be glad when it's healed, for his sake.

Love and lotsa hugs,
Jim and Anita
(alias umuzungus becoming somebodies)

Chapter 79
Anatomy of a Rainy Day

Dear Mom and Pops,

At last. A perfect, miserable, cold, dreary, rainy day. I must say, we have been praying for it, hoping for it, expecting it. And it arrived today with splendor and force, roaring in like a lion, and then staying to cover us like a soggy, grey woolen overcoat. Hooray!

--It all began many weeks ago when the real rainy season should have started and indeed pretended to, with seven days of slosh and boue, mush and sludge. But then it quit. It cleared off. It dried up. The sun came out, and for the first time since we arrived in Ngozi, it got hot.

The first three or four days gave a welcome respite from mush and sludge. But as things continued to dry out and the sky stayed a crystalline blue, the clouds did not return and we began to wonder. Each day we awoke expecting to hear rain beating on our leaky tin roof like a Sousa march on the 4th of July--and each day it grew more still, more stifling, dryer, hotter, dustier...

Days 10...15...25...30.

Just a year ago we would have welcomed such weather, as we were eager then to work, to build, to accomplish. But this year, we awaited February and the heavy rainy season with anticipation; a chance to rest from our labors, stay home, rest, read books, rest, rest, and rest.

You see, our farmers have run crazy amok and they're running us crazy right along with them. One hundred fifty ponds and their associated farmers are working us twelve hours a day, six to seven days a week, and there is still not enough time in the week to do a job well done.

Stop, you say? Great advice. But it hasn't worked. We've refused counsel to the last forty ponds built (at least in the beginning). But when it was obvious they were going to continue with or without us, we couldn't stand to see them doing things wrong, wasting effort, or setting bad examples. We can't prevent our farmers from selling fingerlings to people with substandard ponds or poor management practices, and we worry about the program falling apart from enthusiasm before it's even up and running.

So for now, we attempt to see that as many as possible get started in the right direction. So there you have it. We are not irreplaceable or indispensable, there simply needs to be five or six more of us.

--But, I digress. Back to our story. Each February day dawned hotter and more suffocating than the last.

The garden shriveled and withered, coffee trees drooped, and there was talk of massive crop failure. Apparitions of drought and famine invaded our thoughts.

Is this how it begins?

Now, in Texas or Oklahoma, months without rain occurs frequently. But here, the ancient red soil is different, has no substance. Without rain when it is needed, it dries out swiftly and cracks appear everywhere. Large fissures open up, soil becomes powder and is carried away on the wind, erosion in flight, like a listless bird on the wing.

Each morning saw us up at six with the sun and down in the fields and valleys before seven. By ten, we were dripping wet, but with perspiration, not rain, our clothes saturated and odious. Noon saw dehydration set in and it seemed nothing could quench the thirst.

By mid-afternoon, not even our formidable farmers could work in the lifeless air. Retiring to the nearest shade for an hour's siesta, then back up to finish work around 5:30 p.m., we would drag ourselves uphill the one or two kilometers to the path or road, climb wearily on the motos and head for home.

Day after day with no relief in sight.

Then, on day thirty-five, clouds began to sneak across the horizon, treading lightly on the edge of the sky, like egg shells, fragile, broken, scattered, with only a few wisps and high-flyers.

On days thirty-eight, thirty-nine and forty, a slow accumulation built into massive towers of white and deep blue-grey, but only in the distance. Still, it was too hot to rain. The promise was in the air, we could smell it, taste it, yet no moisture fell to break the spell.

Each evening brought disappointment as clouds raced off into the sunset leaving a solid sky-wide inky black dome lit by a million burning, glittering distant fires.

As day forty-five dawned, we felt something ominous in the air and delayed the start of our day, waiting, hoping. The cumulonimbus puffed and huffed and billowed sky high, overwhelming and dwarfing everything in comparison's reach.

Dazzling white Marie-Antoinette tops with loops and curls cascaded down to serious depths of blues and blacks. The wall of clouds advanced and grew, a dark blue-grayness swelling from the bottom up until it obliterated all of the gleaming white towers.

Swallowing the landscape in monstrous gulps, a cavernous maw of steel blue swept toward our red and white house at the edge of the earth, consuming entire mountains and valleys like some sky-wide tidal wave run awry.

Thunder and lightning crisped the air and rattled the windows, drowning out the chorus of frogs, birds and insects. Then all we could see were shadows, as dusk and quiet fell suddenly in the middle of the morning.

All was still for a hair's breadth.

Abruptly, a fierce wind gusted and swirled. It grabbed the withered leaves from the trees, spinning them up into brown and yellow vortexes to be swept away, scrubbing the earth clean of everything not firmly attached. A few splats, pings, and tings on the tin roof signaled time to seek shelter and with a sudden deafening roar, it arrived.

A solid wall of water pelted, beat, and crushed, coursing out of shadows so fast and furious there was little time for it to soak into the parched, cracked ground. So fast and hard it came, that within minutes, trickles sought ever-lower levels down even the slightest slopes.

They ran together to form rivulets, then joined into streams of ever-cascading violence. They grabbed at the tired earth, pulling and tearing it away, racing with it down, down, down the mountain.

The torrent tortured the landscape, broiling, burning, digging deeper into already jagged scars. It churned red and angry, spilling finally down and out into the rice paddies, inundating and covering them until the mile-wide green valley below us became a flat red basin of roiling water.

Thirty minutes, an hour, two hours. Just as suddenly as it had begun, it stopped. A last few splatters and the dark grey shadows lightened, lifted, and scudded away.

The sun, hot and strong, broke through, and steamy vapors rose off the still hard-packed earth creating a thick fog of breathless heat.

An hour of fierce sunshine. Stillness. The eye of the storm.

Looking eastward exposed another solid wall of deep azure blue racing at breakneck speed toward our perch on the hill. Within minutes, dark shadows, grey and eerie, blocked the sun and again the raucous cacophony of noise, lightning flashes, and rain assaulted the earth, but this time, it mellowed to a steady moderate downpour to nourish and feed a thirsty land. Came. Stayed. Lasted deep into the night.

Day forty-six was overcast but with a band of light on the horizon, as if the last vestiges of rain were winging their way to parts unknown. We waited hopefully until 8:00 a.m., willing it to rain and allow us our first Saturday off in months.

But alas, alack, the sky grew brighter with each passing moment, and regretfully we bid Sylveste and each other goodbye, then headed out in opposite directions, each to our own work and toil; thirty minutes to arrive, fifteen to climb down into a valley, say hello to farmers and begin the day's work.

Another thirty minutes, and what's this? Dark grey shadows materialize out of nowhere, spilling over the edge of the mountains. Enormous white clouds fall from the cliffs like waterfalls on their way down to us, to spread out, consume. Low and racing with the wind, the smell of ozone is strong and fresh as it approaches, thunder and lightning abounding.

You look at your new farmers. They look at you. Eyes get big and in a rush and flurry of gathered tools, everyone runs, scattering for cover and home.

Except you, of course. You are so overjoyed, ecstatic and thrilled beyond measure to be heading home immediately if not sooner, that you don't mind slowly sloshing back alone to the moto.

You are so happy, that when you fall into a sinkhole hidden by tall grass and filled with water, and the opposite bank knocks the breath out of you and the water enters the top of your boots and fills them up, you don't mind.

You are so exuberant and alive with the prospect of a half-day off, that when you slush up to the moto and find your helmet locked to it (as usual), upside down and full of water (not usual), you just laugh, unlock it, empty it, and pull it onto your head, little jets of water squishing out and down the back of your neck.

And you are so intoxicated with the heady idea of almost forty-eight continuous and uninterrupted hours of time off ahead of you, that when a farmer pads up behind you in the rain and taps you on the shoulder, scaring the pee-waddling out of you, you don't even get mad.

And when he asks you to come look at a possible pond site in the rain, you say OK, because you know it will only take five or ten minutes, and then you will be on your way home!

Even when he leads you across three hundred yards of swampy goo and more sink holes to fall into, you don't mind because you are already soaked to the skin. And you just smile and shake it off when you discover the way to his site would have been two hundred yards shorter and dryer by taking the footpath.

You inspect and dig around, then regretfully tell him his proposed site has too much sand and that he should look for clay (ibumba), pass him a soggy fish book from your soggy pack, shake his hand and slush back to the moto, taking the high road this time, lilting and bounding all the way, like a child discovering the joys of mud for the first time.

--Now you're already wet. Soaked through and thoroughly. The squishing noise inside your boots sounds like the agitator on an old-timey washing machine and there's no way you're going to get any wetter.

But you can get a lot colder riding home at even medium speed. So you decide to go all out and put on your new rain pants and jacket (they just arrived in the mail, thank you very much!) to block the wind.

The trouble with putting on rain pants after it starts raining is that your boots have to go into the holes before the rest of you. And the problem with that is that they've been walking around in the muck and mush and are covered with it.

Now you might ask, "So what?"

Well, for the uninitiated and inexperienced, I will elaborate.

When you put a boot covered with sludge and boue into the top of the pant hole to get to the bottom of the pant hole, a whole lot of the gooey part doesn't make it to the bottom. It sort of grabs on and clings all the way down. So, when the rest of you follows, you are not only wet through and thoroughly, now you have lots of nice gooey slimy stuff to soak into the layers of wet, and an impervious pair of plastic pants to make sure it stays there.

But even that's okay today, because you are going be home in thirty minutes, have a cup of hot tea, send employees home, and relish and relax into almost a whole extra day off.

So you pull out the plastic pants, balance on the left foot, and start to put the other through the right hole. But your new Chinese rubber boots are bigger, clunkier and heavier than the old worn-out, holey American ones that actually bent at the ankle, (you have to wear two pairs of socks just to keep them on) and the heel catches on the elasticized waistband. The elastic stretches just enough to keep you from tumping over sideways into a mud puddle, but not enough to keep you from tipping head first into the seat of the moto.

It's a good thing you have your soggy helmet on, huh?

At last, plastic pants firmly in place, (the goo inside assures that), rain jacket zipped and snapped, and your heart bursting into song, you mount your trusty steed, kick start her slowly into life, stretch your legs out as training wheels and slowly slip and slide your way back to the paved road, boots and helmet sloshing merrily in time to the staccato rhythm of the engine.

--I'm not sure if you know this, but there are several problems with wearing a helmet, soggy or dry, in a tropical rainstorm. If you leave the visor down, it steams over from your breath and you can't see. If you raise it even a little, to get circulation and erase steam, rain comes in from the top, runs down the inside where you can't get to it to wipe it off, and again, you can't see. If you raise the visor altogether, the rain blinds and stings your eyes and guess what? You can't see.

So what do you do? You try combinations of all three, say a Hail Mary, and drive blind.

--Something else you never think much about is rain gear or its construction, unless or until it doesn't fulfill its function of keeping you dry. Rain jackets and plastic pants usually work very well as long as you are standing still or walking around upright.

If however, you are foolish enough to ride a moto in the rain with them, there are several peculiarities in their construction that cause you to question the intelligence of wearing them altogether.

Our rain jackets have an inner zipper with an outer flap that snaps to keep the rain from coming in through the zipper teeth. But if you sit on a moto, you find that neither the zipper nor the flap or snaps lay flat. They gather and pooch, creating gaps for the rain to enter.

You also discover that helmets are designed to catch rain and funnel it, either down the chin guard so that it pours directly into the zipper-snap-flap channel, or down the back of your neck into your unmentionables.

You may also discover while sitting astride the moto, that the plastic pants with your legs inside form a U-shaped dam between the gas tank, the moto seat, and your behind.

Therefore, what water isn't absorbed into your interior dryness via the zipper, snap, flap contraption of the jacket, is funneled down to the dam between your legs, collecting in quantities sufficient to permeate the inside seams of the plastic pants, thus slowly infiltrating to the private parts and on down the legs and into the boots.

This is not a particularly pleasant feeling and it's not long before water begins to fill the boots and overflow--like a fountain.

But, speeding for home in the pouring rain, you don't even mind this inconvenience today.

You pull up into your very own driveway and see Sylveste standing at the window watching the rain. You slosh up to the front door and begin to peel off the boots, plastic pants and jacket.

Sylveste wrings his hands and groans when he sees all the mucky, muddy goo clinging to the clothes so fresh and clean just two hours earlier. But you dispel his fears of more washing on a rainy day, thank him for the week's work and send him home with a bonus just for being sweet, and he too, is now happy.

You empty your boots and wring out your socks as Odance wanders in through the rain with enough fresh greens to last the rabbits the weekend. Him, too, you send away into the grey curtain with a bonus, a smile, a "thanks", a "Turabonanye" and an "Au revoir".

You sponge off, change into dry clothes, dry socks, dry shoes, towel dry your hair, make hot chocolate and hot tea, put on music and collapse into blithering giggles of ecstasy just as your mud-covered husband rides up on his moto.

Now--what to do with almost an entire extra day off?

First, think I'll go write a letter...Anatomy of a Rainy Day.

Chapter 80
Washington, D.C.

Dear Folks,

Greetings from Burundi, almost Washington D.C. Yes, I said
Washington! Peace Corps is flying us to D.C. for three days! Why?
Read on!

Each year, Peace Corps selects a current volunteer from each of the
three geographic work regions around the world whose work and
accomplishments reflect the goals, ideals, and visions of Peace Corps in
promoting world peace and progress.

And guess what? We're it. At least for the sub-Sahara Africa
region. Well, I'm it, actually, but we're a team and I wouldn't be here if
not for Jim, so, we're flying to Washington for three days (We have to
pay Jim's way, but I won't go without him) to accept the John F.
Kennedy Volunteer of the Year award at the White House.

And not because we have so many ponds. But because we've
established really good relationships with our farmers under difficult
cultural conditions in a land that doesn't take readily to strangers, and
also because we have incorporated multiple secondary projects that fit
well with the primary, all of which are doing well at the moment.

We weren't even aware there was such a thing until a month ago,
when our APCD, Mona, called us in and said she'd like to nominate both
of us, but that the system only allowed for one and that I was it.

And even then, we hadn't expected anything to come of it. We have
been so busy trying to keep up with our run-away farmers, that we
haven't had time to pay attention to much else. And it was nice just to
be nominated.

--When does all this happen? We fly out the 24th of April, arrive
D.C. the 25th, start whatever it is they want us to do the 26th, finish in
D.C. the 27th, then fly to Dallas that same day for two days of publicity

and recruitment. (Possibly to Oklahoma City or Chicago also?) We will be allowed a few days of our vacation-time to see family, drink O.J., eat tons of apples, some dill pickles, hamburgers and popcorn, then it's back to Africa to work on fish ponds for five months to end of service. Crazy, yes?

Sabena (Belgian) Airlines has graciously donated one round-trip ticket, which helps the Peace Corps budget out, if not ours.

Just a bit of Trivia FYI: In 1985, the annual budget for U.S. Military bands was more than was allotted for all of Peace Corps that same year. P.C. doesn't even have money enough for the housing, transportation or project funding of volunteers, and P.C. staff spends most of their time looking high and low for outside donations and grants from organizations like FICAH (Food Industry's Crusade Against Hunger, funded by the Grocer's of America) to name one, partnership programs, and other business or private organizations just to survive.

If Peace Corps is to continue, and be counted as a professional organization in the International Development field, reliable permanent funding for essential services and support must be found.

The bad news? Unfortunately, the award ceremonies will take another week or two away from our farmers, and they are already concerned we are going to leave before they learn everything they need from us.

The fish are growing by leaps and bounds, much better even than we expected, and growth samples indicate that the one hundred fifty ponds will produce upwards of fifteen tons of fish per year, just in our area!

Now that's something to celebrate! More later on the trip as details are realized and released to us.

Love and lotsa hugs,
The temporarily comin' home gang!

Chapter 81
After Washington

Dear Family,

Just a quick letter of bits and bites to let you know we are back safe and sound in our Technicolor house. Thanks for sending Carol to join us in D.C. It was great to see her, and have a family representative there for the award, just sorry Dad wasn't well for you two to make the journey.

* * *

The trip to D.C. was exciting and the award quite an honor (we met V.P. Bush and First Lady, Barbara, in the Roosevelt Room of the White House–the President was tied up with an unexpected visit from a Prime Minister--Japan, I think?)

One of the many nice experiences: we went to lunch in D.C. with representatives of FICAH (Food Industry Crusade Against Hunger) to let them know how very much we appreciated their support and how important transportation was to our work. FICAH donated enough this year to our fish program to pay for transportation costs; motos and gas, plus the Fish truck, all of which have been essential to the success of our program, so the award is as much their's as ours. I hope we conveyed how grateful we were for their contributions and support.

--A couple of interesting side notes. The U.S. changed another 90 degrees while we were plodding away here in Africa. Example: We both had headaches from 24 hours of nonstop travel) and asked for an aspirin at P.C. headquarters. Five people whipped out different compounds for headaches with names that didn't exist before we left (Excedrin, Advil and Motrin).

New words and phrases have arisen in our absence, like 'couch potato', 'way-cool', RAM and ROM and many more words that have already become commonplace or even passé already, in the year-and-a-half we've been gone.

One of the P.C. folks said it was new movies, another the sudden explosion and growing use of personal computers, of better instant communications.

Either way, we feel like we have been left behind as life moved on without us.

Hardest part? Having to shop for new clothes to wear to the ceremony. Holy Cow, the prices! I realize it's the nation's capital, but, Wow. Especially since shopping is not something either of us enjoys and we had to dip into savings to buy me shoes and a dress, and a suit for Jim, that we will probably never wear again.

Worst part? No time to pick up things we really could use, some more nets for fish harvests, new rubber wellingtons and a few more pair of jeans.

Peace Corps personnel were terrific though, took great care of us, shepherding us here and there with valuable advice and 'catch up' information.

P.C. flew us to Fort Worth for some local P.R. in Dallas, and then gifted us with a few days with family. It was so good to see you again and thanks for driving all the way! We also appreciate Laura, Bill and the boys making the effort to drive in from Midland (they are doing such a great job as parents), and a huge thank you to Dawn for loaning us her Honda for the four days--what a gift! The Zants came through with the fish caps for our farmers, and radios for our employees, well-packed and ready to bring back!

Enjoyed catching up with them, then the rest of the family by phone, then on to Chicago (Jim's folks, brother and family drove up to see us at the airport before we flew back to Burundi. Was great to give and get hugs and appreciated the time and effort they made.

* * *

--We hit the bikes first thing Monday to see our governor, administrators, and farmers. Everyone wanted to hear about the TV, newspapers and award from V-P Bush. They are excited to get some positive press for a change, to have people know some of the many good things about Burundi.

* * *

--We just had a nice interview at our ponds with a reporter from the Washington Post, Blaine Hardin, who covers this region of Africa and wanted to do a follow up to our award. He took photos and everything. More on this later.

--We had expected to jump right back into work, but this trip thing has generated a mountain of paper work, all due for completion before we left (though they actually didn't give us enough time to do that), and P.C. has taken lessons from the IRS in confusing forms in triplicate!

Three late night trips to Buja and we are still not in the clear.

* * *

The next four months will pass all too quickly. If new volunteers don't replace us, it will be especially difficult to leave our farmers. The political climate here continues to be uncertain, and talk is getting stronger that the program will not be renewed, even with all the good results from our ponds and the good publicity. Fooey.

We still are not sure about our life after Peace Corps. Is there any? We need to seriously consider what we are going to be in our next life or when we grow up, whichever comes first.

But better go for now. Have some rats in the attic to chase and catch. A new family moved in upstairs in our absence, and they are a noisy bunch.

--The transistor radios we brought back for our three employees were a big hit. They giggled all day in the back yard, changing stations every five minutes. (Vyance hung around to talk to the other two guys this morning.) Three separate radios going full blast on three different stations doesn't do much for our peace (piece) of mind, so we made a rule: no radios on when we are home. Fortunately we're not here much during the day, so they are quite happy with the arrangement.

Vyance does keep his turned on some at night, thinking the rule doesn't apply after lights out, but it's mostly music, so it's OK.

Tired. Gotta get some shut-eye. More later.

Love and Lotsa hugs,

Hey you and What's-her-face

Chapter 82
Goma Gorillas

Dear Family,

Our poor farmers. They think we've abandoned them, and rightly so. We'd planned long ago to go with friends who will soon be leaving, (former Peace Corps volunteers-- now here with a potato project) to see the gorillas in Zaire (Congo) and though it's only a few weeks since we returned from the trip to Washington (which we hadn't anticipated), Gorilla time has arrived.

Since it's only for a few days and we are not planning to take our second year's allowance of vacation, and we already had our visas ready to go before we learned of the Washington trip, we apologized to our farmers, the Governor and Peace Corps and packed up.

Traveling as passengers in the back seat of their Toyota wagon was an experience. Fitz is one of these wonderfully gregarious, personable, funny types who likes to use his hands and look at you when he talks, never mind if he's in the front seat behind the wheel and you're in the back.

Jim calls it 'digital driving'--head for a cliff and just before you fall off, yank back onto the road, drive straight, yank back--with his wife, Carol, keeping wide eyes on the edge and reaching out to touch him gently and say comforting things like, "Lookout," or "Watch it," or "Fitz!" Frequently.

In a car with super-sensitive steering and a country with hairpin turns and lots of switchbacks, three of us were worn out before we reached Rwanda.

Fitz? He was just fine. And they are both such funny, 'alive' and generous people, with wonderful stories of their time as volunteers in Chad and as ex-pat's here and all the family and time in between, we concentrated on enjoying their company and tried not to watch the road.

We stopped briefly in Butare, Rwanda (to 'spend a penny' at the loo) where we met a man talking wars and rumors of war. He asked how we had crossed the border safely with Rwanda and Burundi shooting at each other?

When we told him we had seen nothing but friendly faces and heard no shooting, it seemed to disappoint him.

Then off in a rush to the other side of Rwanda where we were ordered off to the side while a whole slew of cars pulled up and through the barriers without stopping (turns out they were day workers coming back home and had the proper stickers to pass without question).

We piled out, but couldn't find the border guards as cars kept streaming by. Thirty minutes later we finally roused someone who said, "What do you want?"

"We want to go into Zaire."

"Well, what? On foot?"

We chuckled. "No, no, our car's just over there."

"Well, what are you waiting for? Get on with you!"

We'd driven all the way through the country with no stamp in our passports on either end?

Most unusual. But a hundred feet away at the Zaire border, just as we pulled up to the first swing gate, the new one stuck and the old one in front of it couldn't swing in unless the new one first swung up.

We settled in to watch and wait.

First, the two guys operating the gates sat down and stared at them. As the intensity of their stares increased and the cars piled up behind us, a crowd of guards began to gather, appearing from--well, everywhere. Once they had a sufficient number for a committee opinion, a discussion ensued as to the merits of swing gates along with the possible reasons for them not working. Then it was time for a cigarette while everyone stared and pondered some more.

Grass grew, flies buzzed, sun shone and cars queued up. Just as we decided it was time to lend a little elbow grease to the situation, a customs official roused from his paperwork and looked out the window. A chair overturned, he rushed out, gesturing angrily about the traffic held up behind us and instructed the guards to put their backs into it and get things moving.

So up some jumped, cigarettes sailing in the breeze and hopped up onto the cement counter-weight, while others shook their heads in concern over this unpremeditated move.

Up went the new gate, in swung the old and we were off in a cloud of dust--for a hundred yards. We pulled in and screeched to a halt in front of the Zaire Immigration Office as a line of cars zoomed past us once more.

Pile out, lock doors, climb steps, knock on windowsill, and--no response. Peer in, nobody home. Walk around to side door and--Aha! There is a second desk hidden behind the window that contains a body with its head on the desk, feet tapping to music only he can hear.

"Uh, Sir? Excuse me, Sir?" You say, again, "Sir, Excuse me?"

No response. Walk over and lightly touch his shoulder.

"Aaaggghh," he groans, his head raising an inch and then drops back onto the desk, feet still tapping. You back off, realizing he's not quite present to this world.

Outside again, you speak to a man who has appeared on the steps, "Oh, Sir, Excuse me for troubling you, but we need someone to stamp our passports."

Man looks at you then over at a woman you hadn't noticed under a tree and jerks his head toward us. Slowly, she pulls her considerable self up, ambles over and much to our consternation disappears with all four passports behind the building.

Five anxious minutes later, a giant in uniform slowly and carefully flows around the corner and enters the office. Giant kicks at the spaced-out body, rousing him just long enough to pull two logbooks out from under the lolling head. All this time, one of Giant's hands is cupped tightly closed over something while the other struggles with our four passports and the two large log books.

Giant flows slowly over to the other desk and melts gracefully into the chair, pushes everything to one side, retrieves an envelope, and with very serious concentration brushes contents from cupped hand into envelope, folds over three or four times, places it carefully in a drawer, opens log books, closes each passport (which we'd mistakenly opened to the appropriate pages), folds his hands and at last looks up at us, smiling sweetly and slowly saying in French, "What can I do for you today?"

We explain we want to enter his country.

"Oh, is that all?"

He picks up the first passport, opens it so that all the folds fall out, spreads them out further, and makes much ado of finding the appropriate page, then writes copious amounts of information (more than you knew was in the entire passport) in his log, stamps the passport, identifies its owner and hands it to Fitz.

As this process continues, our friends are accosted by a man whose clothes are in disarray and who looks a bit challenged, in fact, appears impaired, and has great difficulty speaking.

Their French is very good, but unable to understand him, they finally wave him off and disappear into customs with their car papers.

As Jim retrieves his stamped passport, the same awkward man grabs hold of him, pleading with him to come out back. Jim finally figures out that he wants our health cards, and agrees to be dragged to the rear of the building.

It seems splitting us up is part of a plan, because all this time I've been watching as the man outside from the steps and the woman have casually strolled over to the car.

He nods very slightly to her to try the door. She shrugs back that I'm watching. He glances back at me, grins and eases over to lean against the car as if in conversation.

Giant tries to distract me. "That must be your brother you are traveling with as you have the same name."

I smile sweetly, "No, Sir, that is my husband."

"Oh, pity. Will you be staying long in Zaire?"

"No, Sir, less than a week."

"Pity, but perhaps I will see you again, anyway?"

"Perhaps."

Customs man now moves gracefully in front of the window to block my view of the car as man and woman vigorously try all the doors. I ease out of immigration past Giant and step down to car as man and woman innocently resume leaning up against it.

They smile at me, I smile at them, all sharing in the big joke of providing for oneself in an honest world, and we are asked to pay them a 'tip' for watching the car, which in the spirit of International relations, we did.

As we drive away, Jim tells us that the 'Health man' made a big deal of studying our health cards, and finally put two big check marks into his logbook by the day's date, no names, just checks.

We were the only ones that day? With his external infirmities, I am sure he doesn't entice many back to his lair.

And we are still not certain these were legitimate officials or merely some creative entrepreneurs taking advantage of an opportunity during the lunch hour. Everyone else seemed to be just driving on through. But after a short discussion we decided it was much better to have a stamped entry in our passports should any problems arise.

* * *

Safely across the border, we drove at last into the thriving city of Goma for a look-see.

What you see is fields and acres of billows and bubbles of fresh black volcanic rock, black streets, black powdery soil, gray buildings and a monochrome black atmosphere that would be perfect for a science fiction movie backdrop.

At first glance, one would never know it was situated on the shores of Lake Kivu, one of the prettiest and deepest lakes in the world. But on this perfect, clear day, we can see the lake and it has almost no activity on it. We soon discover why.

This is an active volcanic region and the lake harbors deadly layers of methane gas in its dark depths, usually kept trapped by its cold waters. But inversion layers periodically cause the methane to be released suddenly surface-ward, killing living things in its path--fish, people, any and everything, and they lose a dozen people a year from it.

The government has been able to capitalize on the methane in one area by pumping it to the surface and selling it, and they hope to obtain investment and research monies to tap into it further as an alternative energy source. Good for them!

We tried walking on the surface of the fresh lava fields, but quickly retreated back to the car, as the unforgiving undulations of black rock are a perfect place to break an ankle, skin a shin or fall and bump a head.

* * *

We spent a half-day with Trudy and Phil, our Canadian friends, promising to stop for a longer visit on the return portion of the trip, then were up and off early the next day to tour the Virunga National park at the edge of the Ruwenzori mountains, near Uganda. Lions and antelope were plentiful (we got some great photos of lion cubs playing King-of-the-mountain on a termite hill) but a drizzling rain and fog hid most other wildlife from view.

We saw off in the distance a huge cleared area with lots of unusual activity. An old DC-3, a new helicopter and a huge white tandem refrigerated transport truck off-loaded huge amounts of equipment and supplies and before our eyes, erected several enormous 'circus tents', complete with generators, lights, sound-system, air-conditioning and music.

We wondered what kind of display they were putting on, but no one seemed inclined to answer our questions.

The park's hotel rental bungalows were very nice with private baths and good beds that we almost got to sleep in. But loud-pounding knocks at the doors in the wee hours of the night had us fearing the worst. The armed soldier doing the 'rousting' explained we would have to leave immediately because the President was flying in, and his minor staff members needed our rooms.

Not a good idea to alienate the President of the country you are in or argue with folks carrying automatic weapons, so we smiled our cooperation, packed up, moved out and semi-slept in the car. The good news is we were up early to enter the park for animal viewing with the sunrise. I think we got some really good shots of a lion pride with new cubs, and hippos at a mud-wallow.

As the day wore on we were still periodically in sight of the tents, and though the President did not arrive at the lodge, some of his entourage passed us on their way there that morning. By-the-by, it was amazing to see huge colorful blow-up air tents in the isolated and remote golden savannah.

Music, noise and lights filled the still, hot air. A military vehicle approached and we were politely asked to leave the area completely, prior to the President's arrival, so off we went down the track.

* * *

Tired, sleep-deprived and with no breakfast in site, we opted to head on up to the German Zoological cabins maintained for overnight visitors to the Gorilla park.

On the way, we touched the northern shores of a lake we didn't know the name of just to say we had, stared at the beautiful tall peaks of the Rwenzeri mountains of Uganda, just visible way off in the blue haze of the horizon, and searched diligently for food, finding some goat brochettes and peanuts at one stop, and nominal groceries at a small store.

Ordinarily tourists enter from the Rwandan side of the mountains as it is much more accessible, but a U.S. film crew has rented the Rwandan Park for the entire month to film Gorillas in the Mist, so it is closed to tourists. Rumor says they paid Rwanda $17 million dollars for the exclusive use of the park for two months, so hope it helps preserve and protect the park and the gorillas after the filming.

Sadly, rumors are drifting back through local sources that the film crew has been at least temporarily detrimental to some of the habituation work Fossey accomplished by disturbing the gorilla bands to get dynamic shots. Whether true or not (the rumor mills here are as healthy as back home and often wildly exaggerated), we hope to see her work of protection carried on once they leave and that the subsequent showing of the film helps to save them.

These are the last mountain gorillas in the wild (less than 400 remain) and are the ones Dian Fossey was working with when she was murdered in Rwanda our first year here.

Poaching is still severe, but opening the parks to visitors seems to have temporarily ensured their survival. The attention of daily tours and the publicity have done as much to protect them as any laws or game wardens.

Though wardens patrol constantly to fend off the poachers (their own lives and the lives of their families are at risk), they can't be everywhere at once and their job is complicated by the fact that the gorillas move to a new 'bedding site' every night, so it is difficult to keep up with them.

* * *

--Now, a bit about eastern Zaire roads. Did I say roads? While a few are paved, most are not and large-wheeled lorries (trucks) and tropical rains have seen to it that said roads resemble well-mined pieces of real estate. Holes are large enough to swallow entire trucks, and they exist in profusion (holes and trucks).

(Phil told us of seeing a lorry that HAD actually disappeared down into one such hole and never emerged, leaving just the top showing at road level, so they put down logs and used it for the foundation of a bridge--termites can't eat through it don't you know. Still not sure if he was teasing, as he can tell the funniest stories with a straight face.)

* * *

--Following a small sign branching off the main one-and-a-half-lane road, it took three and a half hours to maneuver the next twenty six kilometers, with three of us walking most of the way to give better clearance to the car bottom.

Where we arrived was a dead-end, no signs, no path, nothing but mountains towering above and around us. Kids began showing up by the plenty though, almost as soon as we stopped, along with three men willing to show us the way.

We settled on one strong-looking fellow to help carry our paraphernalia (otherwise known as 'stuff') up the mountain.

(Fitz and Carol had packed enough food and accessories to supply a small army, for which we were truly grateful, though they wouldn't take compensation for our share. One of our own contributions turned out to be not so good--two cans of tuna which upon opening and re-reading the label, was actually a small amount of tuna (well, it smelled like fish) in a large amount of sauce with some unrecognizable vegetables pieces--yum--one should always read the fine print.)

We hiked one kilometer--up and up--to a cabin built by the Frankfurt Zoological Society and found an eclectic collection of eight nice folks also signed up for the tour, twelve half-beds (dormitory style, men on one side, women on the other), clean rooms, clean sheets, cooking utensils, a stove, water and an outhouse! Yipppee! What else could a traveler ask for? (We also discovered how fortunate we were that there were four extra slots for us, as most visitors had signed up months in advance.)

We shared cooking, food, cleanup and backgrounds with our new compatriots then hit the sack for a deep sleep.

We were up at the crack of dawn, breakfasted and excited to begin our journey, then waited till nine a.m. for our guides to arrive (they like to give the gorillas time to wake up, feed, take morning ablutions and enjoy the day before the troupe moves on). Our group of six set out to see Marcel and his family, while the other group of six traveled to see Oscar and family.

* * *

--You hike into the forest along well-worn, volcanic-rock-strewn jungle paths, wondering if the smoke coming from the top of the next mountain over is an indication that it is going to 'blow' soon, while your guides stealthily look for 'sign'.

As you travel deeper, the jungle is not what you expected. No Tarzan-vines, no trumpeting elephants, no enraged leopards charging out of the forest, not even many birds--but thousands and maybe millions of flies. (Flies in Central East Africa are not like their domesticated American cousins. You can't shoo them away even with a fly swatter. They cling and hang around and will crawl right up your nose or into your eyes if you let them, and even if you manage to brush them off or away, they are right back seconds later!)

And Oh! What's this? Step lively now, hup-one-two--army ants-- and can they swarm all over you and bite before you know what you are about! No one looks dignified or 'cool' gyrating in wild circles slapping and pulling the little buggers off.

By now, you are certain you have created enough noise to scare off wildlife within several kilometers (except for the flies and ants, of course).

Then you leave the trail behind and follow guides through foul-smelling plants towering twice your height. The Jungle floor is NOT anymore! Such a tangled mass of plant life you have never seen. Tons and layers of woven, twisting, twining green stuff, and don't step through the holes! You can fall in up to your bum and still not touch bottom, and who knows what lurks in the darkness and shadows below?

And everywhere, the earthy, steamy smell of rotting vegetation. Snakes slither through your mind and you wonder how many vipers you've stepped on, over or under.

An hour later and at last, you're close, (indicated by the very large pile of poo still steaming in a nest of leaves and branches.)

Shhh. Quiet! There they are! Everybody drops to the ground and whispers excitedly. Look! Two juveniles in a tree. Over there--a mama. And all the time your guides are deep grunting in a clear-your-throat-kind-of-way to alert the silverback to your presence, so not to surprise him.

Slowly now--there's the whole group. Everybody stay down. Ow! Oww! Army ants again! Back up quick. Hurry! Shhhh.

Quiet. Try another route. There! Click--Silverback--Whir--Click--Mama and baby--Click--Click--Click. Ohhhh, look!

The best two shots of the day? A pregnant female in a tree, looking down on us, and who seemed to know we were ogling her and were there just for her. She climbed to a tree branch way above us, stretched her arms up and thrust her swollen tummy out for all to admire her soon-to-be-baby--click--click. I swear she posed for us, turning this way and that until everyone had a good photo-op of her.

And the other was of the Silverback watching us intently for signs of danger, then relaxing, lying down on his back, beckoning to the little ones to come play, nuzzling and cuddling them, and lifting them over his head to a tree trunk so they could climb up, down and back into his arms, over and over. A showstopper, as we simply crouched there, barely breathing--and enjoyed.

Such a gift to be allowed to see and experience.

* * *

--Two fascinating hours later, everyone is out of film and our time is way past up (We were allowed to stay an extra hour because we were such a quiet, compliant group, followed instructions, were non-threatening and the band didn't seem to mind us being there. Yipppeee!).

--We walked slowly back in drizzling rain, absolutely enthralled, everyone quiet, reverent and caught up in the magic, overwhelmed with the lovely shy creatures we had been privileged to experience.

Coming back onto the well-worn trail, we spread out, lost in wonder and awe. Hark! What's this? A gigantic mound of poo? Our guides whisper softly that mountain elephants have trodden this very path not ten minutes earlier. Walk softly, slowly and listen close. What was that? It is! A real live trumpeting mountain elephant. Oh, Joy. What a glorious day. Couldn't have been more perfect.

Arrive cabin at 2 p.m. Pack, hike down to car, walk half of 26 km. again to preserve the car, then drive till much past dark to reach Goma, the land of cow cheese and black houses.

* * *

Next day, we bid adieu and bon voyage to our Missouri-bound friends with blessings and hugs, then enjoyed a day with Trudy and Phil, perfect son Daniel and dog, Jake-the-Rake.

One of the fun things we discovered while driving around with them exploring Goma was our first encounter with a round-about, go-around, or rotary, which is like a traffic circle, where drivers on the round-about always have right-of-way over merging oncoming traffic. Glad we don't have these at home. Traffic would be wrecked, snarled and mean forever. We studied it at some length with cars and trucks squealing and whizzing in and out before Phil explained who has the right-of-way, which side to enter from, and how to get off safely once you're on (especially from the inside lane--you can get really dizzy if you don't make the proper lane switch).

SCRABBLE, laughter, talk, love and friendship--then all too soon, we took the long bus ride back to Ngozi to our work-a-day world and wonderful farmers.

Hope all is well with you and yours and thanks for keeping the home-fires burning.

Love and a hug,
Jimani

Chapter 83
Derailed and Betrayed--June

Dear All,

After the chaotic trip to Washington, a week of fast and furious pond work, then the quick trip to see the Goma gorillas, we hit the ground running again and have had great workdays at the ponds.

Our farmers are so excited about the publicity, their fish growth and reproduction, and an announced return of Burundi Television to cover both the Washington award and our upcoming harvests, that they have had their heads in the clouds.

But something has gone suddenly awry and there are rumors from the National Congress meeting (through the ever-present grapevine) that all is not well.

* * *

Please excuse the carbon copies, but the latest news here is just too discouraging to write over and again.

--From the heights of ecstasy to the depths of despair in less than an hour. The summation of our time here. We arrived in from work today to find our P.C. Ad-min., Terry, waiting for us at the house, ready to take all fish-volunteers to Buja for an emergency meeting with our counterparts in the Department of Waters and Forests--to close the program.

It seems the Ministry has refused new volunteers and suggested we find something worthwhile to do for our last four months here, as the program is obviously a failure?

We pressed for reasons from Peace Corps until we finally discovered that the Ministry had used a report from one of our own, a visiting Ph.D. from Washington, to cancel the program.

* * *

He came in January to assess us. We didn't understand why he gave all of us and the fish-program such an immediate hard time, disparaging

us, our ponds and farmers, telling us they would never see results from
their hard work, that we would never see any harvests, the water was too
cold, the altitude too high, that it was all going to fail. It was like being
dragged back into fish training.

We regrouped and responded by trying to show the guy that it was
different here, showing him our sample weights, growth numbers,
elevated pond temperatures, hard-working farmers, farmer exchange
program, well-constructed and hard-tamped dikes with 3:1 slopes, great
plankton blooms, projected harvest numbers and tremendous progress in
such a short time--our farmers even honored him with a banana beer
mini-party to celebrate his being there...

But to no avail, so we 'fishies' collectively shrugged our shoulders
and went back to work--then stewed over it for months, trying to figure
out what we'd done wrong. Didn't write home about it at the time as we
didn't want to comment on something we didn't fully understand and
hoped would blow over. We still don't know how we could have done
any more or different.

And maybe the guy didn't intend for his official assessment letter of
fish culture in Burundi to have such disastrous effects, but it did and has
completely destroyed the efforts of a beautiful, hard-working people
who have never done him a bit of harm. Maybe there is hope for the
project on the horizon and we just can't see it, but it will be too late for
us, or our farmers.

P.C. would not allow us to read the full report (so we suspect it had
negative things to say about us--or maybe there are undercurrents we
simply don't know about)--only the parts that said fish would compete
with rice production, would probably not prove profitable, and definitely
would not survive as a private enterprise.

But we have only 7 hectares of fish against 2200 hectares of rice.
Rice is in the flooded valleys, and fishponds are on the lower sides of
hills and only in heavy clay soil where other things don't grow as well.
Also, fish are selling for $200 FrBu/kilo and rice at $40 FrBu/kilo. Fish
are dense protein and rice is not. The two are compatible and we are
proving they are mutually sustainable.

And to defend our farmers, they not only take excellent care of their
ponds, but of all their other endeavors as well, including communal
labor to support the country's rice production, and all without
jeopardizing food, lives or family provisions.

--Since stability here is both new and fragile and there have been
rumors of program cancellation from the beginning, plus the overall
anti-white sentiment is still strong from the Libya bombing and even

colonialism--all beyond our control--the shutdown might very well have happened anyway. But to have some of our own people give the Ministry the ammunition to pull the plug, well, now we'll never know.

I'm not sure we will ever understand the need to rain unhappiness and misery on the well-being and lives of thousands of innocents when they have the courage to work hard, do a good job and dare to be happy. But I digress, and it doesn't matter now. The damage is done.

* * *

We 'fishies' are all pretty disheartened and have decided to take the offered option of leaving early since we are not sure we will be allowed to stay much past mid-September anyway, much less volunteer for an extended tour, which we were lately considering.

How early we depart depends upon our governor.

He was crushed when we informed him today of the Ministry's decision, as he has been very vocal about how pleased he's been with our work. It made me sad to see him slowly back-peddle for fear he had placed himself in political jeopardy by supporting us so whole-heartedly.

He went from suggesting we train in two special agronomes (extension agents) this last three months, to abandoning the project altogether in the space of five minutes. But then he rebounded within another five, looking for something to salvage and asked us to hang in there (or the equivalent thereof). He has more courage and strength than we at the moment.

He will be journeying down to Buja tomorrow to 'test the waters' and hopefully will return with a better idea of what direction he (and we) can safely take.

So, at the latest, we will leave end of August instead of end of September--at the earliest, the end of July. We will let you know when we know.

Oh, sad, sad day. A good program--a successful one--with great participation and a real future--support from all quarters, including Provincial governors, and we are being thrown out. Bummer! Drat! And Fooey!

It is so hard to face our farmers again with news we are abandoning them and that support is being pulled from the program (they'd heard through the grapevine and knew almost before we did!) Pond construction and stocking has gone so well and we will have proof of profitability from our first major harvests in just weeks. We can only hope we have passed along sufficient knowledge and confidence that some of them will thrive and continue, though typically it takes three or four consecutive groups of volunteers to instill concepts permanently.

Well, Jim's hungry and I'm tired, so it's off to fix supper and early to bed. Hope all is well with you. We are sad and sick at heart and once again looking forward to the end of our contract.

With our program cancelled and our poor farmers lost and out of hope, it is difficult to dredge up day-to-day enthusiasm knowing we'll be leaving them without follow-up in a few months time. Wish we had better news for you, or a better attitude, which here, come to think of it, could come as early as tomorrow, so will write some more then.

* * *

Days later--

Our Provincial Governor continues to be a bright spot in our lives as he's indicated he still appreciates what we and our farmers have accomplished, and he very much wants the program to continue. He has enlisted two extension agents to start training with us immediately (we can't help but wonder if it is at his own expense, but not a good idea to ask).

This support is good news for our farmers (we hope). So we will be staying until around the first of September--and only leave fifteen days early from end of tour, trying to cram as much info into their heads and hearts as possible. But we feel as if our roller coaster has come derailed, and who knows where it or we will land.

* * *

--On another sad note, Sylveste 'fell off his bicycle', mushed his head to concussion size, hurt his knee, and has been off work for two weeks (we have paid for his medications and hospital bills as he wouldn't have had treatment otherwise).

He was back only two days when we arrived home from work to find that he'd given our one good German kitchen vegetable knife (we brought it with us) to the gardener to repair the bamboo fence--for the third time--instead of the machete. (not sure Jim will ever hone a good edge on it again, as it has a permanent hollowed out spot in the center). Poor Sylveste hasn't done any work since his return, and merely sits all day and stares sadly out the window.

We're still not certain he wasn't beaten because of our program being cancelled, or abused by those who resent who he's working for--or robbed for his radio--as he no longer brings it to work...or...we will probably never know, as questioning him further causes him great distress and could get us and him into further trouble, but it feels like he is caught up in 'something not right' and it is worrisome.

* * *

One week later. Sadly, Sylveste's deteriorating work ethic over the last month is only the last in a long chain of frustrations, so we were forced to give him a week off without pay, hoping his energy and enthusiasm would return. He was here yesterday to ask for his job back, but didn't want to start till next week? Said he had some things to do. Wish we didn't fear for his safety and could ask for more details, but it's still not a good idea to know too much here.

In the meantime, we've been doing the laundry and housekeeping rather than train someone else in at this late date, plus we've become really attached to Sylveste and hope he will actually come back to us.

But this, coupled with our regular ten-hour workdays in the field, is wearing us out and down and why we've not written much.

With Love and lotsa hugs,
Temporarily Down and Outa' Luck

Chapter 84
Jamaica!

Dear Family and Friends,

Greetings from Bujumbura! We've just had four days off beginning with the Burundian Independence celebration on July 1st. The fish-emblazoned ball-caps we brought back as gifts from the Washington detour through Texas were a hit with our farmers (Thanks Bill and Theola for making it happen!) We marched with them in the Independence Day Parade in Ngozi with a handmade ten-foot long banner that included each of their commune names, graphics of swimming fish with fingerlings and the project name (Projet Amafi which translates: Project Fish!).

Afterward, we invited our guys over for gallons of banana and sorghum beer, fresh roasted peanuts, and bread (about all we could afford for so many) to let them know how proud we are of them and how we wish them continued success. It was a great day in spite of the looming difficulties.

--Then staff sent word our presence was requested with their blessings over the weekend for a few days on the beach of Lake Tanganyika to boost morale and for our own Fourth of July celebration. Everyone's been down in the dumps over the fish program cancellation. But after talking with the others about their plans for traveling home, we realize that compared to them, we still have a pretty good attitude about the work.

Even though the program is closing, we've met such wonderful hard-working people here on all sides and we hope they will continue on after we've left. At the least we hope we've given them some additional tools they can use in their everyday lives, even if the fish program is no longer supported.

* * *

Speaking of cancellation--sad news--Father Hans (a German priest we've come to respect and love) dropped by for a final visit this week and said he probably wouldn't see us again. He was so disheartened and bereft. He has spent the last fifty years here as a mission priest. He considers this his home and these his people. He has no one in Germany, knows no one and has no place to return to, but his visa has been revoked and he's been given a deadline to leave the country (along with most of the nuns we've met and many other priests).

If we had a home to go home to, we'd invite him to come live with us. We ask for your prayers for the church, the government and the people here.

* * *

--One week later. Surprise--again. We just received a cable from Washington today. It so happens that Peace Corps films its Public Service recruitment commercials every couple of years, and this year it's in Jamaica. Why Jamaica? It looks like many places in the tropical world where Peace Corps works, and it's less expensive than jetting 8,000 miles around the globe to get somewhere with camera crew and equipment or get rained out for days on end.

They've decided to do a segment on fisheries this year to encourage more couples to volunteer, and guess who they want to include? Yep, that's right, yours truly, the Volunteers of the Year from sub-Sahara Africa (that's me and Jim in case you don't remember); all expenses paid for one week starting the end of July.

They've given us the option of finishing our service in Jamaica and coming home from there. This would save P.C. some $5000 in airfare and hotel bills in lieu of bringing us back to Burundi for only two weeks more of work.

It will mean canceling our trip home through India and Asia, but we may consider it. TV stars again! Life as a volunteer certainly has been tough the last three months.

Nothing is final yet, and if details and bureaucracy follow true to form, we will only know the dates and times two or three days after we actually depart, but we are rather excited about it.

After much deliberation, we called Washington to confirm our willingness to sacrifice for the cause in sunny Jamaica.

* * *

--There are six new Peace Corps education and vo-tech volunteers coming in this weekend, which is great for the overall program, but they will be posted in the capital or in schools.

No one will be allowed further work out in the countryside. We think we know now much of the what, who, how and why our successful program was cancelled and with the added betrayal from within, from our own U.S. advisors, we are just saddened.

* * *

To top it off, this Jamaican-film wrench has compressed an already tight time schedule into an impossible one. We are trying to stock and harvest as many ponds as possible before we go, and information meetings with farmers are running us into late hours, usually after dark, which means we travel dangerous roads home.

But we feel we MUST get a good portion of our farmers through an entire cycle before we leave, so at least some of them will have a chance at continuing.

Thank goodness our Governor is still supportive of the program, even if the official government position is not. He and others who have seen the potential may make the difference in the final tally if fish farming is to succeed.

* * *

Surprise again! We just heard the latest rumors circulating, that the government will request our replacements next year--if the harvests go well and reports continue to be positive, so all is not yet lost. (See, told you our attitude would change within a day or two. Not sure I'll ever ride another roller coaster, though–too similar to our emotional time here.)

--And it's still hard to face our farmers with the news that we are leaving them. Everything has gone so well and our first harvests next week will show everyone how profitable fish farming can be.

We arrived here thinking we wouldn't accomplish much in just two years, that what we did would be mostly for own benefit of stretching and growing and making a few lifetime friends.

Then, when we found the farmers to be so terrific, receptive and hard working, and everything looked bright and cheery, to have the rug yanked out from under them just as things were proving out--well, it's very hard to swallow.

We are back to saving our own personal gains out of the experience and pity the poor people.

--The world has grown too small for politics. It's always the little guy who gets hurt, the innocent ones who suffer, and it rarely seems to bother the ones who are making the decisions that alter the lives of a people or a nation. If all the politicians and governments had to actually live by the rules and decisions they imposed on others, there would be a lot fewer rules and regulations made--or better yet, fewer and better politicians--think of that!

(We just read about our own Congress once again refusing to give a cost of living adjustment to social security recipients at the same time they voted themselves another enormous raise. And for the two years we've been here, they've not only given themselves raises, they've delayed signing a balanced budget, which means volunteers don't get paid for months at a time--.)

Well, enough kvetching and pontificating. Gotta' get to work as it seems to be the only positive thing left to do. We promise a better attitude next letter.

Love and lotsa hugs,
Hewe and Aahh-nneeeee-tah
(alias your wandering winsome wastrels)

Chapter 85
Work n' Hurry, Hurry n' Work

Dear Mom and Dad,

Jim here. Hi! Hope things are going smoother there than here. Our celebrity status is almost becoming a burden. Three weeks ago, a correspondent from the Washington Post, Blaine Harden, arrived to do a story about us and our program--due to the Washington award). We found him to be a nice easy-going sort of fellow and had a great time showing, telling, demonstrating and felt we got along with him just fine.

--Later--We just learned that he has a reputation for being tough under that kindly exterior, of not pulling any punches, and it had P.C. worried. A negative article could reflect badly on the program, maybe even be the very straw someone uses to close us down. Thankfully we were totally oblivious to these undercurrents of tension and enjoyed his visit.

* * *

--Later, still, again--Just read the Post article and it was very complimentary to us, Peace Corps and the Ministry, and we've heard they are all pleased, so, Thanks, Blaine!

Our only problem is that all these interruptions take valuable time away from our farmers as we near end of service. When we have a particular day set aside for a group or groups of farmers each week, and we miss their day, it's two weeks lost in work and counseling, and we don't have that much time left.

With no replacements coming, time seems to be compressing, with work growing ever more intense. Any pond issue or problem seems more important than ever before.

* * *

--Good news! The Jamaica filming has been postponed a third time till August 10-14. P.C., Washington has again encouraged us to finish our service in Jamaica and not return to Burundi.

But our first harvests are scheduled during that time. And it is so important to us to be here for instruction, completion of mission, and to celebrate with our farmers by eating farmer-raised fish.

Things just won't be DONE until then. Also, I've been counting on the trip home through India and Asia as a slow re-entry into hectic life at home, so we're being a bit stubborn.

--The fish are doing great and still leaping and bounding up the growth charts. Can hardly wait till harvest. We'll buy some of the bigger ones to give to our Governor, though it's small repayment for all he's done for us.

--One funny thing: Anita and I each tried to give a marketing seminar to our farmers and they laughed at us. They tell us we've done the hard part in showing them how to build ponds and raise fish, but that if there's anything a Burundian knows already, it's how to bargain and sell.

They ARE pretty good at it. I mean, I always leave the market feeling I've just kept my head above water. Time will tell if their marketing skills extend to the fish.

Love,
Jim

Hi again,

Serves me right to finish a letter, seal the envelope, stamp it, and not mail it immediately. Had to steam it open to save the stamp. Our schedule has already changed. P.C. just sent a note up that the Jamaica date has been moved yet again, to August 16th.

Anita is still out working, so haven't discussed it with her yet, but am guessing we'll call it quits after the filming. There's no sense in flying back here for only eight days--jet lag won't even have subsided.

Besides, someone upstairs seems to be telling us something--that maybe we're supposed to come home and skip our trip through the Far East? I was so looking forward to seeing old friends again in India, and they wrote that they were anxiously awaiting our arrival in September, but--?

If we take a week to bask about in the sand in Jamaica after the filming or in Miami near Anita's youngest sister, maybe it will work out for the best in the long run.

--Tick--tick--tick--waiting for her to get home before I seal this up again. Tick--tick--tick.

* * *

Well, as I suspected, we'll probably be stateside bound after the filming. We'll move our harvest schedules up by two weeks and start this coming week, two or three ponds per week as examples, then set up a calendar and a reporting format for them to follow through to February or March of next year, when the original ponds will be ready to harvest again.

Happy Birthday Mom! Hope to see you soon,
Still on the roller-coaster-ride of our lives,
Jim

Chapter 86
Harvests!

Dear Everyone, (please excuse the carbon copies, but best we can do with limited time),

WOW! WONDERFUL! FANTASTIC! AND ALL GOOD THINGS! Guess What? We harvested our first ponds this week and it's better than we ever could have hoped for or dreamed of at this altitude! We AVERAGED 28 kg/are (pronounced 'air' and is defined as 10 meters by 10 meters, which is 30 feet by 30 feet), which is...are you ready for it???? 2464 lbs./acre (1 ton plus per acre!!!!!).

That's double what we were told we could expect two years ago when we started (by the experts from the U.S., and then the 'other guy'), and above even what our growth samples have been showing.

Our best farmers (most experienced and conscientious--the ones we've worked with the longest) got 22% higher with 35 kg/are! If new volunteers could come in and encourage them to use rice bran as an additional food source for the fish, there would be no stopping them or the program! (Using bran would involve a whole new concept of buying bran at a nominal fee to give higher and faster productivity. Up to now, all food: compost--plankton--leaves, etc. has been free and provided by nature. The idea of investing money to give higher yields and thus more profit would take introducing yet another level of learning, and more volunteers.

But then I repeat myself--again--so back to the good stuff.

The coolest thing is that because we are at altitude, the air and water is colder than on the sunny plains, as projected. But not as projected, the fish don't OVER-reproduce from too-warm water temperatures and the resulting harvest (though taking as much as one to two months longer than on the plains) has the perfect ratio of adults to fingerlings. The ponds have the first generation, the adults, which weigh in around a half to three-quarters of a pound, the second generation, at a quarter to a half-pound apiece, (both for sale), and the third generation, the fingerlings, two to three inches long, with enough to restock the pond and sell the rest. Perfect!

* * *

Jim and I spent late evenings last week fabricating a small harvest net for each region, thanks to the skills we learned on the catfish-pond tours of Mississippi during training--nine nets, all totaled! We've left them at central commune offices to be available to each farmer at harvest, with communal administrators agreeing to oversee distribution when needed.

Not the best set-up, (best would be that each pond group had their own nets) but it is the best solution we can think of with no replacement volunteers to oversee the work and no funds to import netting at this late stage.

* * *

This week our farmers harvested four ponds, and talk about a wonderful circus! It drew people from kilometers around and we had difficulty controlling the crowds.

At one of my ponds:

The farmers put the small harvest net in one corner of the deep end, then cut a gradual filtered wedge from the top down, in the dike on the deep end to drain the pond. This species of fish, *Tilapia nilotica,* always swims to the bottom and upstream when there is a current present--always.

The water level fell slowly as farmers deepened the wedge in the dike. We should have seen fish activity in the net in the deep end (seining basin). But the puddle got smaller and smaller and still no sign of the fish.

The crowds pushed and jostled to the dike edges, trying to see, and the poor unfortunates on the front line began to be pushed over to slip and fall down the slippery muddy slopes into the pond.

That's when Jim and I and a few volunteers took over crowd control (to protect the integrity of the dikes our farmers had worked so hard to establish as perfect 3:1's). We grabbed sticks and began jumping up and down, chasing and whacking (very gently).

It was all done in fun and pretty much useless anyway. Sort of like a school of fish when you are scuba diving. You wave your hand and they fall back out of harm's way, but the moment you retreat or your attention is drawn elsewhere, they surge forward and pick up more ground, until they are right back where you started.

Impatient, the crowd began to question our farmers and make catcalls, "Hey, where are the fish?" insinuating there weren't any.

"Perhaps they've all been stolen! Foolish farmers. It has all been for nothing!"

Just then someone in the crowd shouted, "Hey, look at that!"

Everyone turned in the direction of his pointing finger and looked back up at the steep mountain rising high on the other side of the nearby, red-dirt coffee-road. Two men, mounted on one bicycle, were bouncing down a narrow footpath lickety-split, ducking under banana and taro leaves to come see the fish harvest.

What they didn't appear to know was that in preparation for the rainy season, the local communal road crew had just yesterday dug a three-foot-wide trench alongside and parallel with the road, and had removed the several hand-tamped dirt bridges between mountain and road, including the one the bicyclists thought they were headed for.

The crowd waited, breathless in delighted anticipation of the upcoming disaster. And sure enough, the driver saw the open ditch too late. The front wheel plunged in, hit the opposite bank and violently catapulted both men up and over the handlebars, head over tea-kettle, slamming them into the road. They didn't appear to slide well.

Half the crowd fell on the ground laughing and the other half ran over to see the injuries up close and offer help to the infirmary.

All this commotion perturbed my crew, and just to show the hecklers, they hauled up the net prematurely. About half of the three hundred and fifty fish escaped down into the mud, but the other half came up in the net, flopping and flipping muddy water everywhere.

That's where we almost lost the whole thing. The crowd screamed in jubilation and surged forward to partake of the harvest. Our farmers managed to fend the mob off till they settled down, talking, yelling, gesturing and talking until the crowd finally realized that if they wanted fish, they were going to have to pay for them.

--Once the pond was completely seined and three hundred fifty of the perfect-size little fingerlings were reserved and installed in the small, clean, adjacent holding-pond for re-stocking (with guards over them the next three days), we began to count, clean and weigh the rest of the fish, showing farmers how to tabulate their harvest, showing them weights and measures with our scale, then having them find local equivalent alternatives for the weights that they could use to estimate harvests in the future.

They were ecstatic. Since then, they've given the pond three days to dry out (to make sure all fish were collected and none remain buried down in the mud to interfere with restocking numbers.

--Buried, you ask? Yes. These fish are amazing! They can bury themselves down in the mud, slow their respiration to almost nothing and if not removed, when water is added back to the pond up to a week later, will swim and thrive again!)

--Not resting on their laurels or our kudos, my guys immediately went about repairing the dike, hauling and tamping in new clay soil, waited three days for it to dry and settle, added water and new compost to the pit, and re-installed their reserved fingerlings to start the process all over again. And all during that time, you could see the wheels turning in their heads as they truly 'got it'. Their ponds, their fish, their harvest, over and again. And the esteem they are now held in their neighbor's eyes has been worth all the toil, sweat and tears. Wow.

* * *

--Jim's first-pond guys made a small fortune on their harvest, but one of mine surprised me by only (and reluctantly) selling two dozen to me (as our gift to the Governor and to their local administrator) and a very few to neighbors. They said, MAYBE next time they would sell at the market, but this first time, they wanted to eat fish till they were sick. I understand they had a great feast and cleaned all remaining 80 kilos down to the bones.

* * *

To show you how tough these fish are, the ones we bought to gift to our governor, we'd rinsed off and set aside in wet burlap bags in the shade while we finished tabulating the harvest. Two hours later, we packed up, strapped them to the moto seats and carried them the thirty kilometers home.

Once there, we cleaned up, changed, and only then filled the kitchen sink with water to rinse the fish off before delivering them to the governor's house. Surprise!

Dried up, glassy-eyed fish began to breathe again as soon as they hit the water, then came alive, splashing, swimming and trying to jump out. What great fish! We carefully put them in a bucket of water and walked them over to the Governor's house, only to find he was in Buja at a meeting but was expected back that evening. We understand he was very happy with them.

My next week's harvesters have assured me they want to sell their fish (they've already heard how much Jim's guys made last week), so the community has something to look forward to.

I've left write-ups with illustrations on multiple safe fish preservation and preparation techniques at P.C. headquarters to be translated into Kirundi for later distribution through local administration, but really could use another volunteer to follow through with this phase of fish culture and marketing. But there I go again, repeating myself.

* * *

--Two weeks later--our time's almost up and harvests continue to be a dream come true. Productivity and numbers hold steady and everyone is tickled beyond imagination at the results. We've made up schedules for harvests of two per week in the active areas to continue ad infinitum.

Oh, and yes, we purchased one fish just for us, and ate it to the bone in personal celebration of a job well done, in spite of final disappointments. It was great!

Oh, Happy Day and Hooray! These three weeks have made the entire two and a half years worthwhile.

--One week later. As a parting gift this week, Jim and I both came down with the flu (yuck! Too many trips to Buja to clear up old paperwork and start on new stacks!), so we haven't worked nearly as hard as we've needed to in order to wind things up. It's cold and overcast today (it has rained the last three nights--so unusual during the dry season).

Tomorrow we descend to Buja to start end-of-service physicals and--more paper work. Parties through-out the weekend to say goodbye and thanks to our terrific American and ex-pat community, more paper work Monday and Tuesday, then back up to Ngozi Wednesday to pack up, say goodbyes, drink banana beer with our farmers one last time, and then we're off to be TV stars in Jamaica.

--Can hardly believe it's here. Time to go home. If the program were continuing, at this point we would definitely volunteer to stay another year, but we had to say tearful goodbyes to our farmers this week. They don't normally cry in public, but we've all shed plenty of tears in these parting days. (Though to my everlasting regret, I missed several pond gatherings due to the flu.)

We told them the best present they could give us was to have courage and continue to be the best fish farmers they could be; that we were proud of them; that they'd done well and far above what we could have hoped; that they were our friends and had given us much joy; that we'd try to come back someday; and that we hoped new volunteers would arrive in a year from now and find they weren't needed because they (our farmers) had done such a good job in our absence.

The farmers gave similar speeches of thanks back to us and promised to keep up their spirits and remember everything.

We will never forget the lessons of absolute courage, laughter, and light we learned from the people in this distant land.

* * *

--Speaking of lighter sides, there is one single good thing about leaving. We only have ONE more bus ride and we are home free, with no accidents!

(On a side note, I don't think we told you that we finally learned how to pick out which bus to ride. We made friends with a Muslim man, Salamoni, after our first year here. He's friendly, a great guy, and if we let him know when we need a ride, he reserves two places for us, fills up the bus, then drops by to pick us up on the way out of town!

Terrific, yes? I only mention that he's Muslim because he doesn't drink, so it is a very safe and pleasant ride when we are with him, and we only have to ride the smaller mini-vans on his days off, (and most of those are fairly safe, just sardine-can crowded).

Best go now. It appears we have tons of FINAL REPORTS to do before they'll let us out of here. We still haven't cleared up the travel documents from our trip to D.C. It may be years before we're exactly legal and free again.

See you in September!
Love and hugs and full of banana beer,
Hewe and aahh-nneeeee-tah

P.S.

We gave parting gifts to our farmers and the governor, sold or gave our meager belongings to locals and ex-pats, gave our left-over money to P.C. headquarters for our fellow-volunteers to have a party in our name, then stayed up for two days and nights to finish reports and recommendations for the P.C. staff, the two chauffeurs and our employees; followed by mounds of other paper work. We missed saying and hugging goodbye to almost everyone and caught a rush ride to the airport, with four beautiful, color, hard-back books about Burundi arriving as a farewell gift from our Governor at the last second. The slow time never arrived, and here it is already, Time to go Home.

Chapter 87
Winding Down

Peace Corps made a great recruiting commercial in Jamaica. The acting was fun and we enjoyed working with both the U.S. film crew and the Jamaican 'extras'. We were filmed in a jeep instead of on motorcycles (the jeep was actually pushed from behind out of camera view because we weren't allowed to drive--the jeep or the motorcycles), but if it encourages even just one person to sign up, it will have been worth it. I should mention that the entire U.S. film crew, including their award-winning director, donated their time and energy and paid their own expenses to and from Jamaica to support the Peace Corps effort. As did the voice-over actor, Mr. Harry Belafonte. Many thanks and kudos to them all! And thanks to Peace Corps' PR representative, Deedie R., who made our time there great fun and helped us begin a slow decompression from the two years of focused work.

* * *

In the fall of 1987 I was chosen as an Outstanding Alumna by my Alma mater. The acceptance address gave a sense of closure to our work in Africa, a way to bring back all that we had learned to people here at home.

* * *

Address:
I don't know if I can convey to you what an honor it is to have been selected to be here today. Especially when I look back on my academic career. I feel in a very tiny way like the Nobel Prize winning Physicist, Richard Feynman, who, after receiving his prize in Stockholm, stopped in Queens, N.Y. on his way home and looked up his old school records.

"My grades were not as good as I remembered them," he said, "and my I.Q. was only 124, considered just above average."

But his wife said he was delighted with this discovery.

He said, "To win a Nobel Prize is no big deal, but to win it with an I.Q. of 124--now that is really something!"

* * *

"For me, to be here today is really something, considering the many really outstanding folks chosen before me. While my grades were not as good as I remember them, this is where my real education in the world began; the first time away from the farm and my small home town, where I encountered new ideas, new people, possibilities, opportunities, new horizons, a place for dreams to begin their journey to reality.

Of the years since graduating from Southwestern, I've worked at a variety of occupations: as a surgical scrub tech/circulator, a florist's assistant, a chemical lab technician, technical supervisor, environmental specialist, bronze foundry technician, a professional artist, and as a Peace Corps Volunteer.

And each of these experiences has helped propel me toward today, the beginning of the rest of my life.

--Because Peace Corps Volunteer of the Year, or SWOSU Alumna of the Year are only the results of ordinary choices and challenges, recognized as opportunities and acted upon.

Some of my successes I can attribute to a positive attitude and some to a willingness to step out and take risks. But more of them, I believe, are due to the support and encouragement of a few key people:

--My parents, who always told me I could do or become anything and anyone I wanted--with hard work, ethics and a sense of humor.

--An industrial employer, who gave me an opportunity for which I had no experience and few qualifications.

I worked hard...and they said, "Hey, you did good. Now, here's a chance to be a supervisor."

So I did. And I worked hard. And they said, "Hey, you did good. Now, here's a chance to be an Environmental specialist."

And I did. And they said "Hey, you're doing good, we're going to move you up and on to bigger and better things."

And I said, "Thank you, but, no. I'm going to quit and become an artist--something I've always wanted to be."

And half of them said, "What? You're going to give up all of this? A chance for security, your future? Vested rights? To be an artist? Are you crazy? You did BAD!"

But the other half said, "Good for You! Wish I could go do something like that. Go for it!"

And I did. And I did good. Thanks in great part to:

--My spiritual advisors and mentors, Jesuit and Diocesan priests who helped me find the center within and bring that joy into everyday living.

--And another employer and mentor, who taught me the bronze art industry, launching me into a career in the fine arts, answering a driving quest to create beauty from the heart.

--Then I met this good fellow who became my husband, and we wondered what with no children and everything most people dream of obtaining, if there wasn't some way we could go and do something for somebody else.

We didn't want to preach or sell anything or give away things with strings attached--we just wanted to teach by example, teach someone to help themselves, and let them know, "Hey, you did good! You can do it! Go for it!"

So we did.

* * *

In East Africa, we introduced modern intensive fish culture to humble, subsistence farmers.

We showed them how to select pond sites and how to build ponds.

We labored and sweat alongside them with blisters and callouses and aching backs to show for it.

We laughed and cried with them through their efforts. And we learned to laugh a lot at ourselves, to not take things so seriously.

We jumped up and down for joy on the days that water went into their ponds for the first time...and stayed there.

We celebrated the days we transported and installed their first fish.

And we celebrated again with their first harvests when they sold and ate, farmer-raised fish.

We said, "Hey look, you can do this. This is yours. Now take it and run with it." And they did. And they did good.

--Now an average fisheries volunteer may succeed in building anywhere from two to twenty fishponds in a two-year period.

We left one hundred and ninety with an expected harvest of over fifteen tons per year, just in our province.

We tried to stop giving council or help to new farmers after the 40th pond because we found ourselves spread much too thin. But they built ponds anyway, with or without our help. And rather than see them build poor constructions or set bad examples, we capitulated and tried to give support and council to them all.

I tell you this not to say, "Look how great I am or we were", but to say, "Look what can happen when you give a little encouragement and support to people who have never had any."

They go wild! And they do things they never dreamed of or thought they could do.

Each of us has that gift and responsibility, and you don't have to go to Africa, or win the Nobel Prize to do it.

Even someone with average grades, or an I.Q. of less than 124 can make a difference.

* * *

I'd like to ask you to think about something with me. Did anyone ever support you, give you a chance, teach you something or say, "Hey, you did good! Now go for it?"

How much difference did it make? Or would it have made if you'd had it at key points in your life?

Each of us has that opportunity every single day of our lives.

How long has it been since you told your wife or husband that they're doing fine and that you appreciate them--within the last week--the last month--or year?

Have you ever told your children, "Hey, you can accomplish anything you set your mind to and I'll try to support you in any way I can?"

Now you may not understand or agree with their choices, but in this world of opportunity, they deserve the chance to become the most of whom they choose to be.

You may never hear it from your parents (perhaps because they never heard it from theirs?) or from the person or people you love most in the world, but there is nothing--nothing to stop you from saying it to them.

And that goes for employers, employees, colleagues, friends and family, and the world at large.

* * *

If our time in Burundi taught me anything, it is that I can positively affect and bring about everyday change in people's lives with simple life choices--and it is becoming the center and focus in my life.

We can affect and bring about change in the world. We can have an affect on poverty, disease, hunger and repression--through innovation and a willingness to come together to solve humanity's problems--to 'work the problem' until we've solved it.

We can improve education, politics and the quality of life itself.

Sometimes this has been done by marching in the streets or throwing stones at the system. But we can also do it by simply standing up to what is wrong, with patience, hard work and working within or around the system for positive change.

I can.

I have

You can. You have. You are doing it right now.

By being here today--by taking time away from your family and friends to be here, by taking time out of your life to hear about something that's important to another person.

You have each made my life richer and fuller today by your presence here, and I appreciate it. You did good.

Thank you.

Chapter 88
Epilogue

The roller coaster ride in East Africa continues. The week after our departure from Burundi there was a relatively peaceful, bloodless coup, and we heard it was a 'positive' change in the government. Months later, we learned that the new government had asked for fifteen fish volunteers to continue the program where the six of us had left off.

A survey team from the Food and Agricultural Organization (FAO) found our farmers and ponds to be doing relatively well, but in need of supervision, and they too, recommended that P.C. fish volunteers be brought back in to continue with our initial efforts.

But the spring of 1988 saw horrendous genocide in the northern provinces (ours among them) with an estimated 5,000-20,000 dead (officially). Unofficially (through the grapevine) we heard double or triple that. We looked for and grasped at every morsel of news or information from international sources, praying that our farmers and their families, our teachers, neighbors, Governor and administrators had been spared, but alas, we heard nothing.

An uneasy peace followed as new fisheries volunteers arrived in the summer and fall of 1988, and while faced with the problems of starting over, the outlook was promising. Peace Corps quickly expanded the program to twenty fisheries volunteers, but they were soon evacuated when conflict and hostilities forced all foreigners out of the country, and still no word of our farmers, as no volunteers had been posted to Ngozi or Kayanza.

* * *

The horrific intervening years of genocide and misery has torn at our hearts as we've seen all the potential good in these people buried under thousands of acts of hatred and bloodshed, perpetrated by extremist Tutsi, Hutu and interlopers alike, upon one another and those that come between them--while the suffering has expanded deep into the

Democratic Republic of the Congo (formerly Zaire) against all life, and continues moving westward.

--We requested help and intervention multiple times from the Clinton and Bush administrations, calling for unilateral international blockades, weapons embargos and economic sanctions on Burundi, Rwanda and the Congo to bring them to peace talks, fearing that if the world ignored the repressed tensions, they would erupt into violence against millions.

Tragically, that since has come to pass. Even sadder, our U.S. State Department has admitted that mass genocide was a probability and that sanctions might have been effective--but their (unofficial, verbal only) response then and now, continues to be that neither country has enough to offer to warrant interference (i.e., nothing we can take advantage of in the form of minerals, natural resources or strategic defense that would merit our involvement).

What a sad reflection on our own government and our lip service to equality, freedom, justice and peace.

* * *

To the People of Burundi: We have seen your courage, the bright light in your eyes and in your hearts, your laughter and your joy. We know you have the capacity to forgive one another the terrible actions and great loss each of you has suffered in the last decades, because we have seen into the greater heart of your people.

With respect, we offer our deepest wishes for healing and reconciliation to this day, and to those many we came to know and love.

For the repose of all the souls lost in the years of conflict (most of our farmers, their families, our teachers, supporters, neighbors and friends), we offer our prayers.

Author's Note

We hold a quiet hope as reconciliation occasionally takes root in small pockets of Central East Africa, even while hostilities continue to ebb and subside in the region.

--Rwanda recently joined the British Commonwealth and adopted English as their language of commerce, and as such they have rules of democratic and human rights to abide by in order to remain a member.

In Burundi, Rwanda and Uganda, schools, cell phones, computers and fiber optic networks are becoming more commonplace and global information more affordable to the masses. Micro-loans to entrepreneurs and co-op leaders are slowly reshaping torn, disrupted family units in the cities and the countryside.

Land rights, political affiliations, education and equality for families and women, and feeding millions of people are still the greatest challenges for peaceful progress. Though incursions by rebels harbored in the Congo are still ongoing and spreading westward, and though both Burundi and Rwanda still experience rumors of periodic violence, repression or threats of instability, we witnessed a 2012 YouTube flash-mob of dance and music in downtown Bujumbura, and our hearts soared with joy at sight of it, and we dared to hope once again.

In 2014, the YouTube video in Burundi of '*Happy*' was released and we saw joy and restoration through the camera's eyes. But lately, rumors of a descent into violence once more have surfaced.

* * *

We continue to ask ourselves what will work, what will help these people who became our friends and made such an impact on our lives, who have so much spirit and such vast potential--to break free of the past?

Our permanent hope is that they--and all African nations--will stand tall and choose to rise to their potential greatness, to find the grace and peace of solutions from within; that they will choose wisely among development agencies offering appropriate assistance, education and guidance, rather than arms, weaponry and interference; and that they will fully embrace the concept of bettering the lives of all their diverse peoples through education, acceptance and peaceful actions.

We hope that they will choose to support representative leaders who respect human rights and sustainable societies, resisting the short-term gains of control or absolute authority.

And finally, from our hearts to yours, that the call to peace, freedom and equality for all life will ring in as fresh, bright and new as the light we have seen shine from within each of you.

With love and a hug,
jimani

Acknowledgements:

Our deepest thanks to Peace Corps for allowing us the opportunity to serve as good-will ambassadors of the United States--for their support and willingness to stand with us as we fought for our program and the Burundian people we came to know; to our fellow volunteers and the American and Ex-pat communities who made our experiences so much richer, who gave us good friends and memories strong enough to last a lifetime; and to family and friends who supported us, then and now, we thank you.

Jim and Anita Pauwels

**If you enjoyed this book, please consider rating and writing a positive review for it on the site where you purchased it or redeemed a coupon).

Also, please consider recommending this book to others for purchase, as 20% of royalties will be donated to support on-going positive development projects in Burundi that build community and promote stability and peace within the nation. Thank you for caring.

* * *

--Jim Thorne is a space scientist, singer-songwriter and all around good guy. He is also the husband of Mary, our fellow fishie PC volunteer in Turtle Tushies in the Land of Banana Beer. He wrote this song for their returned Peace Corps friends and as it reflects our own first nine months as volunteers, he agreed to let us share it with you. Enjoy!

https://soundcloud.com/jimthorne/we-had-mud

About the Author

Anita Pauwels walked out of the dust in a semi-arid desert seeking a wider Universe beyond the beyond. She has worked in surgery as a scrub tech, a nurses' aide, in a flower shop, a chemical plant, a bronze foundry, and for almost 30 years was a successful bronze artist and writer of prose, showing and selling in venues and galleries across the greater Southwest.

In mid-careers, Anita and her husband took a two and a half year sabbatical with Peace Corps to work in Burundi, East Africa, where she earned the JFK Volunteer of the Year award, and has written a memoir, Turtle Tushies in the Land of Banana Beer, about their adventures in fish farming among a heart-warming people.

Under her pen name, Cooper Hill, she has published six dystopian, future-fiction/sci-fi space opera action-adventure novels, replete with strong female protagonists, sidekicks, heroines, heroes and an abundant and appropriate number of villains.

She hopes to continue deciphering the bewildering world of social media.

She enjoys writing-reading, on-going projects, gardening, community, family, ballroom dancing, friends, cooking, long walks with the dog, painting, kayaking and good movies.

Cooper currently greets the sun each morning with her fun-loving Mom and their latest rescue dog, a bundle-of-energy-and-joy black-cock-a-poo, Cricket. They reside on a beautiful tree-covered hill above a quiet valley.

* * *

Discover other titles by this author (dba Cooper Hill) at Amazon.com
https://www.amazon.com/-/e/B00925MJY4

The Spidy Chronicles
Spidy, Recluse's Revenge Bk 1
Escape to the Billows Bk 2
Stones of Fire Bk 3

The Entity Chronicles
Leaving Earth Bk 1
Phoenix Rising Bk 2
Chasing Nyrlkas Bk 3